VISUALIZE THIS

COLLABORATION, COMMUNICATION, AND COMMERCE IN THE 21ST CENTURY

JOE CLABBY

Prentice Hall PTR
Upper Saddle River, NJ 07458
www.phptr.com

ISBN 0-13-066255-0

Library of Congress Cataloging-in-Publication Data

Clabby, Joe.
  Visualize this : collaboration, communication, and commerce in the 21st century / Joe Clabby.
      p. cm.
  Includes index.
  ISBN 0-13-066255-0
  1. Human-computer interaction. 2. User interfaces (Computer systems). I. Title.

QA76.9.H95 C53 2001
004'.01'9—dc21

2001036922

Editorial/Production Supervision: *Donna Cullen-Dolce*
Acquisitions Editor: *Karen McLean*
Marketing Manager: *Jim Keogh*
Manufacturing Manager: *Alexis Heydt-Long*
Cover Design Director: *Jerry Votta*
Cover Design: *Anthony Gemmellaro*
Interior Design: *Gail Cocker-Bogusz*

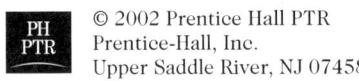
© 2002 Prentice Hall PTR
Prentice-Hall, Inc.
Upper Saddle River, NJ 07458

Prentice Hall books are widely used by corporations and government agencies for training, marketing, and resale.

The publisher offers discounts on this book when ordered in bulk quantities. For more information, contact: Corporate Sales Department, Phone: 800-382-3419; Fax: 201-236-7141; E-mail: corpsales@prenhall.com; or write: Prentice Hall PTR, Corp. Sales Dept., One Lake Street, Upper Saddle River, NJ 07458.

All products or services mentioned in this book are the trademarks or service marks of their respective companies or organizations.

All rights reserved. No part of this book may be reproduced, in any form or by any means, without permission in writing from the publisher.

Printed in the United States of America

10 9 8 7 6 5 4 3 2 1

ISBN 0-13-066255-0

Pearson Education LTD.
Pearson Education Australia PTY, Limited
Pearson Education Singapore, Pte. Ltd.
Pearson Education North Asia Ltd.
Pearson Education Canada, Ltd.
Pearson Educación de Mexico, S.A. de C.V.
Pearson Education—Japan
Pearson Education Malaysia, Pte. Ltd.

In memory of those who lost their lives and those who have suffered from the terrible events of September 11, 2001. May the advent of the forthcoming new virtual society help us all communicate more effectively across state and religious boundaries and help us live together in peace forever.

Table of Contents

Preface   VII

Part I   **The Premise**   1

    Chapter 1—Take a Virtual Journey   13
    Chapter 2—The Opening Argument   27
    Chapter 3—Virtual Worlds: Today's State of the Art   45

Part II   **Technology Roadmap**   61

    Chapter 4—The Sensory Virtual Internet Roadmap   65

Part III   **Human Interfaces**   77

    Chapter 5—Speech Recognition and Artificial Intelligence   85
    Chapter 6—Navigation/Manipulation   111
    Chapter 7—Receiving Sensory Data from Your Computer   121
    Chapter 8—3D Graphics   137
    Chapter 9—Sound, Scent, Touch, and Taste   163

Part IV INFRASTRUCTURE 173

Chapter 10—Networking: Overcoming the Biggest Obstacle to Realizing the Sensory Virtual Internet 183
Chapter 11—Personal Computing Devices 217
Chapter 12—Back-End "Peer-to-Peer" Systems 235
Chapter 13—The Role of Data Compression 253

Part V WEB SERVICES 265

Chapter 14—Web Services 269

Part VI COLLABORATION 283

Chapter 15—The New Age Virtual Applications 291

Part VII WHERE DO WE GO FROM HERE? 321

Chapter 16—Summary Observations 323

Bibliography 331

Index 335

Preface

Just Suppose for a Moment

Just suppose for a moment that I were to tell you that I believe that human interfaces, application development technology, computer/network infrastructure, and collaborative applications are rapidly converging—and that these technologies will soon enable Internet users to experience a sensory-rich Internet that can deliver 3D visuals and audio, scent, touch, and taste sensations right to their very homes. Also suppose that I were to claim that great improvements in the way that we interface with our computers were imminent—improvements such as speech recognition for greater command and control of our computer environments, as well as vastly improved computer screen navigation and manipulation. And further suppose that I were to state that these technologies will soon change the way we humans conduct business, shop, socialize, worship, learn, and otherwise collaborate—replacing the need for physical presence with electronic virtual representation. Would you believe me?

When I put forward this scenario to business executives, the comments I usually get are "No way," "This won't happen for at least a decade," or (and this is my favorite) "You're way out there, man." But after explaining my theory—that the convergence of five technologies is already enabling the formation of a new, sensory-enabled Internet—something strange starts to happen. The business executives (usually CEOs, CIOs, and line-of-business managers) or Information Systems (IS) executives start to nod their heads in agreement. They recognize that some of what I'm saying is possible. Usually within five minutes, these executives not only get it, but they actually start contributing their perspectives to my general thesis. They start to get enthusiastic. They start to extrapolate. They get into it.

This book is about what I call "the Sensory Virtual Internet." It describes how certain technologies are coming together to change the way we communicate electronically. When we communicate with each other electronically today, we primarily use unimodal approaches such as the telephone or e-mail. When we communicate tomorrow, we'll be using videophone services and videoconferencing complete with 3D visuals, sense-around audio, scent, and touch.

When we interface with our computers today, we primarily use a keyboard or some other physical device (such as a stylus) to input data and commands. Our computer environments of tomorrow will be speech-activated command-and-control systems complemented by speech input systems.

Even more exciting is the fact that as sensory technologies come online, you can expect to see a new generation of collaborative, virtual world "colocation" software evolve that will create the illusion that you, I, and other people are coresidents in metaphorical virtual meeting places—be it a conference room, a shopping mall, a place of worship, or some other virtual place. By using this new breed of collaborative colocation software, we will be able to eliminate the need to be physically present to conduct collaborative activities such as learning, socializing, shopping, worshiping, buying, or selling. Figure 1 serves as a synopsis of this idea, and of this book.

This book contends that when all is said and done, we have entered a new age in human communication—the Sensory Virtual Internet age—wherein we will be able to communicate electronically in a sensory-rich manner, and wherein we will

WHAT:

Better Human Interface
to Computers
Speech Recognition
Artificial Intelligence
Improved Navigation and Manipulation

Better Sensory Interface
from Computers
Three-Dimensional Visual
Three-Dimensional Audio
Scent, Touch, Taste

HOW:

Improved Infrastructure
Faster High-Speed Networking (Broadband and Wireless)
Greater Access to High-Speed Networking Services
Computationally Oriented Processing (Peer-to-Peer)

Improved Architecture
Very Powerful Computationally Intensive Graphics Handling
Faster Bus/Switch Architecture
Faster Central Processing Units

New Application Development Approach
Object-Oriented Programming Combined with Web Services

RESULTING IN:

A New Generation of Collaborative Colocation Applications
The Formation of Virtual Worlds and Metaphorical Meeting Places
Reduces or Eliminates Our Need to Be Physically Present to Meet, Collaborate
Will Permanently Change the Way We Conduct Business, Socialize, Learn, and Are Entertained

WHEN:

3D Video and Audio, Scent, Touch—Now
Speech Recognition/Artificial Intelligence to Computers—Now
Peer-to-Peer, PC Architecture Improvements, Web Services, Taste—Over the Next Two to Five Years

FIGURE 1
What This Book Is About

have vastly improved human interfaces with our computers. This will result in the ability to electronically collaborate with one another in a location-independent manner.

WHY WAS THIS BOOK WRITTEN?

This book was written for two reasons:

1. To make business executives and IS executives aware of the subtle convergence of certain technologies that will soon greatly influence the way that business will be

conducted. It includes a lot of information about the role computer systems and networks will play in the formation of a new, computationally intensive (as opposed to transactionally intensive) Internet. It describes a major shift in the way that future applications will be developed and how the next generation of collaborative applications will help us work, learn, socialize, and otherwise collaborate together without having to be physically colocated.
2. To bring order out of chaos. Most people have been overwhelmed by the barrage of technical information that they are receiving—and they don't know how all of the pieces fit together into a grand plan, a big picture, or an overarching strategy. This book focuses on showing you how certain key technologies and industry trends relate to each other, such that when you see a bit of information on one particular technology you'll understand how that information relates to other technologies and the bigger picture in general. Essentially, the goal is to help you understand how various technologies are interrelated in order to help you implement the right strategy to exploit the evolving Sensory Virtual Internet for your business, educational, or social needs.

As an example of bringing order out of chaos, after reading this book I'd like you to be able to understand how a relatively new technology—fixed wireless technology, for instance—relates to the grand scheme of enabling the Sensory Virtual Internet. After reading this book, you'll understand why fixed wireless communications has come about (because the telecommunications industry is having trouble providing direct high-speed wiring to some homes and businesses); what it does (fixed wireless provides for high-speed connection for a certain class of business or home users); and how it relates to the big picture (fixed wireless is important in the grand scheme of the Sensory Virtual Internet because you need high-speed connections to deliver complex graphics and sensory data to virtual users). In other words, by reading this book you'll understand how technologies interrelate; you'll be able to characterize and categorize that information more effectively; and you'll understand how certain technologies are contributing to the formation of the next-generation Internet. You can then, accordingly, base your own individual or professional strategies on how to make use of this information to exploit the Sensory Virtual Internet.

Hidden Purpose

This book also has a hidden purpose—to get business strategists, application developers, product marketers, and individuals to recognize that, with the convergence of five technologies, we have the opportunity to radically change the way that we interact with other humans (moving away from having to be physically colocated to conduct business, or to socialize, or to learn—to being virtually present). It is my hope that this book will jump-start Sensory Virtual Internet projects by encouraging businesses to start offering sensory-rich, virtual experiences to customers and business partners. I hope that business success with these technologies will lead to a broader move by consumers and educators toward sensory-rich virtual worlds on the Internet.

Who Is This Book For?

While I'd like to say that this book is for the common reader of technology and business books, I don't think that the common reader is going to pick this book up and get it quite yet. Most consumers of business and technology books are focused on immediate issues related to e-business (electronic business), i-business (Internet-business), or m-business (mobile business and commerce)—and are not ready for the v- (virtual) discussion quite yet. This book is for the uncommon reader—someone a little bit ahead of the pack—the strategic thinker and planner who is looking to understand what certain technologies will make possible from a virtual worlds perspective, and who will be able to exploit these technologies for his or her enterprise's strategic business advantage. It is for the reader who wants to look beyond the pale at the next big thing—the forthcoming "v-" trend.

This book is also for application developers, consumers, investors, marketing professionals, and educators. It is especially crucial for application developers to understand the big virtual world picture presented herein. Developers need to understand how applications need to be developed and assembled to create the virtual collaborative environments of the future. Without aggressive application development, the description of the technology convergence in this book will amount to nothing more than an interesting write-up on interfaces and infrastructure. It is equally important that marketing professionals understand how their products relate to those of other enterprises (since they may need to structure relationships with other application suppliers in order to rapidly build rich virtual world product suites). And because of projected high growth in the field of e-learning (also known as distance learning), educators need to become familiar with the technologies covered in this book in order to build (or rebuild) effective distance learning curricula.

How Should You Use This Book?

This book should be used in several ways:

- For readers new to the idea of "virtual you" (an electronic representation of you in virtual space), I'd like to help you become familiar with the PC and graphics products, applications, and tools that you will have at your disposal to enter and participate in new and forthcoming collaborative virtual world environments. I'd like to save you some money—don't buy that brand-new bargain PC unless it has an extremely powerful graphics card, a fast bus or switched architecture (to be explained later in the book), fast network conection hardware, and a very powerful central processing unit (CPU). Otherwise, you may find that your PC or like device will not be able to capture or present the kind of rich sensory data that you will soon have access to on the Sensory Virtual Internet!

- If you are a savvy *marketer* looking for new ways to reach consumers, this book will provide you with a foundation for understanding how to use new sensory and virtual technologies to reach prospective consumers of your products or services—and how to use these technologies to engage and retain existing customers.
- If you are a *professional services provider* (doctor, lawyer, sales representative, consultant, etc.), this book will make you aware of how new technologies will enable you to provide your services to consumers electronically. The next-generation, sensory-based, virtual Internet has the potential to enable you to reach more people, provide better service (e.g., eliminating waiting lines in doctor's offices), and collaborate more effectively with other professionals—all without having to meet physically with consumers, patients, or prospects.
- For *investors,* many of the technologies described in this book represent the next big things—and at present there are plenty of opportunities to get in on the investing ground floor at many fledgling technology companies that will lead the Sensory Virtual Internet charge of the future. Further, expect these evolving sensory virtual technologies to kick start and spawn new markets, which will present additional opportunities for strong portfolio growth. For instance, according to IDC (a computer industry market research firm), the market for e-learning content, software, and services is expected to grow from $2.2 billion in 2000 to over $11.4 billion in 2003. The use of virtual technologies combined with pedagogical

software will help to further spur this meteoric rise. According to other research studies, the Internet 3D game market is expected to more than *triple*, reaching $17.2 billion in 2003. These two statistics indicate clearly that there is a public thirst for sensory-rich virtual software. Investors should be aware of the technologies that will drive this market and should expect that Sensory Virtual Internet technologies will play a big role in making these dramatic rises in revenue happen.

- For *applications developers,* this book should be a *wake-up call* that drives you to create Web Service applications. Web Services will enable you to rapidly build sensory-rich applications on-the-fly—for instance, using a speech recognition application service from one vendor and maybe a scent producing service provided by another vendor. Your contribution is critical to the success of the Sensory Virtual Internet—and this book will help you understand the big picture and your prospective contribution to it.
- For *enterprise strategists and planners,* this book should give you a heads-up on technologies that are coming your way so that you can properly plan for deployment.
- For *product marketers,* no matter what your product, your strategic plan needs to support the ideas of better human interfaces, faster networking/processing, or more efficient applications development. All of these technologies will make it possible to present data in other-than-just-character format. You need to be the first on the block at your company to start sounding the wake-up call for products that are designed for the Internet of the future: the Sensory Virtual Internet. Start looking for new business partners with whom to collaborate on delivering highly integrated, sensory-driven applications and solutions. If you don't get moving, your company may lose its competitive edge as your competitors will get there before you.

- For *educators,* this book will describe the advent of virtual schools and universities as well as discuss how the forthcoming Sensory Virtual Internet will help you teach and collaborate more effectively.
- For *students,* there is a substantial body of proof that the addition of sensory data—including sight, sound, and smell—will help you learn better. Written theory has its place, but actual experience is a better teacher. This book will serve to explain how certain technologies are converging to help you become better educated—no matter where you are physically located.
- For *Information Systems (IS) managers,* this book is technology-focused and describes how systems infrastructure and application design will change to support the development of sensory-rich virtual environments of the future. This perspective, and the products that complement it, should help you make infrastructure and product decisions today that will accommodate the advance of these technologies in the future.

How Is It Organized?

This book is organized into seven parts:

1. Part I—*The Premise*—examines the background for the argument that we have already entered the Sensory Virtual Internet Age. It describes the five technologies that are converging to create a Sensory Virtual Internet. It also examines the current state of the art in virtual worlds and describes the changes that need to be made to enhance virtual world technologies in order to sensory-enable these worlds for collaborative purposes.
2. Part II—*Technology Roadmap*—frames the problems and issues that we face as we attempt to build a sensory-driven, Sensory Virtual Internet. It explains how Internet users will use certain technologies to experience this new

Internet, and it projects when such technologies will mature over the next several years.

3. Part III—*Human Interfaces*—examines the technologies that Internet users will use to better interface with our computers, and it examines the technologies that our computers will use to provide better sensory data to us. This part is divided into five chapters: speech recognition and artificial intelligence, navigation and manipulation, output technologies overview, 3D visual technology, and audio/touch/scent/taste technologies.

4. Part IV—*Infrastructure*—takes a close look at the computer systems and networks that will provide the "virtual you" with access to the sensory-rich 3D graphics, enriched audio, scent, touch, and taste sensations that will be made available to you in Sensory Virtual Internet worlds. It examines the changes that are taking place to systems platforms (workstations, PCs, handhelds, and servers) to enable the sending and receiving of complex, large, sensory data files. It also looks at what is taking place on the computer back end (at the server level) to handle the computationally challenging task of displaying, animating, and motivating virtual you in virtual worlds.

5. Part V—*Web Services*—describes how the use of Internet standards will enable developers to easily construct sensory-rich applications and link sensory-rich modules to collaborative applications. As a result, applications will come to market more quickly than ever before. The availability of new applications is crucial to making the Sensory Virtual Internet a reality.

6. Part VI—*Collaboration*—examines the new applications and new 3D worlds that the virtual you will have access to. More specifically, this section focuses on business-to-business collaboration; e-learning; entertainment; and social-collaborative applications that will evolve using

7. Part VII—*Where Do We Go from Here?*— provides a wrap-up of all of the previous sections plus a look at distant-future but relevant technologies such as holography.

The Use of Sidebars

Throughout this document you will find a series of sidebars—short anecdotal breakout sections (separated from the main text) that serve to illustrate the point being discussed. These sidebars are intended to illustrate how a particular technology is being used or describe some point of interest. Here's an example:

> Get ready: The next catch-letter that will be introducing every business, educational, entertainment, and social experience ranging from activity through zoo will be preceded by the letter "v-." The "v" stands for "virtual," and "v-" signals the move beyond "e-(electronic) everything," "i-(Internet) everything," and "m-(mobile) everything" into the virtual world environments where we will conduct business, learn, socialize, and be entertained in a virtual reality mode.

The Birth of a New Medium

As the world of the Sensory Virtual Internet becomes a reality, you will likely find that the biggest payback of this new Sensory Virtual Internet will be that it saves you, as an individual, *time*. The Sensory Virtual Internet will provide you with the ability to interact with others without needing to be physically present. If you are a service provider (a lawyer, an accountant, even a doctor) you may no longer have to keep office hours and appointments in your physical office. If you are a consultant, you may no longer have to travel long distances to work with clients—instead your services will be hosted at Internet vistas that offer virtual office space, where you will use sophisticated collaborative software to work in a virtual mode. If you are a sales representative, the Virtual Internet will provide you with a new way to interact with your customers—enabling you to provide high-touch in a virtual fashion, even from remote locations. Expect the Sensory Virtual Internet to save you commuting and travel time and provide you with more time to do other things with your life (perhaps providing you with more leisure time to engage in recreation, sports, family activities, or even 3D Internet game activities).

As you read this book, you will realize that you are witnessing the birth of a new medium: not print, not broadcast, but a virtual and multimedia-enriched medium that will eliminate geographical boundaries and constraints and change the way we will interact with each other on a global basis. You are wholeheartedly encouraged to read on; to become enthusiastic; and to share your enthusiasm with others!

Part I: The Premise

The Goal: Multimodal Electronic Communications

The next big step in human communications will be to make our electronic communications multimodal—in other words, it will be the use of electronic media to provide three-dimensional visuals and audio as well as scent, touch, and taste sensations. When we achieve this objective, we will be able to see each other electronically in three dimensions (height, width, and depth). We will be able to hear objects pass us by when we're stationary or become louder or quieter as we get closer or more distant. And we will be able to collect new sensory information such as touch, scent, and taste while being located remotely. By gaining access to multiple modes of input, we will be able to learn better and communicate and collaborate more effectively.

If you look at the historical progression of electronic communications, you will find that previous electronic communication inventions changed the way that we conducted business and how we socialized.

In the mid-1800s, the telegraph was introduced, thus allowing people to communicate electronically across great geographical distances. At the time, it was used primarily for improving business communications and also served as the first form of electronic messaging. In effect, the telegraph was the e-mail of the 1800s!

In the early 1900s, Alexander Graham Bell introduced the telephone—enabling humans to again communicate over a physical wire, but this time with a better human interface. Speech, rather than dots and dashes, was used to allow humans to communicate with one another. The telephone was also quickly adopted for business and for social use.

Adding a wireless touch to communications, short-wave radio soon followed the telephone, providing yet another means to communicate electronically for business or social purposes over great distances. Only in this case a wireless short-wave radio wave is used as opposed to physical telephone lines.

Note that if you examine the state of electronic communications for the past 125 years, you'll find that human-to-human electronic communications has been dominated by a single sense—sound. Yet, in the real world, most of us gather information about our environment and communicate with others using multiple senses—including sound, but also including sight, touch, smell, and taste. For us to communicate more naturally using electronic medium, it logically follows that we need to find ways to enable that medium to accommodate sensory feedback in our electronic communications (see Figure 2).

The next age of communications that we will experience will be an age where we can communicate in multiple modes (sight, sound, scent, touch, and taste) over physical wiring or via wireless technologies. I call this age the Sensory Virtual Internet age.

The Move Toward Multimodal Communications Is Underway

Believe it or not, we have already entered this new multimodal Sensory Virtual Internet age—only few people know it. Today, we can communicate in two modes simultaneously—audio and video—using videophone or videoconferencing technologies. And the technologies needed to produce touch and scent sensations already exist today—commercially available touch and scent devices can be used to provide haptic and olfactory experiences over the Internet. With the imminence of new multimodal peripherals and the broader availability of high-speed networks, we are now poised to enter new, sensory-rich electronic worlds where we can meet and collaborate without having to be physically present.

Note the word "poised" in the previous paragraph. We currently have access to the basic technologies that can present 3D audio and visual representations or replicate touch, scent, or

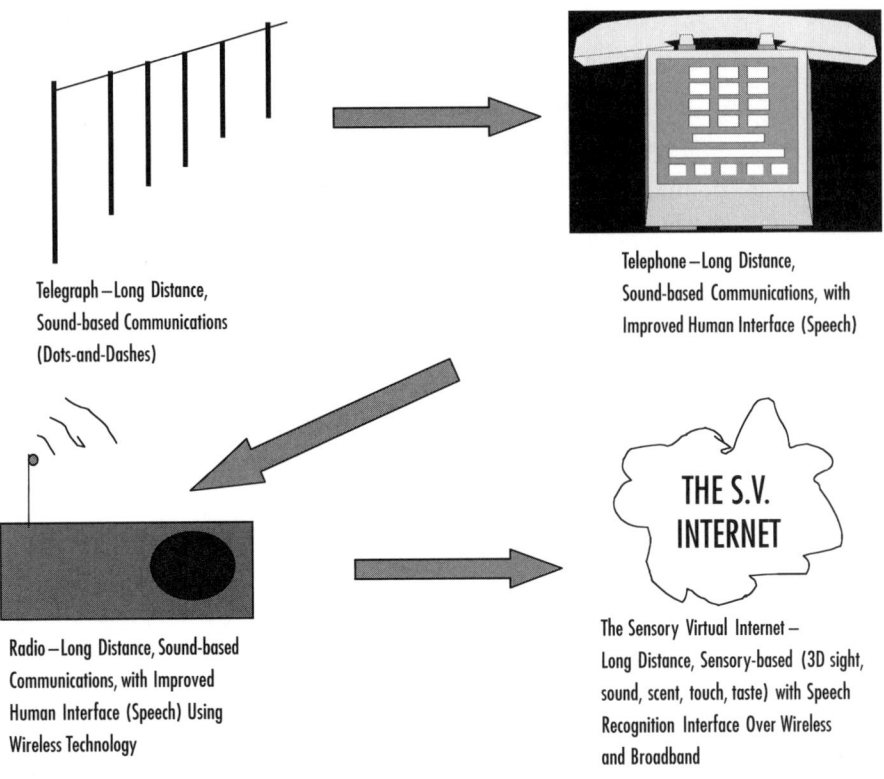

FIGURE 2
The Evolution of Electronic Communications

sound—but what we need in order to create a true multimodal experience is *greater integration* between these technologies. We need these technologies to work in unison together to help create immersive, three-dimensional virtual worlds in which we can conduct business, socialize, learn, or be entertained.

Inability to Exploit Multimodal Communications

There are many reasons that most Internet users have failed to recognize that we have entered a new Internet age:

1. Most Internet users do not yet have access to high-speed networks. Because the Sensory Virtual Internet relies

heavily on the sending and receiving of large sensory files, low speed links (less than 56,000 bytes per second) are inadequate.
2. Most PCs (PCs are the most common access points to the Internet) are not equipped to handle the presentation of rich sensory data. Hence many Internet-connected PCs are not capable of reproducing detailed 3D images, sense-around sound, or scent and touch experiences.
3. Most of today's applications have not been written to exploit sensory technologies.
4. Back-end servers are not configured to handle the huge computational workload involved in creating virtual world environments.
5. Few applications exist that exploit complex sensory technologies such as 3D, visual and audio, scent, touch, and taste.

When the integration of sensory technologies into mainstream applications becomes more commonplace, and when people have sufficiently upgraded their computer systems and networks to send, receive, and process large sensory files, the computing world will then recognize that a new medium—the Sensory Virtual Internet—has been created.

Good News/Bad News

The good news is that the hardware and software integration work needed to architect the Sensory Virtual Internet is now taking place (most prominently in game application development). But, integration of sensory data is also underway at companies that provide access to virtual world environments, such as ActiveWorld, blaxxun Interactive, and Worlds.com. These virtual world companies are starting to integrate voice with 3D visuals so that people can see and talk to each other in virtual reality. And integration is taking place at companies that build videophone and videoconferencing solutions and at companies that provide e-learning solutions. Eventually the software offerings of all of these types of companies will start to blend together, creating rich sensory environments that provide realistic virtual world experiences for Sensory Virtual Internet users. It is reasonable to expect that eventually hundreds, even thousands, of sites will be created that will offer scent, touch, and even taste sensations over the Internet.

The bad news is that, at this juncture, *much of the integration effort that needs to take place to build a sensory-rich virtual Internet seems to be completely disorganized.* Few software developers or enterprises have an overarching plan or even a common roadmap. Without such common ground, nothing is driving the convergence of technologies around a common idea such as the Sensory Virtual Internet. Solution providers are stumbling and fumbling in that direction—they just don't know what the ultimate goal is. Hopefully, this book will help people see the big picture and encourage application and system designers to work together toward building an immersive Sensory Virtual Internet environment.

THE PREMISE

It is the premise of this book that five technologies are converging to create a new, multimodal, sensory-rich medium—the Sensory Virtual Internet. These five technologies involve advances in:

- *Human Interfaces to Computers*—Advances in speech recognition and artificial intelligence are now making it possible for people with limited computer skills to make use of computers in a more natural manner using their voice to operate their computer system. At the same time, new devices that can accept natural human input (such as motion detection devices) are being developed that can replace or augment mouse and cursor movement and enable manipulation of objects in virtual 3D space.

- *Computer Interfaces with Humans*—Already, computers are capable of sending and receiving rich, three-dimensional visual and audio data—making it possible for us to conduct videoconferencing activities from geographically dispersed locations. But in the very near term, computers will be able to provide back to us sensory-rich haptic (touch) and olfactory (scent) data. Perhaps in under five years it will become practical for our computers to deliver realistic taste sensations as well.
- *Computer Infrastructure, Architecture, and Computing Techniques*—Advances in high-speed networks, peer-to-peer processing, and compression/decompression algorithms are helping to create the high-speed highway and the computational processing power needed to deliver sensory-rich files to a wide variety of devices over the Sensory Virtual Internet.
- *Collaborative Applications*—For almost a decade, software developers have been building applications using component models to create applications as reusable objects. The maturation of certain application development standards—and the commitment of major system and software manufacturers to the use of those standards—will now enable application developers to rapidly assemble the kinds of common language between virtual applications that will be needed on the Sensory Virtual Internet.

   Advances in human interfaces to and from computers, computer/network infrastructure, and application development design and deployment based on Web standards can be expected to lead to the development of a new generation of sensory-enabled, collaborative colocation applications that will change the way we conduct business, learn, socialize, and experience our entertainment.

The primary benefit of this convergence will be a form of location freedom. We will soon be able to communicate with each other and with our computers using natural speech and motion, to see each other in three dimensions, to pick up scent and touch clues, and to interact as if we were there—all without having to be physically present. We will soon be able to share a whole new range of sensory experiences in virtual space.

For those who have access to the Internet, life will get easier. In most cases, we will no longer need to physically travel to an office, a classroom, or other locations in order to receive the services we require. We will most likely be able to use the time we save for other activities, such as leisure, more revenue-producing work, family life, other social activities, or for entertainment purposes—spending time on things we want to do rather than wasting it.

For businesses, new Sensory Virtual Internet applications will provide new avenues for marketing and delivering products and services. And these new virtual worlds will allow for new business efficiencies, such as cutting down on travel and improving the quality and timeliness of business training.

For educators, the new Sensory Virtual Internet will expand the opportunities for marketing existing intellectual material (or coursework) globally, not just locally or regionally. Immense revenue opportunities may exist for leaders in their respective fields to market their courses worldwide. The use of sensory technologies will improve the effectiveness of this electronically delivered course material.

When Will This Convergence Take Place?

This convergence is already taking place. Today, we already have access to functional virtual worlds that can produce three-dimensional images of a "virtual you" in a three-dimensional electronic venue. This virtual you, or avatar, can converse with other virtual people that you meet. You can live in virtual neighborhoods, locating your dwelling near people with the same likes and dislikes, interests and disinterests that you have. You can go virtual shopping. You can attend concert events (and if you're lucky, you can even go backstage). If you've got the right equipment and a high-speed network, today's virtual worlds can be quite exciting.

However, you should be aware that today's virtual worlds have several shortcomings. For instance, some do not currently support the simultaneous use by virtual visitors of voice and 3D graphics. This means you cannot talk to the virtual people whom you meet in some 3D virtual worlds—you still need to input conversation in typewritten chat mode, and none of today's leading virtual world sites provides scent, touch, or taste support.

Still, it is my contention that these shortcomings will soon be addressed by the convergence over the next three years of faster graphics processing, higher-speed networking, more powerful processors, better interfaces, and richer collaborative applications. And this contention, in a nutshell, is what this book is about.

What This Part Is About

This part describes the premise of this book: We have entered the Sensory Virtual Internet age, an age that will radically change the way we communicate with our fellow human beings. This part describes in detail certain specific technologies that are converging to lead to this observation and how we will make use of this new Sensory Virtual Internet once we get there.

Chapter 1 focuses on what is possible on the Sensory Virtual Internet—what's in store for us as five critical technologies converge. It talks about what this convergence of technologies will enable you to do and why you should care.

Chapter 2 focuses specifically on clearly stating the premise of this book and justifying the position that the evolution of a Sensory Virtual Internet is already underway. The next few years will be all about how five technologies will be fine-tuned to deliver a radically new sensory-rich Internet experience.

Chapter 3 focuses on the current state of the art of virtual worlds. It identifies the strengths and weakness of today's environments and it observes that every weakness is being addressed.

What I Hope You'll Learn

After reading these chapters you, too, should conclude that there is a major shift underway in how we will use the Internet—and that this shift is going to greatly affect the way this and future generations will work, play, socialize, and learn. You should understand the basic technologies that are converging to form the Sensory Virtual Internet and what those technologies will enable you to do. You should also gain a basic understanding of the state of today's virtual world environments and of how the convergence of various technologies are going to affect the way you conduct business, learn, socialize, and experience entertainment in the future. You should take away a solid understanding of what will be possible in these worlds, and how you will be able to use these worlds to your personal or professional advantage.

CHAPTER 1
Take a Virtual Journey

The new virtual Internet worlds that you and I will have access to in the future will be vibrant and alive. These worlds will be fun. They will lure and attract Internet users to virtual malls and virtual venues by the millions. The "virtual you" who visits these venues will use a 3D persona, or "avatar" (electronic representation of yourself), to conduct commerce, play games, recreate, gather information, and collaborate with others. This new Internet will be driven by human voice and motion. Virtual you will use your natural senses—sight, sound, and smell—to navigate, transact, experience new virtual landscapes and vistas, learn, and socialize with other "netizens" (members of the Internet community) in virtual 3D space.

For the virtual you lucky enough to have access to high-speed Internet connections and decent 3D graphics technology (which require powerful graphics cards and specialized 3D displays), you will be able to enter rich virtual worlds on the Internet where you will find interesting landscapes and developing communities. Fellow explorers represented by avatar likenesses may approach you and engage you in conversation—perhaps providing you with directions to other interesting sites.

Other changes heading our way include the arrival of sensory-rich videophone services. In the new computing world, people will be able to conduct real-time, live conversations while viewing three-dimensional images of each other because the major performance obstacles and technical limitations of the past that have hindered such simultaneous voice/visual communications over the Web are now being overcome. As a result, people will be able to pick up visual as well as audio clues when communicating with each other, leading to a richer form of communications than today's audio-based telephone or character-based e-mail options.

Scent-based sensory technologies are also being added to the Internet communications environment, enabling people to smell facsimiles of the goods they are going to buy. These technologies will enable marketers to promote new products or venues (like tropical vacations—complete with the piña colada and coconut oil scents), or store owners to lure visitors into their Internet storefronts using bakery scents, candy scents (like chocolate), perfume scents, and much, much more.

Other sensory-data such as touch and taste—will also be Internet-enabled in the not-so-distant future. (Today touch sensations can be delivered over the Internet using force-feedback game peripherals; tomorrow sensory information such as the coarseness or smoothness of an object and other sensations will also be deliverable.)

On the application side of computing, huge strides will be made in collaboration software—enabling business people to work cooperatively on a grand scale as they architect products or share ideas, thus allowing virtual you to easily convene meetings and share ideas with members of your favorite Internet communities.

Finally, the way we learn will change: Access to richer sensory data—data that will provide us with heretofore unavailable sensory information—will stimulate our senses and help us learn more quickly, accurately, and experientially.

How Is This Possible?

A close look at the state of sensory technologies in today's markets reveals that:

1. *3D visual technology* is now used heavily in several markets including engineering, entertainment, and medicine. The Sensory Virtual Internet will help 3D visual experiences permeate other business markets and expand further into our individual lives. Visual 3D technology is ready for prime time and just keeps getting better and better as hardware and software continue to improve.
2. *Audio technology* has moved from analog to digital sound over the past 10 years. And, it has also improved in quality, producing sound that is almost identical to original sounds in the natural world. The next step for audio will be to create 3D Audio: audio that surrounds us, immersing us in virtual world environments. Such audio would be able to duplicate the Doppler effect—the sound of a car approaching and then passing us by. The ability to produce such 3D sound is here today. The challenge ahead will be to find ways for games and business applications to capitalize on this surround-sound technology.
3. *Touch technologies* are available now—but are currently in a rudimentary stage. Today you can experience vibrations on joysticks and like devices (such as steering wheels) when playing video games. Soon "electronic

gloves" will become commercially viable, enabling the virtual you to feel textures and shapes of objects in three-dimensional worlds.
4. *Scent technologies* have only recently come to the forefront. This topic is currently the butt of many jokes—skeptics doubt the applicability and usefulness of the sense of smell in electronic computing environments. Nonetheless, scent technologies will be used in the future to enhance our travel through virtual worlds, providing us with exotic scents when visiting exotic places or augmenting our shopping experience with bakery, chocolate, flower, and other scents relevant to the items we are seeking to purchase. They might even provide scent clues that will help us in e-learning or business situations.
5. *Taste technology* is still on the drawing board in terms of product readiness, but there are several very interesting research efforts taking place. One of the most interesting involves impregnating a bland substance (such as a potato- or rice-based card) with flavors (bitter, sweet, salty, etc.), then surrounding that substance with appropriate scent data and tasting the result. Scent is very important to our taste experience—initial experiments that combine both scent and taste have been very encouraging—but a lot of work still needs to be done to make this technology commercially viable.

What's in Store for Us Beyond Sensory Improvements?

Some of the areas that promise to greatly improve our Sensory Virtual Internet experience over the next few years include:

- *Speech Recognition*—One area that looks particularly exciting. As speech recognition modules start to front end traditional character-mode applications and databases, one of the biggest changes you'll notice is how using keyboards and keypads to input data will start to recede. You'll see this first in the mobile computing world, but eventually you'll find that the need to use keyboards to interface with your personal computer will also diminish. Instead of character-driven keyboard-like interfaces or handwritten shorthand notes on static palm computer viewscreens, we will see our PCs, Palms, and mobile computing devices become capable of taking and acting upon speech commands. The move away from the keyboard is a huge shift in computing. For the past 50 years we have been forced to deal with our computers using complex code sequences and keyboard input devices. But as new human-to-computer speech recognition modules combine with Web-based or traditional applications, we are very close to moving away from tethered keyboarding toward a more human-oriented, sensory-driven approach to computer input and output.

- *Navigation and Manipulation*—In the same way that speech recognition and voice commands enable us to input commands and data into our computers, we humans will be able to use new biofeedback devices such as touch-gloves or retina-driven navigation devices—or even magnetic "dots" on our foreheads—to input screen navigational data into our computer.
- *High-Speed Networking for the Masses*—Distribution and service problems in providing access to high-speed networking have beset the telecommunications industry. Over the next three years, expect these problems to subside. Better service planning, a different attitude from service providers, and competition among wireless local area network (WLAN), cable, and satellite vendors will soon give consumers more options and help alleviate this inadequate services situation.
- *Virtual Shopping*—In three years, expect to transact business with 3D personae on the Internet who may or

may not be real people. In fact, many avatars that you will interact with will really be computer programs designed to help you locate products or information, execute transactions for you, or otherwise do your bidding. The virtual shopping experience as we know it will change radically, thanks to the use of sensory technologies. Shoppers at virtual Internet shops and malls will be able to see, hear, smell, and touch products. Businesses will gravitate to this new Sensory Virtual Internet as a means of establishing a competitive edge, capturing new customers, and serving and retaining existing customers.

- *Videophone Service for the Masses*— Over the years, there have been numerous attempts to create videophone service. Promotors have long advocated the ability to both talk to and see the person you are communicating with. These services have been plagued with technical difficulties related to compressing voice and graphical data and sending that data over low-speed links between computers. However, thanks to better compression/decompression techniques and faster processing, soon more and more of us will move beyond using simple telephone services, adding simultaneous video/audio videophone services. As other sensory technologies mature, we will see greatly improved videoconferencing that will make use of additional sensory information to provide richer learning, social, and business collaborative experiences over the Internet.

One new approach to conquering the videophone problem is presented by First Virtual Corporation, the maker of Click-to-Meet. This is an Internet portal that allows users who have high-speed broadband access to participate in high-quality, decent-resolution two-way voice/video calls.

At the present time, First Virtual lists Cisco Systems, CUSeeMe Networks, EDS, Ezenia!, France Telecom,

Ideal Technology Solutions, Nortel Networks, Polycom, Qwest Communications, SBC Communications, Shanghai Telecom, Telestra, and Verizon Communications as its strategic business partners.

Source: http://www.fvc.com

- *Virtual Collaboration*—The biggest changes in application environments will be in the integration of sensory data with applications that allow for videophone/videoconferencing, virtual space collaboration software, e-learning, and electronic commerce (specifically Web-based retailing or e-tailing). The new Sensory Virtual Internet will enable us to talk with and see the people with whom we choose to communicate and collaborate in a three-dimensional mode. We will be able to share complex product design information with our business partners, touch objects in remote locations, and use our sense of smell in certain appropriate situations. Businesses as well as traditional colleges and universities will be able to deliver high-quality training in 3D mode over the Internet.

What Will These Changes Enable You to Do?

As these changes come about, the way we deal with computers and humans over the Internet will also change—quite profoundly. *Computers will become devices for creating, sending, and receiving sensory data—not just information processing and retrieval systems!* Depending on the computing device that you decide to use (desktop, handheld, Palm, mobile phone, portable computer, or other, yet-to-be-invented device), you will be able to receive character, graphical, audio, video, touch, and/or scent data whenever you want it from wherever you are.

Over the Next Three Years...

Three years from now, you will no longer be completely bound by the physical world. You will be able to use the Sensory Virtual Internet for shopping, consulting, collaborating, learning, socializing, developing relationships, game-playing, experiencing entertainment, and for a wealth of other activities. You will suddenly be logistically free. You will be location-independent!

> In January 2000, Mitch Maddox of Dallas, Texas, USA, decided that he could rely solely on the Internet to meet his needs and set out to prove the point. For one year, Maddox used the Internet to obtain food, furniture, and other commodities—as well as to obtain noncommodities. He managed to meet his fiancé in a chat room on the Web. Twenty cameras monitored "DotComGuy" during the course of his stay at home. His expenses were paid by sponsors.
>
> He was successful. In January 2001, Mitch Maddox ended his self-imposed exile at his Dallas townhouse, having helped prove the point that there is much one can do to sustain life and socialize while using the new Internet medium. This situation makes one wonder, if Maddox had had more 3D, sensory, and virtual tools and worlds at his disposal, would he still be at hanging out at home?
> Source: http://KVIQ.com/now/story/0,1597,260872-338,00.shtml

On an individual basis, expect 3D and sensory technologies to enter your entertainment world as well as your social world. If you are handicapped, 3D and sensory technologies and improved human interfaces may help compensate for issues of mobility, visual impairment, and other handicaps.

In three years, expect Internet users who have access to high-speed communications to have the ability to casually make videophone or videoconference calls as a matter of course. Today, sending voice and visual traffic over low-speed Internet lines is cumbersome. Picture quality is poor and voice synchronization is often choppy. Tomorrow, with high-speed Internet access combined with better data compression/decompression techniques, using video and audio simultaneously will be possible. Person-to-person communications will be smooth, fluent, and—with the addition of 3D visual effects—realistic.

In the business world, expect 3D and sensory technologies to become integral parts of mainstream applications such as Enterprise Resource Planning, supply chain, or Customer Resource Management (CRM) applications. These technologies will be integrated by large suppliers to form complete, sensory-based business application solutions.

Over the next three years, expect to see the development of new "virtual space" collaborative applications, which will present all Internet users with ways to work together, shop, socialize, and otherwise communicate and conduct business in virtual space.

As virtual worlds mature in the future, virtual you will be able to use your full complement of senses to learn about the electronic environment that surrounds you. You will eventually be able to see 3D likenesses of your friends in these worlds (and they will see a similar likeness of you). You will be able to go places with fellow virtual companions—perhaps to parties, to classes, or to religious services—places that are virtual metaphors of real-world meeting places. As the Internet is adapted for multimodal communications, the way that we conduct business, socialize, learn, and are entertained will undergo radical change.

Why Should You Care?

Whether you are a business person, a professional (doctor, lawyer, consultant, etc.), an educator, a consumer, or just an interested observer, this new Sensory Virtual Internet will eventually touch your life in some way. The following are examples of how.

For Business Executives

If you are a business person, you should care about this trend because the use of sensory technologies and collaborative software is going to help you find new ways to:

- *Attract and retain customers*—There are numerous industry examples of how 3D technologies are being used to increase Internet site "stickiness" (the amount of time a customer or prospect stays online at your site). There is a correlation between the time a customer spends at a site and the possibility that he or she will find the information they need or buy something.

    Also, automated programs that present human-like avatars will be able to provide a friendlier and higher degree of customer service than many of today's character-driven CRM applications without incurring the cost of hiring a human. This approach will result in greater customer satisfaction and retention while still keeping overhead low.

    An *Information Week* survey (May, 2001) showed that by using collaboration software, business executives saw increased sales and marketing opportunities; improved collaboration; new ways of innovating; the development of more efficient processes; an increase in customer satisfaction; and, in some cases, reduced costs. This survey was based on using today's two-dimensional collaborative applications!

    Imagine what would be possible if businesses could provide more personalized human-centered services to their customers and business partners. The Sensory Virtual Internet will help businesses achieve this goal.

- *Improve productivity while reducing costs*—By creating sensory-rich environments for employees, employers will spend less money sending employees to distant locations for meetings or for training purposes. By reducing the amount of time that employees spend on the road, em-

ployers will find that they can save money (travel and expense costs) while improving productivity (less travel time translates into more "work" time). By making use of new collaborative computing software, employers will find that meetings will be run more efficiently—again resulting in improved productivity.
- *Broaden the hiring pool*—One of the most important evolving sensory technologies is speech recognition. As our computers adapt to speech-driven commands rather than typewritten commands, employers will find that they can hire less-skilled individuals to perform computer-related information processing tasks. Imagine being able to hire workers who need only to be able to use a mouse and speech commands to fill in forms. New, less-skilled employees could be hired to address worker shortages. Needless to say, such workers would be easier to find and their wages would not have to be as high as more skilled computer professionals.

For Professionals

Consultants are frequently called upon to visit customers in person; to listen in on telephone briefings; and to contribute advice *in person* to marketing, development, and strategic planning personnel.

Now imagine a scenario where consultants could attend meetings virtually. These consultants could:

- Cut down on wasted time traveling (and use that time to handle more customers).
- Provide personalized customer service by being able to more frequently deliver "high-touch" services. In this case, high-touch refers to the ability for a consultant and his or her customer to see the other's reactions in three dimensions and hear each other clear as a bell.

- Reduce travel time and expenses and related scheduling overhead.
- Service more clients, thus potentially significantly increasing revenues.

For Consumers

Consumers of professional services (such as legal, medical, or other services) will benefit greatly from the arrival of the Sensory Virtual Internet. Look at the following example.

> A new branch of medicine is evolving, thanks to advances in 3D and imaging technologies combined with the availability of the Internet. This new branch—Telemedicine—allows doctors and other healthcare workers to provide remote diagnosis and treatment for health problems. Telemedicine makes use of Internet-enabled diagnostic equipment (such as a variety of physiological monitoring devices) to help monitor and determine a person's state of health and (if needed) provide treatment. Computer hardware and software is used to gather such information and forward it on to a physician or healthcare worker, who then undertakes the appropriate action.
>
> In the United Kingdom, the current National Health Service (NHS) Direct telephone service allows UK citizens to obtain a diagnosis and advice on minor ailments without trips to the doctor's office. This telephone service has been extended to 65 percent of the UK's population. It will be complemented by a new NHS Online service. NHS Online will initially only be available to those with Internet access at home (about one third of all UK households have Internet access), but over time will likely be made available at public Internet kiosks found in supermarkets and pharmacies. The UK plan is to allow for doctors and other healthcare professionals to participate in online consultations with their patients, as well as potentially participate in community-based health discussion groups.

What is important about this trend is that people no longer need to go to the office and frequently wait for hours to be examined. The new Internet monitoring devices will some day be complemented by visual technologies that will enable doctors to do visual assessments as well as physiological assessments of their patients without requiring an office visit. This will be done virtually, potentially in a 3D mode, using technologies that will run over the Sensory Virtual Internet.

Another similar example is Dr.Goodwell.com. This company's major objective is to help workers cut down the time they are away for doctor's appointments. Microsoft is one of Dr.Goodwell's first major clients. Think about this. No more exasperating travel time to doctor's offices (or law offices, or accountant's offices, etc.); no more waiting in lines or sitting in offices waiting to be served. This concept can be applied to many professional service organizations (except maybe dentistry and some other "must touch" services). For instance, if you want the services of a lawyer, find one on the Internet and go visit that lawyer in his or her virtual office—you no longer need to meet face to face.

On the flip side, the Sensory Virtual Internet will also change professionals' business model. They may be able to service more people in less time (potentially increasing revenue opportunities) while consumers of professional services will be able to get access to the services they need when they want them, with less time wasted traveling and waiting for such services. The Sensory Virtual Internet is about to provide us with a whole new dimension in human communications as certain technologies converge to make it possible for us to communicate effectively, but virtually, with each other without having to be physically colocated.

CHAPTER 2
THE OPENING ARGUMENT

The next iteration of the Internet—the Sensory Virtual Internet—will be characterized by the way it changes our ability to communicate electronically with each other in a multimodal fashion. We will be able to communicate using 3D visuals and audio, scent, touch, and taste cues over long distances and over wired and wireless networks. By being able to communicate in this sensory-rich manner, the next Internet will greatly change the ways that we collaborate, conduct business, socialize, learn, and experience entertainment.

The Advent of Multimodal Communications

The telegraph, telephone, and short-wave radio comprise our first three generations of devices enabling us to communicate over long distances. By using these devices for almost 125 years, we have been constricted to only one mode of electronic communication: sound-based. But in the 1980s, companies like PictureTel started to liberate us from single-mode electronic communications. At that time PictureTel was a leading maker of hardware and software platforms that enabled users to send and receive video and audio data simultaneously over long distances. The company used videophone and videoconferencing technologies to provide users with dual mode (sight and sound) communications. For businesses that could afford to put in place dedicated high-speed communication links and that could afford the then-expensive platforms and cameras, multimodal communications for the purpose of videoconferencing had finally arrived.

Although the videoconferencing systems and videophone technology have been available for over twenty years, there has been limited mass-market acceptance of these technologies. Even though people in general have a thirst for multimodal communications, videophones and videoconferencing have not yet become common for small business and home use. The primary reason for this is that videophone and videoconferencing technologies have traditionally required high-speed network lines and expensive processing and camera equipment in order to send the large, complex audio and video files between user environments. This has made these technologies unfeasible or too expensive for the mass consumer and small businesses.

The videoconferencing scenario is now changing. Over the past decade, high-speed networking technology has greatly improved and become more broadly available to homes and offices. These technology and infrastructure improvements have laid the groundwork for the broader use of videophone and videoconferencing technologies at the small business and consumer level. Video cameras can now be purchased for less than $50 that can, when hooked up to a computer, provide the electronic eye needed for videophoning or videoconferencing. Video conferencing software has also become more efficient. Compression and decompression techniques help to shrink the size of large audio and video files, thus improving the overall performance and quality of videophone and videoconferencing systems. As high-speed Internet connections have become more widely available, either through the phone company or from other sources such as cable or satellite communications providers, they have paved the way for greater use of multimodal videophone/videoconference services.

Videophoning and videoconferencing represent only the first step in multimodal communications. Research and development advances in the areas of electronic smell and touch have now enabled these sensations to be sent over Internet connections. Advances in taste research will also some day enable sensations such as bitter, sweet, sour, and salty to be sent to receiving devices over the Internet. All of these sensations are being designed to use the same high-speed Internet pathway that videophone and videoconferencing systems are using today.

For us to communicate more naturally, we have needed to find ways to include other senses. Yet to date we have not had the infrastructure in place to facilitate multimodal sensory communications. With recent infrastructure improvements such as the availability of high-speed networks and faster wireless technology, as well as research and development efforts in 3D sight, sound, and sensory technologies, it looks like the days of multimodal electronic communications will soon be here.

How Are We Going to Get to This Multimodal World?

Moving to this world of multimodal electronic communications involves quite a bit more than just faster networks and more efficient videophone/videoconferencing software. It involves the convergence of five technologies: human interfaces to the computer; human interfaces from the computer; infrastructure improvements in the transmission and processing and of large graphics and binary files; new standards for application architecting; and improvements in collaborative applications.

At first glance, all of these technologies seem to be unconnected, dissimilar, disparate—they just don't seem to relate to each other. After all,

- What do human interfaces have to do with networks?
- What does peer-to-peer computing have to do with three-dimensional (3D) graphics processing?
- Why are application component modules so important to collaborative applications?

To the naked eye, these technologies seem, at best, loosely related. Or are they? Look closely and you will find that these technologies are highly interrelated and rapidly converging. This convergence will help to bring about a new age in computing: the *Sensory Virtual Internet* age.

Observe that

1. *Human interface technologies* (human-to-computer and computer-to-human interfaces) *are rapidly maturing*—From a computer-to-human perspective, the use of speech recognition to communicate with computers and databases is becoming more and more prevalent. This technology is now showing up in many enterprises' voice messaging systems and in customer service applications. Speech recognition is also showing up in mobile-device-to-computer applications. IBM recently introduced tech-

nology that enables voice interaction with data files using voice-driven mobile devices such as cell phones.

2. *From a human-to-computer perspective, new navigation and manipulation devices are coming to market*—These devices will make it possible for us to move more easily through three dimensions on our computer viewscreens as well as to pick up and manipulate objects in 3D space.

3. *The high-speed network backbone is in place*—Bandwidth is a term for the amount of data that can be sent simultaneously over a network connection. I'll familiarize you more with this concept later in this book. Today there is actually a bandwidth glut in many major metropolitan areas. What is missing is the ability for most of us to hook up to that big bandwidth backbone. But new advances in satellite technology, fixed wireless, third-generation wireless, fiber-to-the-home, networking using existing power lines, and other approaches will soon provide options for all of us to get the access and amount of network bandwidth that is needed to send and receive rich 3D, audio, touch, and scent information over the Internet.

4. *Improvements in systems architecture and processing techniques are now making it possible to efficiently compute and transmit large, binary, sensory files to and from networked users*—One of the biggest obstacles to sending and receiving sensory-enriched data (such as files containing speech commands or real-time video) has been that these sensory-rich multimedia files are huge. For instance, hundreds of megabytes—or even gigabytes—of information can be contained in a short video clip.

Over the past 50 years, producing, playing, and displaying such files on computers in a high-quality fashion has been a real challenge. Advances in raw computer processing power, new techniques for harnessing that power (such as peer-to-peer computing), and new compression/decompression techniques are now making it possible to process large, complex, sensory-rich data streams between thousands if not millions of virtual yous in virtual vistas of Internet virtual worlds.

As of late, dramatic improvements have been made in PC power and graphics, in peer-to-peer computing that can provide supercomputer-level power, and in the development of switch-based "fabrics" in computer servers and (soon) in PC and workstation devices. Previous generations of these technologies simply did not yield the processing power or network speed necessary to deliver high-quality sensory data to a large population of Internet users. But new and improved technologies will soon make it possible to deliver 3D, audio, haptic, and scent sensory data to millions of simultaneous users in future virtual computing worlds.

5. *A new Web Services-based model for application development and deployment is evolving*—In the early 1990s, most applications were developed in a tightly coupled, monolithic manner wherein all of the modules that make up an application are tightly integrated with each other. Using this traditional model, modifications to one aspect of an application often had a ripple effect on other modules within the same application. To ensure that all application modules continued to work harmoniously together required changes throughout the entire application. The resulting application's code was often called "spaghetti code" because if you modified one part of the code you would most likely affect some other part of the code—just the way that if you pull on one end of a spaghetti strand, the other end will surely move.

Over the past six or eight years, a component-based mode of application development has emerged—one that enables applications to be loosely coupled (loosely, interrelated) such that they can be easily assembled in an "object-oriented" modular fashion. This approach makes it possible to rapidly assemble applications from discrete modules while reducing the risk of breaking the entire code base when modifying applications.

However, this component model isn't the news. The big news is that by making use of these components and the Internet, applications can start using components hosted by other sources on the Internet—creating a vast universe of new application modules that code developers can use to build applications. This concept is known as "Web Services" because application modules can be offered as services to core applications and they can be delivered to these core applications over the Internet. For example, a Web-based speech module could be used to provide speech access to an existing character-oriented application.

This Web-Services approach will greatly accelerate the development of sensory-rich applications—enabling the arrival of sensory-rich applications far more quickly than most people expect.

6. *Collaborative applications* (business, commercial, e-learning, social, and entertainment) *are becoming integrated with each other as well as becoming sensory-enriched*—Teleconferencing is a one-dimensional experience—you listen to someone or a group of people over a sound-based telephone link. Videoconferencing to date has also been static in nature—but at least it has been two-dimensional (for most videoconferencing users you can see dimensions such as height and width but not depth). Videoconferencing is rapidly moving toward creating three-dimensional experiences that include height, width, and depth. When combined with a new generation of collaboration software that focuses on program

and project management and mixed with virtual colocation software, virtual you will soon find yourself able to work collaboratively with fellow workers in sensory-rich virtual environments in virtual space as if you were physically colocated.

Now, take these six data points and link them together:

1. If interfaces to computers become more natural for humans to use; and
2. if computers become more adept at presenting sensory data; and
3. if high-speed networks become more broadly available; and
4. if computational processing speed increases tremendously; and
5. if the application development model changes so that sensory services can be added easily to new and traditional applications; and
6. if new applications are developed that allow us to collaborative more effectively while making use of sight, sound, touch, and scent in a virtual environment . . .

then you, too, may agree that these technologies are actually interrelated, and that their *convergence* could create a new type of Internet: a Sensory Virtual Internet. This concept is illustrated in Figure 3.

No Way Say the Doubters

Is this trend analysis believable? To quote one business executive that I interviewed, "You're way out there, man." In other words, "I doubt it."

Many people will tell you that they don't believe that a sensory-driven Virtual Internet will be possible in the next few years. They scoff when the topic of scent technology is mentioned (calling it "smell-o-vision"), doubting that it will have

CHAPTER 2: THE OPENING ARGUMENT

HUMAN-TO-COMPUTER
- Improved Speech Recognition
- Improved Artificial Intelligence
- New navigation and manipulation devices

INFRASTRUCTURE
- Broader availability of high-speed networking
- New peer-to-peer "supercomputers"
- Better compression/decompression techniques

COMPUTER-TO-HUMAN
- Improved sensory output including greatly improved 3D video, sense-audio, new haptic (touch) technologies, improved scent technology, and some-day taste technology

CONVERGING TO CREATE THE SENSORY VIRTUAL INTERNET

COLLABORATIVE APPLICATIONS
- Improved Speech Recognition
- Improved Artificial Intelligence
- New navigation and manipulation devices

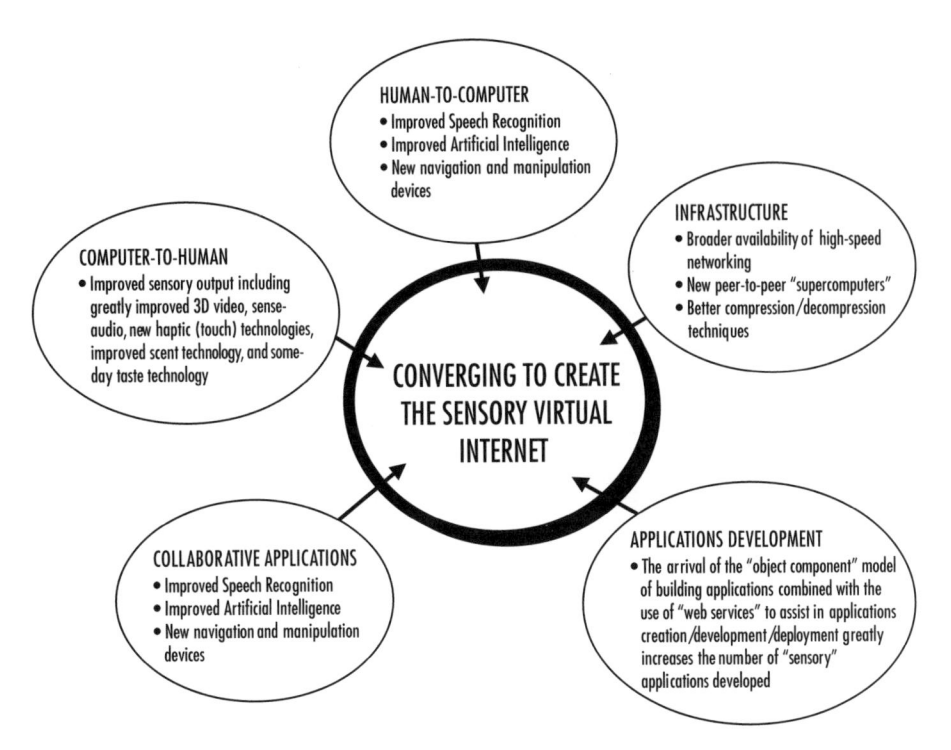

APPLICATIONS DEVELOPMENT
- The arrival of the "object component" model of building applications combined with the use of "web services" to assist in applications creation/development/deployment greatly increases the number of "sensory" applications developed

FIGURE 3
Convergence of Factors Leading to the Sensory Virtual Internet

any real-world practical application. They are dubious that touch and taste technologies will ever work over the Internet, much less have any practical use.

Further, there are plenty of other reasons for doubt. As this book is being written, the United States, one of the premier players in information technology, is flirting with economic recession. Information Technology (IT) spending is flat or decreasing (except for certain initiatives such as business-to-business, system security, and a number of other immediate-return-on-investment projects), and some technology stocks are at an all-time low. A strong argument can be made that this economic malaise will forestall the creation of the Sensory Virtual Internet.

Yes-Way Say I

If you start looking at the rapid pace of application and technology development in human interfaces, high-speed networking, system power, Web Services standards, and collaborative application development, you'll be hard pressed to find how the world's economic woes are slowing down the advance of these technologies. For instance, by some counts there are over 300 *start-ups* involved in speech recognition research alone. The world's economic engines may be idling but there is little evidence that the research and development in the areas of sensory interfaces, faster networks/systems, and the development of Web-based application services have slowed. The same holds true for the advance of the next generation of collaborative computing. These technologies are continuing to advance at a startling pace. One venture capitalist I recently met described six different and distinct collaborative computing start-ups that he had been asked to consider for financing.

What are the factors that lead to the conclusion that the Sensory Virtual Internet is alive and well and continuing to be funded and developed? Observe that:

- *Sensory input is improving*—Most people would agree that using speech and gestures to input our thoughts and desired actions into computers would be far more natural than using a keyboard. Thanks to very significant advances in speech recognition and artificial intelligence as well as new developments in human-to-computer input devices, great strides in speech—enabling our computers to respond to voice commands—are being made. And new devices that aid in navigation and manipulation of objects in 3D worlds are also coming to market. As speech technologies (and other supporting technologies such as expert systems) improve, we will soon find ourselves able to communicate with our computers in a natural manner by using voice commands, speech, and motions as opposed to using complex and cumbersome keyboards.

Speech recognition works—and it is advancing dramatically every year in terms of accuracy and usability. Eventually, using speech recognition and new navigation and manipulation devices, we will be able to input data more easily and more naturally.

- *Sensory computer output is improving*—Advances in 3D display rendering, in speech output (the ability for computers to talk to us), and the arrival of scent and touch technologies are now delivering richer sensory experiences to computer users lucky enough to be able to afford the peripheral devices needed to deliver such sensations.

Due to advances in computer graphics accelerators and graphic programming techniques over the past year, there have been tremendous improvements in the quality of graphics delivered over the Internet.

It is hard to imagine how digital sound can be improved further. Today's digital sound quality is excellent and can already rival the experience of natural sound. Advances are still being made in getting sound to mimic the Doppler effects of the real world (such as reproducing the changing sound of a car passing you by when you are standing on a virtual sidewalk).

Thanks to the use of a printer-like peripheral device that burns various oils to create aromas and scents, scent technology has arrived. The challenge here is broaden the library of scents that can be delivered over the Internet.

Touch technology is already being used by gamers to feel the vibrations of a virtual roadway in a racecar game or to feel the sensation of an enemy plane strafing the gamer's aircraft. Today the touch sensation is primarily used only in such vibration-based applications that are received through our hands, but someday we may be able experience hot and cold or other sensations delivered through body suits to the rest of our bodies.

Eventually taste technology will also become commercially viable. One approach that is being researched is the use of bland potato- or rice-based cards imprinted with taste sensations such as sweetness, bitterness, or others. You just pop a card in your mouth and voilà—you can taste sensations such as salt, bitterness, sweetness, etc. Note that our sense of taste is also greatly influenced by our sense of smell, so expect taste and scent technologies to be used together to deliver a realistic taste sensation. Also note that duplicating texture, or warmth and coldness will also be challenging.

All of these technologies are in various states of maturity, but soon continuing improvements will enable these technologies to enrich our online experience.

- *Computer architecture is being adapted*—Note that sensory technologies create complex data streams (very large files) that place new demands on our computer architecture and infrastructure (systems, platforms, and networks). PCs and workstations are going to need to be modified and optimized for 3D graphics input, capture, and display. Back-end systems will need to be architecturally redesigned to allow for the processing of computationally challenging workloads.

  Now look at the product roadmaps of companies like Intel and AMD. You'll find that PCs and servers are being rearchitected to support the sending and receiving of richer graphics and very large files—files comprised of sensory-rich data. Major changes are underway in PC bus architecture, memory, and graphics capabilities.

  Meanwhile, on the back end, a method of computing known as peer-to-peer processing now allows for the creation of commodity super-computers, which will be needed if our computers are to process sensory-rich data and heavy computational workloads.

Servers are large computers that process data for client PCs or other personal devices—as well as for other servers. Issues related to computing vast amounts of sensory data may force systems architects to configure their servers to handle vast computational versus transactional workloads. Instead of relying on a single server to handle all of the calculations needed to project our movements and provide us with sensory data in virtual space, we are likely to see computer design shift toward the use of hundreds or thousands of computers to handle these calculations. We'll need this combined power to recreate virtual movements or virtual sensations and provide us with rich sensory data as we move about in virtual worlds.

Balancing workload and synchronizing databases have long presented technical challenges to the computing industry, but advances in workload balancing and peer-to-peer processing are evolving to help accommodate the processing of computationally challenging data. Also, a new standard for enabling peer-to-peer computing and networking to take place, known as "InfiniBand," is evolving. Sponsored by Intel and supported by a number of systems, software, and networking companies, InfiniBand creates a platform for networked storage devices, computers, and other network components, knitting them together into a "fabric," wherein computational workload can be readily shared among multiple computers. Initial InfiniBand products have already made their way to market and dozens of new products are set to roll out over the next year.

- *High-speed networking technology is available*—High-speed network connections to the Internet play a vital role in enabling us to send and receive sensory data. *The high-speed interconnection technologies already exist that are needed to deliver a Sensory Virtual Internet.* The real issue in high-speed networking has to do with delivering these technologies over the last mile to users' homes, which has proven to be difficult.

Better access to high-speed services will help speed the delivery of sensory data to our computers and to back-end systems. According to Jupiter Media Metrix, among Internet users in the United States, a cable connection remains the preferred choice for their Internet access, with 3 million people using cable, compared to 1.2 million using DSL and 50,000 to 100,000 using satellite services. Fortunately for those of us who don't have (or won't soon have) access to high-speed broadband services in the near term, other alternative high-speed options are rapidly evolving. These high-speed communications options include wireless communications, satellite communications, fiber to the home, and even powerline.

The primary problem with telephone wire-based broadband services is availability. The companies that own the wires have had some difficulty providing quality installation and maintenance services to many buyers. But this situation is starting to improve as telephone companies improve service practices.

Given these advances and the fact that broadband services are becoming more broadly available, from my perspective it is reasonable to expect that over the next three years the number of people who can and will connect to the Internet using high-speed technologies (including new wireless options) will double.

- *A new way of building applications is evolving*—One important lesson that computer makers generally understand is that hardware and operating systems are meaningless without viable application software. Several companies have learned the hard way that having the world's greatest hardware platform, or even have the world's fastest network connection—even having a huge, state-of-the-art room-sized graphics display system—is not enough to ensure market success. Without worthwhile applications, all of this great technology goes for naught.

A new model for application development—more specifically, application delivery—is evolving. It is known as Web services. Using this model, application writers will be able to pick and choose applications from anywhere on the Internet. After negotiating certain legal distribution and technical connectivity issues, they can integrate these applications easily with existing core applications. This means that application writers will be able to rapidly acquire and integrate new application modules into existing or newly developed applications extremely easily—greatly hastening the delivery of sensory-based applications to the marketplace. This is a profound change in application development. This impending move to Web Services is one of the strongest reasons that I believe that a rich suite of sensory-enriched applications will make it to market more quickly than most people expect!

- *Collaborative applications are being adapted*—The Internet was originally established around the concept of collaboration—making it easier for the early adopters at the Defense department and institutions of higher learning to communicate and work together more effectively. But for the most part, the Internet has since its inception been based on collaboration through character-driven communications (typewritten memos, e-mail, and content). With the addition of new sensory technologies such as touch and scent, and the expansion of existing sensory technologies such as sight (moving from two-dimensional views to three-dimensional views) and sound, the older text-based collaboration applications are about to undergo a radical face-lift as applications become more visually and vocally oriented.

Further, today's state-of-the-art online videoconferencing and meeting software (which represents the first wave of sensory-based virtual collaborative applications) is starting to combine with other collaborative applications—such as project coordination, collaborative product design, e-learning, and workflow management—to create a new category of *collaborative virtual space* or colocation applications. This new generation of applications promises to change the way that humans interact socially with each other, the way we conduct business, the way we learn, and the way we are entertained.

- *Computer systems are becoming easier for the masses to use*—Changes are happening in the human interface, computer design and infrastructure, application development, and collaboration software. The Sensory Virtual Internet will become easier to use thanks to the development of more intuitive, natural human interfaces. And we will have greater accessibility to the Internet than ever before thanks to huge advances in mobile computing and the development of new devices such as wearable computers, new types of handheld and laptop devices, and especially new mobile phone devices. Improvements in wireless and broadband communications will greatly aid the sending and receiving of sensory data. The next generation of sensory-enabled collaborative virtual space applications will greatly enhance our ability to conduct business and commercial endeavors, to learn, to socialize, and to be entertained on the Internet.

Why Do We Need Richer Output?

Why do we need richer output? Because we learn better—and we can make better judgments—when we have multiple sources of stimuli (sight, sound, touch, scent, and taste). The more stimuli, the richer our learning and the better our assessment of computer data will be. This is the long and short of why we need to be able to get more sensory data from our computers.

A Closer Look at Why Sensory Virtual?—The Answer Is . . . Stimuli

Numbers, letters, and two-dimensional graphical data are fine in written reports, but scientists and researchers have long known that deeper human learning and retention occurs when we can make use of two modalities. This can mean using both vision and hearing, for example, and/or additional senses (scent, touch, and taste) to evaluate the information that we are receiving, rather than relying on just one modality. It has long been documented in scientific texts that, other conditions being equal, more learning occurs when information is received simultaneously rather than in a single modality.

So, why do we need more intuitive, natural, sensory data from our computers? The answer has to do with how we learn and assimilate information. Simply stated: *We learn by being stimulated*. Simple forms of learning involve stimulation from a single stimulus—for instance the sound of a voice on a telephone stimulates our audio sense. More complex forms of learning involve the stimulation of multiple senses. For instance, someday when making a routine telephone call we will see the people to whom we are speaking, and we will learn not only from audio stimulus but also from visual stimulus. By receiving more stimuli, we will be able to gather more information and more diverse information. By gathering additional information, we will be able to make more accurate and informed decisions. Making more accurate and informed decisions is good—especially in medical, business, and interpersonal environments.

So, if we learn most effectively using multiple stimuli, how much longer will we be satisfied using computer systems that offer us only static output in character form? Many high-speed Internet users are already being tantalized by the ability to download multimedia streams, by videoconferencing, by 3D games, and by 3D collaborative software. How much longer will the general Internet populace need to wait until we can receive richer visual, audio, olfactory, and haptic data from our computer systems?

This, in a nutshell, is why the availability of increased sensory data is crucial as we look to embark on our journey to future electronic virtual worlds.

The Bottom Line

The multimodal technologies, the network and systems infrastructure, and the application development methodologies needed to build the Sensory Virtual Internet are here today—but in various stages of readiness. The challenge ahead is to find new ways to integrate these technologies with collaborative applications such that we humans can use our computers to communicate and collaborate more easily and in a more natural manner.

CHAPTER 3
Virtual Worlds: Today's State of the Art

Make no mistake, virtual worlds are here today—thousands of them. These precursors and prototypes are, for the most part, implemented as two-dimensional vistas that offer entertainment, socialization, community services, and other activities to constituents and visitors.

One way to examine the state-of-the-technology in virtual worlds is to go to sites such as AOL, Microsoft, or Yahoo! and search on the term "virtual." Each site yields different, but interesting results. The Yahoo! site, for instance, found dozens of virtual site categories with numerous subcategories. Here are some favorites:

- Virtual art galleries (like the Smithsonian Renwick Gallery)

- Virtual beer and brewing (this one will be great some day when scent technology allows virtual you to smell the hops in the virtual concoctions they are making)
- Virtual communities
- Virtual cow-tipping (a practice of sneaking up on a sleeping cow and giving the animal a "little push")
- Virtual kisses
- Virtual labs
- Virtual libraries (there are hundreds of these)
- Virtual malls (there are hundreds of these located around the globe in places like the U.S., China, Eastern and Western Europe, Asia, Africa, and Australia)
- Virtual pets
- Virtual pool (played with other contestants over the Internet)
- Virtual pubs
- Virtual tours (one of Antarctica!)

Source: http://search.yahoo.com/bin/search?p=virtual

If you visit some of these virtual vistas, you'll note that the majority of these virtual worlds are two-dimensional, character-driven, static, and noninteractive—designed primarily for the sharing of information. For instance, hundreds of libraries have listed their inventory on the Internet in text form and have made that inventory searchable—but few provide an interactive 3D avatar assistant to help with queries. Another example would be shopping sites. Again, inventory is listed in character form (occasionally a picture or graphic of a product is included), but for the most part Web-based shopping is a flat, static event.

However, both libraries and shopping sites are moving toward becoming sensory-enabled, starting with 3D virtual world services. Occasionally, advanced implementations of library services can be found that allow visitors to click on various icons, such as library buildings (virtual metaphors) or books, to view data or information in two-dimensional and sometimes three-dimensional modes. Some of these sites call on you to imagine yourself inside a building (a library, a school, a city hall) or some

Chapter 3: Virtual Worlds: Today's State of the Art

other metaphorical place. You can actually see yourself moving through three-dimensional worlds. You can even pick a book off of a shelf and perhaps find a multimedia file attached to it.

Soon you may be able to verbally ask your computer to find information for you.

> One Voice Technologies, a California company, recently announced the general availability of a voice interactive human interface for computers and the Internet. Users can talk to the company's Intelligent Voice Animated Navigator (IVAN) and IVAN will bring you to any Web site. IVAN can find Web sites for any given topic and will guide you through the site and help find requested information using intuitive voice commands.
>
> Source: http://www.onevoicetech.com

The important point to be made here is that rudimentary virtual worlds do exist. Most are two-dimensional, but many are moving toward three-dimensional site structures. People are visiting these sites. The major motivation for these visits today is to gather information or to shop. However, as technology matures, that reason will most likely change to include work, shop, play, socialize, learn, and otherwise collaborate.

More Advanced Virtual World Sites

In the less mature, two-dimensional worlds (characterized by primitive virtual malls) you can move from shop to shop in character mode and look at two-dimensional graphics or photographs of the objects you may be considering for purchase. Clicking on objects or text on the screen dictates your movements. There is no concept of the virtual you moving through virtual vistas to get to the location you desire.

The more mature worlds are spatial, characterized by advanced 3D graphics handling, virtual people and places, voice-driven (not character-driven) chat, and the ability to pick up and manipulate objects in 3D space. As the virtual you visits these sites, you will find serious and/or wild-and-crazy vistas through which to traverse. You will find avatars (virtual representations of yourself and other people) with whom you can speak. You'll find stores where you can pick up and examine objects in virtual space.

My three favorite advanced sites include Worlds.com, blaxxun's Cybertown.com, and ActiveWorlds.com. These sites represent the most mature examples of virtual world sites in the industry today. If you choose to visit any of these sites, look closely and you will find that people are already congregating in 3D virtual environments on the Web, sharing thoughts and ideas, engaging in idle conversation, flirting with members of the opposite sex, building 3D vistas, and otherwise using these sites as a source of entertainment and socialization.

These community-based sites (so named because they encourage membership) allow members to explore, find, and live in virtual communities with people who have like interests and enjoy discussing topics ranging from religion to politics, from science to the weather, and a whole lot more. Interestingly, these people are starting to co-reside in virtual reality, sharing virtual real estate together. Virtual real estate is actually just disk space on some computer somewhere, but people are using that disk space to store virtual homes with virtual artifacts in virtual neighborhoods.

Visit these sites and you will find thriving communities that operating in a 3D-like mode complete with interesting vistas, shopping, and chat sessions. People love these experimental-experiential environments. These environments are novel, interesting, and represent prototypes of what the Sensory Internet of the future will become. These new 3D virtual reality worlds are fun to explore. And because they are novel, they have a characteristic that Web site developers refer to as "stickiness," which means that they encourage people to come and stay for a longer time than they do on sites with collections of static Web pages. Often visitors stay two and sometimes three times as long as they would on a visit to even the most popular portal sites like Lycos and Yahoo!.

> Initial surveys by Jupiter Media Metrix of 3D community sites versus some of the most popular 2D portal sites revealed that visitors are likely to stay two to three times as long on 3D sites as they are on portal sites like Yahoo!, or even on game sites like that of Electronic Arts, or information sites like CNET. At one point, Media Metrix, a trend measurement firm (part of Jupiter), found that virtual visitors remained on virtual sites much longer than on character-driven sites. My conclusion is that people prefer having access to richer graphical information and voice-driven chat over character-driven conversations and flat, static screens.
> Source:http://www.worlds.com/aboutus/investorsinfo.html#valueprop

If you extrapolate a bit, it is pretty clear that these communities will become hubs that attract demographically and ideologically identifiable visitors. This in turn will attract advertisers and retailers—and trade will thus enter the virtual Internet. Once you have explored some of these sites, you'll quickly understand how easy it will be to build shopping venues, business meeting places, doctor/lawyer/consultant offices, and other commercial/service facilities in virtual reality. Before long, you will be spending less time in traffic and waiting rooms. Soon you will obtain virtually from your own home or office the same types of services that you used to spend hours trying to obtain physically. In short, the basic technology foundation exists for the formation of a full-blown Sensory Virtual Internet. The business model that will help make this Internet a reality is also starting to come together.

As exciting as the newly evolving virtual worlds will be, there is still a lot of technological advancement that needs to take place for these worlds to reach what I would call a truly Sensory Virtual state. If you have had the opportunity to visit any of these 3D virtual worlds, you may have found certain obstacles that made your 3D virtual world experience less than optimal. You may have noticed network performance problems (manifested in choppy movement through 3D worlds). Or you may have observed that some sites can only handle character-driven chat sessions as opposed to voice-driven sessions. You may have found navigation and manipulation complex and unnatural. You most definitely would not have experienced touch, scent, or taste sensations—even at the most advanced commercial virtual world sites.

The Virtual Worlds: Plenty of Room for Improvement

If you could compare a visit to today's virtual worlds to a visit to the most advanced 3D world environments of only one year ago, you would observe how much networking, graphics, and application programs have improved. You will also understand how much they can improve over a very short period of time.

Last year,

- From a networking perspective, most Internet users only had low-speed access (less than 56 Kb line speed) to virtual world environments. Although 56 Kb modems are rated to provide 56 Kb speed, it is highly likely that most users were receiving substantially less than 56 Kb line speed—most probably in the 30 Kbps to 40 Kbps range. At this speed, 3D data file delivery for many virtual visitors was more than likely quite choppy.
- Most PCs (or other receiving devices such as handhelds and surprisingly laptops) could not adequately present rich 3D graphics. Often this would limit user access to a barely satisfactory two-dimensional graphical display of 3D world environments. Last year, the lack of good graphics accelerators built into PCs or other devices made many 3D worlds visually unimpressive and, at times, difficult to navigate.

Do you want to see the combined effects of slow network speed, mediocre graphics handling, and lack of application selection on the Internet today? If you've got access from work to a high-speed Internet connection, but have a low-speed connection from home, try this. If your home computer processes data on a CPU with less than 500 MHz and is connected to the Internet at a speed of less than 56 Kb and has a graphics controller with less than 16 Mb of memory, try connecting to Worlds.com, ActiveWorld, or Cybertown. You'll find the experience to be a bit protracted. Now find a high-speed Internet connection and use a PC with plenty of memory, at least a 750 MHz processor, and a decent 3D graphics accelerator. The difference is night and day—the more powerful PC will experience richer graphics and better overall performance (less choppiness as you navigate through the site you chose) thanks to better graphics and systems processors on many commercial systems and faster network connections.

- Navigation and manipulation of 3D objects in virtual worlds was cumbersome.
- The mixing of voice and graphics creates large files that, when sent over the Internet, can be network-intensive—bogging down network connections, resulting in poor application performance as well as quality degradation. Last year's virtual worlds had not yet deployed Voice over IP (VoIP) technology—the technology needed to drive voice over the Internet. Even today, at several sites the virtual you will still need to converse with other virtual world members using character-driven chat sessions because many virtual world sites have still not mastered sending voice and complex graphics over the Internet simultaneously.
- Not many applications existed that would allow visitors to work together collaboratively in a sensory-rich fashion. At best, you could see an avatar of a person with whom you were having a discussion in a public forum—

a situation not well suited to private business meetings nor classroom education.

If you evaluated virtual world sites last year, you would have found that they were primarily organized around social and entertainment activities. Few commercial or collaborative applications were in existence. Commercial usage of virtual worlds to create floor space at virtual malls, entertainment events like concerts or pay-per-view activities, or collaborative environments like schools were all in their infancy.

In short, last year virtual worlds were an amusement—a place where people could go to socialize or to be entertained. Only those visitors with high-speed connections and good graphical interfaces were able to have optimal experiences. Because most applications and services (such as shopping, video streaming, and other forms of entertainment) lacked maturity, most visitors treated virtual worlds like glorified Internet 3D chat rooms—something to experiment with but not something viable for commercial use.

This Year: Demonstrable Progress

Having identified many issues and obstacles that could obstruct our path to a sensory-rich, Sensory Virtual Internet, it would be easy at this point for a reader to put this book down and conclude that correcting these technical deficiencies will not occur in our lifetimes. *But don't despair. Every one of these shortcomings is in the process of being addressed.*

For instance, over the past several months advances in high-speed networking have taken place (especially in 802.11 wireless communications); strategic plans have been announced for the next generation in graphics accelerators (and consolidation has taken place in the graphics processing industry); a roadmap has been developed for the complete architectural redesign of the personal computer; and a number of advances have taken place in speech recognition and artificial intelligence that improve overall speech recognition accuracy and computer response. Additionally, new products have been announced in the areas of screen navigation and in the manipulation of 3D images. Processing speed continues to improve—and peer-to-peer processing is making a comeback (this time as a way to help create supercomputer-like computing complexes, which could offer the processing power needed to help millions of virtual avatars move through the virtual worlds of the future).

In short, high-speed network access is becoming more broadly available; graphics processing is advancing rapidly; PC architecture is changing to accommodate the processing of complex sensory data streams; back-end systems are joining together to process large volumes of computational data; and new collaborative applications that can take advantage of these technologies are evolving!

High-Speed Networking: The Primary Obstacle Is Being Overcome

The biggest obstacle to our enjoyment of virtual worlds is related to high-speed networking. It is, in my opinion, the primary complicating factor that prevents the greater use of 3D and sensory technologies today. Most Internet users have access to the Internet at speeds between 28.8 Kb and 56 Kb (which happen to be the most common dial-up speeds). Transferring large files (as sensory data files tend to be) frequently leads to poor, choppy, cumbersome, and visually disjointed performance on the receiving computer. If you are lucky enough to already have access to high-speed broadband Internet service (with network service in the millions of bits per second[1]), your sensory Internet experience will be markedly improved.

---

1. Quick note: A bit is an on or off signal. These on or off signals, when combined in groups (usually groups of 8, 16, 32, or 64), comprise a "byte" of data. A bit is like a character, a byte is like a word. Bits or bytes can be sent over communication networks at speeds ranging from the low thousands of bits per second to millions of bytes per second.

On the positive side, high-speed networking is becoming more broadly available to prospective users of the Sensory Virtual Internet. And, as network access becomes faster, computers will be able to send and receive rich sensory data far more easily than they can today.

On the negative side, instead of prices moving downward as the volume of users increases, cable and high-speed phone connections are starting to move up in price in certain areas of the world. In the United States, Digital Subscriber Loop (DSL) connections (high-speed telephone wire connections) to the Internet are moving from around $49 per month to $59 per month at many high-speed Internet service providers. This trend does not bode well for getting high-speed access into middle- and low-income homes.

The technologies needed to provide high-speed data transfer are available today. The bottom line is that the industry has a distribution problem related to trying to provide high-speed services to the people who want to buy such service. This is called "the last mile" problem and is covered in depth in the networking section of this book. From a networking perspective, several technologies will help provide high-speed networking to home and mobile users. Home-based Internet users will soon have greater access to DSL and Asynchronous Digital Subscriber Loop (ADSL), fixed wireless 802.11b, and satellite technologies. Over the next five years, mobile users will find that connection speeds for Internet access will reach well beyond the 2 megabytes per second range, up from only thousands of bytes (9.6 or 19.2 kilobytes per second) today.

The Need for New Navigation and Manipulation Devices Is Being Addressed

Another obstacle that has inhibited the growth of the Sensory Virtual Internet is related to navigating around and manipulating objects within virtual 3D worlds. Input peripherals (such as mice or joysticks) were originally designed to provide screen navigation in a two-dimensional world. This makes many existing virtual reality sites cumbersome and awkward to navigate. Although these devices may suffice in the short term, improved navigational devices—such as sensor-driven hand controls and body suits and other new 3D immersion technologies—need to be further developed to enable three-dimensional movement (up/down, forward/backward, in/out) in a more natural, human manner through electronic 3D environments. Several innovative approaches that involve navigation in virtual worlds and the manipulation of 3D objects in those worlds are covered in Part III.

Graphic Handling Issues Are Being Addressed

If you got beyond performance issues related to slow network access speed last year, you were likely faced with another constraint related to graphics presentation. In order to take advantage of 3D visual effects and some of the new sensory-enriched multimedia applications, you need a good graphics accelerator in your PC or mobile device. For most new PCs, 3D graphics cards now come standard. But for those of us with older PCs, it is likely that we will have to upgrade our computer's graphics processor. This means that we will have to buy a new graphics accelerator PC card—or like accelerator card for other devices—to handle the 3D graphics requirements in the future.

Very significant advances in graphics acceleration (as well as improvements in compression and decompression techniques) have been made over the past year. At the same time, major consolidation of vendors has taken place in the industry. Both these changes greatly improve the 3D effects that virtual world companies can deliver to Internet visitors. Dramatic improvements have also occurred in the ability of PC graphics accelerators to process graphics as evidenced by the following:

> Look really closely at a picture in a newspaper, and you'll see tiny little dots called "pixels." When shaded or colored, pixels make up a picture on your PC's monitor. Today's PC graphics cards are doubling in performance every six months. One of the hottest commodity PC cards today, the nVidia GeForce2, can process 800 million pixels per second, 1.6 billion texels per second (whatever those are), and 25 million polygons per second (polygons are used for color and texture effects). This performance and graphics presentation range is starting to approach the performance of dedicated game consoles. For instance, the brand-new Sony PlayStation 2 can process 20 million polygons when using lighting, texture, z buffering, and alpha blending effects. Compared with nVidia's 25 million polygons per second, the PlayStation 2 can still process more raw polygons per second—up to 75 million. The key point is that PC technology is getting closer to the processing speed of dedicated game consoles.

This year's advances were eye-popping. Future graphics accelerator roadmaps promise graphics that are even more astounding!

The Voice over IP (VoIP) Picture Is Changing

In the past, IS managers have found that sending voice and data over the same communications lines has been inefficient. Often voice quality suffered. New data compression techniques combined with better network utilization and bigger network pipes are already leading to acceptable levels of performance and almost-equivalent-to-analog quality within enterprise Intranet environments. At some future point the cost delta for running voice and data over the same network will shift in favor of digitized voice, making digitized voice a preferred technology for audio communications. For many voice/data network managers today, the cost to rebuild the physical network to accommodate voice can be prohibitive. This will change as costs for digital switching equipment come down and as networks gradually improve to accommodate additional digital (as opposed to analog) data traffic.

A Shift in Configuration and Optimization to Handle Complex Computational Tasks Is Underway

Since its beginning, the primary commercial focus of computing has been on transaction processing—the processing of information related to recording transactions at a cash register, balancing bank accounts, or even providing access to a commercial Web page. On the other hand, colleges and universities, oil explorers (using geographical information systems), and pharmaceutical companies have used computing to handle advanced computational tasks involving modeling and rendering of information.

Virtual worlds today make use of both types of computing—transaction-based to handle subscriber's requests (for instance, to process the purchase of items at a virtual store) and computationally based to render 3D images of virtual visitors in 3D vistas.

To handle the thousands, and ultimately millions, of individuals that are going to be accessing the Sensory Virtual Internet, computers will be required to adapt and optimize for computational processing tasks. Back-end computers will need to be capable of processing very large files (instead of small transactions) efficiently and then packaging those files for delivery over the Internet, sometimes to receiving devices such as PCs, laptops, Palms, or handheld devices. In other words, back-end computers will have to do a tremendous amount of graphics, manipulation, and navigational processing while front-end devices will largely be concerned with decompression and presentation activities.

The reason that running sensory-rich virtual world environments is computationally challenging is that millions upon millions of calculations need to be performed to represent objects in 3D spatial environments. Add to this task the need to include speech, scent, and touch data and you can easily see how files could become large, unwieldy, and computationally complex.

New ways of configuring computer systems to optimize them for computationally heavy tasks are now being perfected. Improvements in distributed computing architecture—and the rebirth of something called peer-to-peer computing or "grid" computing—hold the promise of enabling enterprises to create virtual supercomputers by linking hundreds of servers together to process computationally intensive tasks. Peer-to-peer computing is covered in greater depth in Chapter 12.

A lot of this complex sensory data processing will have to be performed by back-end servers—servers that the virtual you will connect to on the other side of the Internet. Today we are used to running our graphically rich PC applications locally. We are all going to have to think seriously about moving our graphics and navigation/manipulation processing to a service provider model, where many of our applications will run on back-end servers rather than on our desktops. A complete discussion of the changes in computer design and infrastructure is included in Part IV.

Collaboration

Last year, advances in collaboration at virtual world sites were a big surprise. In 2000, few sites were doing anything particularly interesting in e-learning. But in 2001, colleges, universities, and other educational institutions as well as business began to invest and experiment rather heavily in virtual learning environments. ActiveWorlds, for instance, had few e-learning customers in 2000 but now boasts over 100 distance learning or e-learning customers. Also in 2001, businesses started to make heavier use of Virtual World sites to provide training and education to workers and customers over the Internet. In 2001, prototypical collaborative Sensory Virtual Internet learning-oriented sites had clearly arrived.

Chapter Summary:
Positive Changes on All Fronts

Virtual worlds are here, but there are several shortcomings. These have to do with the human interface, performance, VoIP, navigation, manipulation, and others. These shortcomings must be overcome in order to provide the rich sensory experience that the Sensory Virtual Internet is being designed to deliver.

The good news is that the basic technologies that we will need to make these improvements already exist—albeit not in a unified, integrated form. You can, today, hop on the Internet and visit virtual vistas, chat with other people while viewing them in a 3D-like mode, go shopping at virtual stores, and even consult with knowledgeable techies while residing in virtual worlds located in virtual space. You can play 3D games that let you to feel the sway in your virtual car as you take a turn too quickly, or that simulate a little of the impact of bullets on the fuselage of your plane as you fly through enemy territory. You can smell the heady aromas as you prance through a field of poppies with Dorothy, the Cowardly Lion, the Tin Man, and the Scarecrow. The task at hand will be to find ways to integrate these basic sensory technologies with useful applications—most specifically, collaborative applications.

Still, how do we address these technology readiness/accessibility/design/infrastructure issues to allow us to get high-quality access to the Sensory Virtual Internet? To get to where we need to be in building a sensory-enabled virtual Internet, we:

1. *Must find alternative-to-keyboarding ways to input* instructions and content into computers. In other words,

we need a more intuitive, natural, speech-driven human interface to computer systems.
2. *Must make our computers capable of providing us with sensory-enriched output* (visually rich 3D graphics, improved audio, touch, and scent) so that we can use all appropriate senses to gather, assess, and act on the data we receive.
3. *Must improve high-speed access to the Internet.*
4. *Prepare to adopt a different computing architectural model* based upon use of back-end servers (servers that belong to a company that hosts applications on the other side of the Internet for us). We need these high-end servers to handle the very complex computational load created when generating rich sensory data. We'll have to optimize our front-end devices (such as desktops, laptops, Palms, handhelds, mobile phones, and specialty devices) for graphics presentation and other sensory presentation services. Back-end servers will be responsible for dealing with the huge amount of computationally intensive application processing, data stream compression, storage, and delivery of 3D and sensory services to front-end devices.
5. *Need to encourage the development of applications that integrate sensory technologies with core, mainstream applications.* We need more sensory-rich applications.
6. *Need sensory information to be integrated with collaborative applications.* Remember, without applications, all of the preceding technological improvements will go for naught.

Now that you understand how virtual worlds operate and what their strengths and weaknesses are, the next part will examine how and when we'll see the improvements needed to build a sensory-enabled virtual Internet.

Part II: Technology Roadmap

The Sensory Virtual Internet age in computing is near. Virtual worlds already provide decent 3D images of virtual visitors in virtual vistas. And simultaneous voice and 3D graphics are available at some virtual world sites. These technologies, if available, work pretty well together, provided that the user has a high-speed network connection.

But there's more to virtual worlds and creating a Sensory Virtual Internet than 3D imagery and sound. Human interface technologies need to be improved and computer architecture and infrastructure need to be redesigned and reconfigured to accommodate the processing of very complex sensory data streams. Network speed needs to be improved. Once the network pathways are put in place to efficiently send and receive sensory data, applications need to be developed that will accept and deliver rich sensory data. When this happens, we will then use this new sensory-rich virtual Internet environment in a collaborative fashion for business, entertainment, learning, and socializing.

So, you might ask, how do we get to the Sensory Virtual Internet age? What are the technological milestones that must be achieved? In what timeframes will I see which products impacting the market? When will these changes take place? How?

What Is This Part About?

To get to a sensory-rich implementation of the Sensory Virtual Internet, advances in the following technologies need to take place:

- *Human Interfaces*—From an input perspective, advances in speech recognition, navigation, and manipulation need to take place. From an output perspective, new sensory peripherals (scent devices or haptic devices) need to be developed and integrated with sensory-enabled applications.

- *System Architecture and Infrastructure*—Computer architecture (how, for instance, PCs are built and optimized for the handling of sensory data) as well as support infrastructure (e.g., high-speed networking, peer-to-peer processing, etc.) have to be modified to optimally process sensory data. High-speed Internet access will have to become more broadly available.
- *Web Services and Collaborative Applications*—A new generation of applications needs to be designed that uses the new Web Services approach to application development to provide the virtual you with sensory-enriched data. These Web Services will drive the creation of a new generation of virtual space collaborative colocation applications.

Chapter 4 represents a possible roadmap of when the technologies that will help form the Sensory Virtual Internet will become "market viable."

What I Hope You'll Learn

I hope that by showing you what changes to expect, and when to expect them, this section will at a minimum help strategic planners figure out how to best exploit the new Internet technologies for their enterprise's benefit.

I also hope that by studying this roadmap, you will be able to learn where various technologies fit in the big picture so that when you hear a product announcement or read an article about a new technology or service, you'll understand where it fits and how it contributes to the building of a fully realized Sensory Virtual Internet.

CHAPTER 4

THE SENSORY VIRTUAL INTERNET ROADMAP

Improvements in human-to-computer interfaces, infrastructure (especially high-speed networking and back-end processing), and application development (including the advent of Web services and the creation of colocation-capable collaborative applications) are leading to the creation of the Sensory Virtual Internet (as illustrated in Figure 4).

How and when are these changes going to happen? When will the market move from plain old dial-up service (low-speed connections to the Internet) to alternative, high-speed, broadband solutions? When will collaborative colocation applications be available? When will Web Services take off? What applications will be hot in what year?

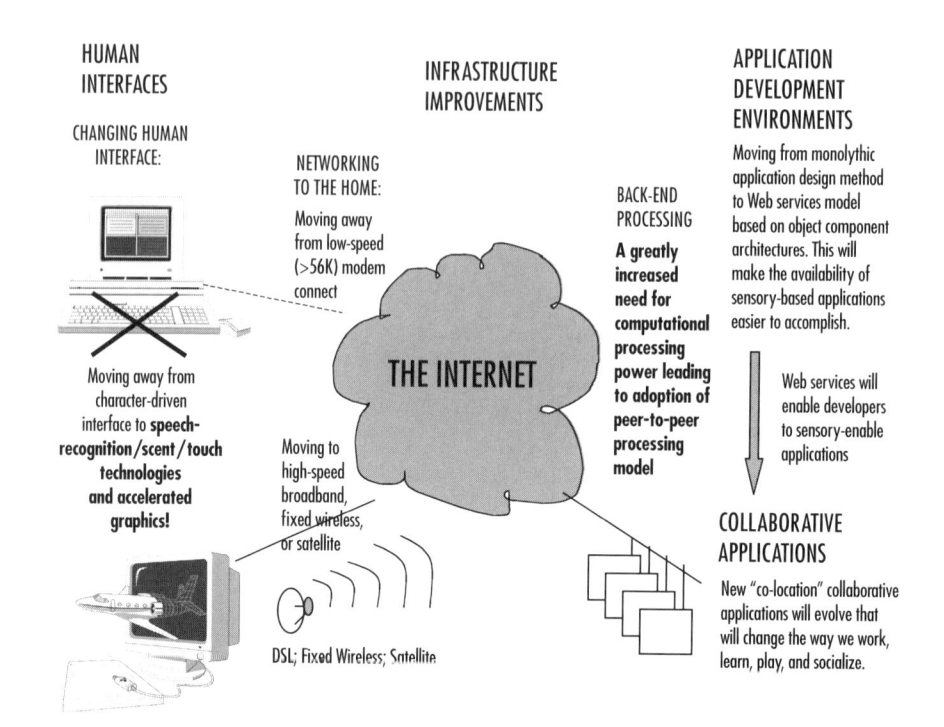

FIGURE 4
The Creation of the Sensory Virtual Internet

How and When Will This Happen?

How will the Sensory Virtual Internet be rolled out to the market? What technologies will become popular—and when? When will fully sensory virtual applications be available? These and related questions are the topics of this chapter. These projections represent my best guess, and the logic behind these projections are expanded upon in depth in subsequent chapters throughout the rest of the book.

Projected Roll-out of the Sensory Virtual Internet

Figure 5 represents the various developments that can be expected over the next few years as improved human interfaces, improved infrastructure, improved application development

Figure 5—Sensory Virtual Internet Roadmap

	TODAY	2002	2003	2004
Human Interfaces to/from Computer Systems	Command-and-control speech recognition; Voice over IP (VoIP).	Speech recognition—mobile devices; new navigation and manipulation devices.	Command and control of PCs and servers (manageability); arrival of commercial scent technology; new touch devices.	Dictation systems are perfected; commercial taste technology starts to arrive on the scene.
Infrastructure Improvements	High-speed networking.	Massive upgrade of graphics subsystems; back-end peer-to-peer grid architecture evolves.	Ongoing cycle of faster networking (with big advances in mobile high-speed technology); continued peer-to-peer upgrades; PC power/graphics upgrades.	Ongoing infrastructure improvements.
Application Development Environments	The onset of Web Services.	Web Services start to take hold; key sensory technologies that will be adopted will be 3D visual and audio.	Web Services applications start to adopt scent and touch technologies. Traditional application environments adopt speech and 3D video.	Web Services applications start to adopt taste technologies.
Collaborative Applications	Already making use of video and audio services today (in games and videoconferencing).	Extensions for "co-location." Aggressive adoption of 3D audio/video in retailing. Continued integration of program/project management.	Automated camera control. Integration with other sensory technologies (smell and touch). Continued integration of program/project management.	Full sensory experiences.
"Hot Applications"	Games; videoconferencing.	Games; videophone; videoconferencing; streamed media; e-learning.	All preceding plus "Collaborative Virtual Business" and "Collaborative Virtual Commerce," and V-Learning.	V-everything.

techniques, and new collaborative applications create the Sensory Virtual Internet.

The State of the Sensory Virtual Internet Today

User Interfaces

Today, from a user interface perspective, you can already have a pleasurable sensory experience at sites like Worlds.com, ActiveWorld, or blaxxun's Cybertown. Gamers can play any of a number of interactive 3D games at sites such as Microsoft's Gaming Zone. Virtual you can visit 3D virtual vistas, build virtual homes and businesses on virtual real estate, and socialize in a wide variety of virtual venues. Businesspeople can use these networks to conduct videoconferencing. It is possible today to make use of 3D sensory output from computers. Voice over IP (VoIP) is available for videoconferencing (and even game-playing). In addition, you can use speech commands to control your computer's command-and-control systems (for instance, phone answering systems or some customer service systems). The first round of user interface sensory technologies have already made their appearance!

Infrastructure

Today, high-speed networking is readily available in large metropolitan areas. It is also becoming more broadly available in suburban and rural settings.

The mass availability of high-speed networking is a vital part of making the Sensory Virtual Internet a reality. High-speed networking is crucial to the formation of the Sensory Virtual Internet because as the "pipeline" into your home becomes bigger, more and more sensory-rich data can flow through it from Internet sites including rich 3D graphics, audio, and streaming media (such as movies). Additionally, Internet users will finally be able to make use of videophone services to send high-quality images of themselves to others over the Internet complete with high-quality audio—as opposed to today's videophone/videoconferencing services, which often suffer from the limitations of home low-speed network connections.

Worthy of note is that most high-speed networking today is based on broadband wiring—either via cable or telephone line. Satellite high-speed service is just now starting to take off as upload and download speeds are increasing to the point where they can be competitive with wired solutions. Also, note that wireless communication speed is orders of magnitude behind landline solutions, generally not exceeding 19.2 Kbps. Without higher-speed wireless technology, mobile devices will not be able to provide rich sensory experiences to mobile users.

Collaborative Applications

At this stage in the development of the Sensory Virtual Internet, collaborative applications are largely text-based workflow type applications, videoconferencing, or e-learning-related. E-learning is expected to see strong growth during the remainder of 2001 and throughout 2002. However, the big changes that need to take place to enable collaborative colocation applications that include rich, sensory-enabled sight, sound, touch, scent, and taste are still a few years away. High-speed network access, better graphics handling, and computationally oriented computing need to go mainstream in order to advance the state of collaborative applications.

In 2002

User Interfaces

In 2002, user interface design will continue to improve with the development and commercial availability of new biofeedback input devices. This year will also see the rise of speech-driven access to the Internet using mobile phone devices to access character-oriented information that resides in databases. In fact, IBM is already delivering this type of speech front end for their back-end WebSphere Internet application servers.

Infrastructure

The year 2002 will bring great advances in systems infrastructure. Peer-to-peer processing, a newly revamped form of distributed computing, will start to make inroads in enterprises that are looking to exploit computing power they have already purchased but are not using effectively. And it is reasonable to expect that much of the additional computing power gained by using peer-to-peer methods will be dedicated to providing the computing power needed to enable a virtual you to travel and shop in virtual venues.

2002 will also bring incredible advances in graphics processing as graphics accelerators continue to double in processing power every six months. This phenomenon will assuredly lead to the ability to generate extremely realistic 3D imagery in games and in virtual venues.

One of the biggest obstacles to building integrated multimodal solutions has been that low-speed networks cannot support the large data steams that are generated by the creation of rich sensory files. As high-speed networking is more broadly adopted, this issue will subside.

Application Development

The next obstacle to be overcome is the lack of expertise in the development community in constructing multimodal applications. Few developers have a solid working knowledge of how to integrate sound, scent, touch, and 3D video technologies. And fewer still can build systems from scratch that can present a completely integrated multimodal experience.

This is where the concept of Web Services comes into play. Newly evolved Web standards known as UDDI, WSDL, and SOAP (covered in depth in Part V) are expected to contribute greatly to enabling applications to work cooperatively in a program-to-program and data sharing mode.

> Web Services are application connectors that enable applications to work cooperatively with other applications. They do so using newly evolved Internet standards: UDDI, WSDL, and SOAP.
>
> - Universal Description, Discovery, and Integration (UDDI) is a "directory standard" that allows applications to be listed and located from public or private directories.
> - WSDL (Web Services Description Language) is a *descriptor standard* that allows applications to describe to other applications its interface and interaction rules.
> - SOAP (Simple Object Access Protocol) provides the basic program-to-program "middleware glue" that enables applications to bind together and commence program-to-program communications.
>
> These standards are important because they enable applications to share data over the Internet more easily than traditional approaches. By so doing, they have the promise of enabling a new model for computing, where applications can use other freely available application modules to perform services for the main application.

The basic concept is that developers will be able to assemble sensory-rich multimodal applications from application components that can be found in public libraries on the Internet. If used properly, these assembled components will result in the creation of a myriad of sensory-rich applications. We will see a flood of these sensory-rich applications hit the market—a renaissance unparalleled in the history of previous application development.

In 2002, expect the concept of Web standards to begin to take hold, standards that enable applications to work cooperatively with one another over the Internet. In subsequent years, large libraries of sensory application components will be made available to application developers. And these libraries will enable developers to easily assemble sensory-rich applications.

Collaborative Applications

E-learning will continue to be one of the strongest growth areas for collaborative applications, but a new class of business software will also make a strong showing in 2002: colocation software. Colocation software uses metaphorical programs to create places of business, places of worship, or other meeting places that people can easily identify and navigate. For instance, colocation software would allow a virtual organization of geographically distributed workers to convene in a virtual business location, complete with a reception desk, conference rooms for meetings and briefings, and individuals' offices. The availability of collaborative colocation software will have a huge positive impact on the acceptance of the Sensory Virtual Internet.

V-commerce

In addition to colocation software, 2002 will bring out the early adopters of "v-commerce" software—software designed to leverage colocation software to create virtual shopping malls or professional locations (for lawyers, consultants, and other professionals). V-commerce applications will allow you to see, hear, touch, and smell in virtual venues. V-commerce also includes transaction software to conduct business. However, the real pick up in v-commerce software adoption will not happen until late in 2003.

In 2003

User Interfaces

From a user interface perspective, 2003 marks the timeframe when the operating system software arrives that will enable us to verbally issue commands to our PCs and mobile devices and have those devices respond accordingly.

Meanwhile, speech recognition and Artificial Intelligence will not be standing still. It is reasonable to expect that speech recognition technology will improve in accuracy as well as in packaging, moving to a component model in order to be more easily deployed as a Web Service. This will enable it to be used in thousands of different applications.

Infrastructure Development

2003 will see peer-to-peer infrastructure development become more prevalent as system security concerns are mitigated. On the personal level, PCs should be approaching 4 to 6 GHz speeds with commensurately faster bus architectures and graphics processing capabilities.

Application Development

If 2002 was the year for early adopters to experiment with Web Services technologies, 2003 will definitely be the year when Web Services become more mainstream. In 2003 expect to see sensory-enabled applications gain in popularity as hundreds of sensory components become available to application developers, and as developers integrate 3D visual, audio, and scent applications with core user interface components. Still, it won't be until 2004 that Web Services see broad market acceptance and increased utilization by the smaller businesses.

Collaborative Applications

2003 will usher in the age of Collaborative V-business—a term that will refer to the ability to conduct business in virtual person with your customers and business partners in sensory-rich environments. Collaborative v-commerce will see rapid adoption rates as competitors vie for new ways to delight and entertain their customers.

In late 2003, the first commercially attractive (from a price perspective) intelligent robotic cameras and related software will arrive. These cameras will help orchestrate meetings, switching from speaker to speaker as dictated by spoken and motion cues.

In 2004

User Interfaces

2004 will be the heyday for the Sensory Virtual Internet as most sensory output technologies will have matured to the point where 3D sight and sound, smell, touch, and (this is a strong maybe) taste peripherals will become broadly available and commercially affordable. Clever packaging by the makers of sensory technology hardware and software solutions will enable the widespread use of these technologies over widely available high-speed Internet connections.

On the human-input-to-computers side of the equation, speech recognition will reach a level of sophistication that will enable people to dictate to their computers with a high degree of accuracy and manipulate text more easily than today. Additionally, computer operating systems that respond to spoken directives will have also improved, making it vastly easier for people to command, control, and manage their own personal computing devices.

Infrastructure

Expect to see personal computers in the 7 Ghz range with incredible amounts of local storage (over 100 gigabytes in the average new PC). These will allow for capturing, manipulating, and sending large files—the kind of files created by sensory technologies.

On the back end, expect to see very large server/storage/network farms develop using the industry's newly evolved Infiniband standard—a standard that helps form a networking/computing/storage fabric for the sharing of available computing power, storage, and networking bandwidth. As this standard is adopted, expect the resulting increase in processing power to allow greater support for large populations of avatars in sensory-rich virtual world environments.

Application Development

The Web Services approach to application development will be in full swing by 2004, with all segments of business (small, medium, and large) adopting this approach to expand their application offerings and to open new business opportunities. Speech-enabled applications will start to become commonplace. Scent-based applications will also gain in acceptance—especially with shoppers and gamers. It is, however, unclear at this point whether taste technology will be mature enough to enter mainstream applications.

Collaborative Applications

By 2004, collaborative applications will have matured to the point where colocation functionality will have become a standard feature. This type of technology will enable businesses to find new ways to conduct commerce, it will enable new forms of entertainment, and it will be heavily exploited as an approach to e-learning.

By this time, prices for the hardware, software, and related deployment services needed to establish virtual offices should start to come down, making it possible for individual businesspeople to run their own virtual offices. It is more likely, however, that virtual you will start using collaborative applications hosted by application service providers (ASPs) because ASPs can amortize the cost of deploying and managing complex virtual environments across many customers and manage virtual environments more effectively than individuals or small businesses.

Are These Projections Believable?

Getting to this new Sensory Virtual Internet is going to be quite a challenge. It will require upgrading network infrastructure such that the virtual you can get access to high-speed networking at home or in a mobile setting. It may require systems/platforms and other Internet device upgrades to handle complex 3D graphics and sensory data. Furthermore, a slew of new applications will need to be built in order to attract and service millions of virtual avatars in 3D worlds.

Can It Be Done?

Read the following chapters on human interfaces to and from computers, infrastructure, application development, and collaborative applications—and you, like me, may find yourself believing that the Sensory Virtual Internet is not only achievable, but also imminent.

Part III: Human Interfaces

Lesson 1 from Biology, Anthropology, Psychology, and Sociology 101 courses: Humans are social animals. We have a strong need to communicate and interact with each other. When we communicate, we rely on visual clues, audio inflections, and even scent and touch to help us determine whether the information that we are receiving is accurate or illusory.

So here's the problem. As we increasingly use computer technology as a means of communication—whether it be through voice mail, electronic mail, or some other form of written or character-driven communications—we lose *context*. For the most part, we interface with today's computer technologies through character-driven screens—screens that deprive us of the ability to make use of all our senses to gather additional information. From a graphics perspective, images that we view are often two-dimensional (possessing height and width but lacking depth). Hence we can't use our visual senses to determine accurately an object's size, depth, or distance away. A typical e-mail lacks inflection (is the sender happy, sad, angry, sarcastic?). Hence written e-mails can only deliver literal meaning. Yet in normal conversation we humans hear a great wealth of inflections that conduct the speaker's tone, mood, and intent (so we know if that person is displeased, happy, or whatever). If we're talking with someone, we pick up visual, often involuntary clues. If the speaker constantly looks away, is he or she lying to you? Simply stated, today's computer technologies lack important visual, audio, olfactory (scent), and haptic (touch) clues that allow us humans to communicate more effectively. What we need to receive from computers is *additional sensory output* so that we can better interpret the information that we are receiving.

Compounding this problem is the fact that most of today's *computers cannot understand sensory input from us!* Consider that humans communicate with each other using the senses of sound, sight, and touch as well as gestures, body language, and facial expressions. Our evolution has optimized our communication processes around these senses. When we communicate with computers and other devices, we are forced to use keyboards, touchpads, or other unintuitive input devices that are often quite subject to error and inaccuracy. To communicate with a computer, we must convert language into keystrokes, translate our thoughts on the fly into characters, and be able to organize our thoughts on electronic viewscreens. No wonder there is such resistance to the use of computers by so many individuals. Typing, abstract thinking, and composition are not skills and abilities possessed by everyone. Most of today's computers do not include the components needed to interpret voice commands or facial and body expressions. In other words, computers cannot understand us when we talk, give visual clues, or gesture—the natural ways that we communicate. With computers, everything is literal, binary (yes or no), digital.

The good news is that the next generation of interface, networking, computing, and application technologies is under development. It will help us realize our desire for improved sensory services. In the next two to five years, we will, in essence, be able to talk to our computers and have them understand what we are saying or seeking. They will be able to provide us with rich sensory responses to our inquiries.

If we can find a way to overcome these user interface problems, the world of computing will take a quantum leap forward. First, we will be able to get more meaningful data from our computers. Multimodal data will stimulate multiple senses—not just sight as the reading of characters and charts does now. This will result in a richer flow of data to us, allowing us to learn more about the subject and in an easier way. Second, people who are disabled, computer-illiterate, or computer-resistant will now be able to use computers because computers will no longer require keyboard input and the use of convoluted command sequences in order to interact with humans. Instead, computers will be able to respond to speech and motion commands. Third, sensory input and output will lead to new efficiencies when dealing with computers. People will be able to input and retrieve information more quickly because that information will be presented in a more natural, consumable fashion. Fourth, by using sensory input and receiving sensory output from computers, we will be able to enter new "virtual worlds" as easily as we go for a stroll in the park. We'll be able to use our natural senses to visit worlds that will present us with a myriad of opportunities for education, collaboration, socialization, commerce, and so on.

What This Part Is About

This part focuses on how our human interface *to computers* is in the process of changing and how new technologies and peripherals will be used to deliver sensory data *from computers* to us.

More specifically, this section focuses on:

1. Human-to-computer speech recognition
2. Human-to-computer navigation and manipulation devices
3. Computer-to-human 3D graphic output
4. Computer-to-human audio output
5. Computer-to-human scent output
6. Computer-to-human touch output

Chapter 5 examines how applications will make use of technologies like speech recognition and Artificial Intelligence to understand and interpret information from the user.

Chapter 6 focuses on new devices and peripherals that are being developed to help us navigate our way through 3D virtual worlds, as well as devices that will help us manipulate objects found in those worlds. These new developments also include devices that will allow us to feed information into our computers.

Chapters 7, 8, and 9 examine how new technologies will be used to enable computers *to output richer sensory information to us* using new visual, auditory, tactile, and olfactory approaches. Chapter 7 provides the background information you'll need to familiarize yourself with sensory output technologies. Chapter 8 focuses specifically on the state of the market in 3D visual output, while Chapter 9 examines the state of the art output to the other senses.

> Although frequently used interchangeably, the term "speech recognition" is often confused with "voice recognition." Voice recognition has to do with voice verification and security. Speech recognition has to do with the input of, and recognition of, the spoken word, vocabulary, as well as computer interpretation of other variables. The two technologies are often used interchangeably in press reports and public presentations. You may even find me doing the same in this book. . . . (*Mea culpa.*)

What I Hope You'll Learn

In the past, speech recognition has had a bad rap. Some of this criticism has been well deserved—for instance, many people are still not happy with the accuracy of their speech dictation systems. What you have to understand is that there are four categories of speech recognition systems: command-and-control, continuous dictation, dialogue, and transcription. Some of these technologies work very well. In particular, command-and-control as well as dictation systems have made strong progress over the past two years—and the strong growth of companies that create such products is testimony to how well these technologies do work. Dialogue systems—speech systems where your computer interacts with you verbally—are just starting to make their way to market. Expect powerful and accurate dialogue systems to become commercially viable around the year 2005. In the past it may have been true that speech recognition technology is not ready for prime time, but now this reputation is, depending on the category of speech system being used, often undeserved.

Another human interface concern has been how to navigate and manipulate objects in 3D worlds. New devices that will follow body motions are being developed to provide easier navigation in 3D virtual worlds. They include the ability to pick up and examine 3D virtual objects. When you complete this chapter, you should have a good understanding of the current and future state of the art for computer screen navigation and manipulation systems.

From a computer-output-to-user perspective, we will soon see a spate of new computer-to-human peripherals capable of delivering improved 3D graphics, touch sensations, and scent sensations. These peripherals will serve to greatly enhance our virtual Internet experiences, making these experiences far richer than most of us have ever considered to date. This part of the book discusses the development path of these peripherals.

The forthcoming advances in human-to-computer and computer-to-human interfaces will make our computer far easier to use than today's models. The next big challenge we will face once the new peripheral devices come to market is, Who is going to write the application code that makes use of these devices? When you complete this part, you should have a good understanding of the new types of peripherals being developed as well as of the issues and obstacles that must be overcome to enable these peripherals to enter the mainstream market.

CHAPTER 5
Speech Recognition and Artificial Intelligence

In the very near future, you can expect to see a new generation of intelligent speech products making their debut. These products will make use of Artificial Intelligence, expert systems, knowledge databases, and the like to provide you with new human-to-computer input options other than keyboards, touchpads, and shorthand handwriting techniques. These new input products will consist of more natural-to-use peripherals that will help you to more naturally input data, navigate through virtual venues, and manipulate objects in virtual reality in the very near term.

The changes being made to the human-to-computer interface are extremely important in the development of the Sensory Virtual Internet. If computers can be made intuitive, and if they can provide feedback in a natural, multisensory manner, more and more people will be able to use computers—and these people will thus be able to expand their professional and intellectual horizons.

Before entering into an in-depth discussion of speech recognition and Artificial Intelligence, it is probably a good idea to come to a common perspective on their definitions. To this end, I offer the following.

Speech Recognition: The Basics

The aim of speech recognition technologies is to reduce our need to input thoughts and commands into computer systems using a keyboard interface and a mouse (or similar device). The goals of speech recognition technologies are:

1. To enable you to issue voice commands to which your computer (or more precisely: your operating environment or application environment) can respond.
2. To foster the development of a dialogue capability between humans and computers.
3. To enable voice-input-to-character-output dictation (a creative and iterative process done in a first-person, human-to-computer mode).
4. To transcribe voice (a second-person activity that takes audio input and literally transcribes that material into written form).

The Types of Speech Recognition Systems

There are four modes or types of speech recognition systems:

- *Command-and-control systems*—Command-and-control (C&C) systems are exactly what they sound like: They respond to the limited list of commands that control or navigate the computer or application environment. C&C technology is probably the easiest speech recognition technology to develop because it has a very limited vocabulary of commands and numbers. For instance, when using AT&T for long distance on a pay phone, you are asked by a C&C system to provide a payment method (credit card, collect, or operator-assisted) by speaking or using touchtone keys. This is a simple speech recognition application that makes use of a limited vocabulary and a few numbers.

- *Continuous dictation products*—The commercial continuous dictation market is led by three companies: Dragon with Naturally Speaking; IBM with Via Voice; and Lernout and Hauspie with Voice Xpress. These products require an enrollment period, during which a user teaches the system to understand them by dictating words, phrases, and stories. This allows the application to get a lock on the user's pronunciation patterns. Also characteristic of these commercial speech recognition programs is that each has its own voice-activated editing command-and-control system that allows users to edit documents using speech commands. The idea behind continuous dictation is to allow professionals to input letters, reports, and other documents without being constrained by a keyboard interface. Accuracy rates are frequently very high (depending on the speaker)—95 percent to 99 percent accuracy rates are common using today's technologies.
- *Dialogue systems*—Dialogue-based systems are where speech recognition technology is definitely headed. As an example, a company by the name of OneVoice has created a program called myIvan that enables users and computers to establish a dialogue based on conversational speech back and forth with the computer system (as if the user were having a conversation with the computer). Users can, for instance, verbally instruct myIvan to conduct an Internet-based search for words or phrases

without typing a single command or typing a single character on the keyboard. Other examples include dialogue-based speech recognition systems that are used to run railroad and air travel booking systems, to operate stock quote systems, and even to provide tourists directions at specially designed information kiosks.
- *Transcription*—Transcription services are available today that hold the promise for streamlining speech-to-print in medicine, news, entertainment, law, and other areas that have a need for accurate transcriptions of audio input into character output. One of the more exciting applications for this technology has to do with using transcription in tandem with translation software to translate speeches, seminars, or other audio events into the written word. Conversely, the U.S. Weather Bureau employs technology that takes the latest character-oriented weather reports and translates them into computer-voice-driven audio broadcasts.

There is also a potential fifth type of speech recognition system—a sort of reverse speech recognition, software that translates text into speech also known as speech synthesis.

> In February 2001, Audible, Inc., a provider of spoken word audio content delivery systems (systems that can read digitized information such as electronic books, written news, and other content to consumers and businesses) announced that Microsoft had invested $10 million in the company (adding to previous cash investments). Audible will use the investment to add wireless delivery services to its content delivery systems.
> Source: http://www.audible.com

ARTIFICIAL INTELLIGENCE: THE BASICS

According to ZDnet's Webopedia, Artificial Intelligence is a term coined by John McCarthy of the Massachusetts Institute of Technology (MIT) as "the branch of computer science concerned with making computers behave like humans." Artificial Intelligence (AI) is a computing discipline that covers a broad spectrum of sciences including robotics (the study of how to program computers to see, hear, and react to external sensory stimuli); neural networks (the process of simulating on computers the physical connections of human and animal brains); expert systems (more on this in just a second); and natural language analysis (the programming that enables computers to interpret natural language usage).

One of the more important AI disciplines germane to this book is the field of expert systems. Expert systems are computer applications designed to complete tasks—or assist in the performance of tasks—that would otherwise be done by a human expert. For instance, expert systems are used to help schedule airline travel and to help develop weather forecasts. Some expert systems assist their users. Expert systems are used in air traffic control to assist their flight controllers in traffic management. Other expert systems are used to completely replace the need for a human. For instance, various expert systems have replaced the need for human telephone operators. By linking speech recognition and expert systems, computers gain the ability to hear, interpret, and respond to queries or requests.

What is important to understand about Artificial Intelligence is that AI disciplines (particularly expert systems, and natural language interpreters) are now being linked with speech recognition and knowledge databases to enable computers to respond intelligently to human instructions and queries. Finally, after decades of waiting, we are on the edge of reaching our goal of having computer systems that can understand what we say, what we mean, and respond intelligently. We're not there yet, but we're getting close.

One of the bigger challenges when adapting human speech and intelligence to computers has to do with natural language processing. Natural language processing refers to the ability of a computer to adjust speech input into a proper syntactic form.

For instance, one might say when filling out a ledger or an expense report, "fifty-three dollars and forty-nine cents." The computer would have the ability to change this natural language expression into "$53.49" for numerical input into a spreadsheet. Natural language processing is a form of intelligence that computers will have to have to interact successfully with human beings.

Now that we have common definitions for speech recognition and Artificial Intelligence, let's examine the issues faced by user interface designers and how speech and AI technologies can work together to solve these issues.

THE HEART OF THE HUMAN INTERFACE TO COMPUTERS PROBLEM: PHYSICAL INPUT DEVICES

We use the following devices to navigate and manipulate objects on our computer screens today: Touchpads (found on some portable, mobile, Palm, handheld computing, or telephone devices). The infamous mouse (circa 1975 technology). The joystick (and variations such as the game pad and steering wheel). The pointer (the functional equivalent of the mouse—an annoying red or gray trackpoint placed by some computer makers in the middle of the portable computer keyboards to help the user navigate the viewscreen). The pen, the stylus . . . But will these be the optimal devices for navigation and manipulation in the 3D worlds of tomorrow?

Furthermore, how intuitive and natural is it for human beings to transcribe thoughts into structured character streams and type those thoughts into a computer rather than using speech? How convenient is it to pull your mobile phone away from your ear or out of your pocket to key in telephone number sequences rather than use voice commands? How natural is it for you to push a mouse pointer to the top of your viewscreen in a virtual environment in order to look up—or to the right of the viewscreen to look to the right—rather than just turning your head? Wouldn't using voice combined with body motions be a more efficient and effective way to instruct your computer?

In addition, consider that today's keyboard interface is simply archaic—and fraught with usability issues such as:

- *Proximity*—Most computer input devices require close proximity to the computer being used.
- *Body positioning*—It's difficult to interface with a personal computer in any position other than sitting. For example, try typing on your personal computer using a keyboard while standing or lying down.
- *Health challenges*—Carpal tunnel syndrome, an affliction that causes pain in the hands and arms of some computer operators as a result of repeating the same motions in the same position over a long period of time, is just one of many ergonomic-related injuries that affect 102 million workers every year. Carpal tunnel causes an average workday loss of about 35 days per incident.
- *Control sequence memorization*—Memorizing keyboard command sequences can be confusing and frustrating, and can require a highly skilled individual as an operator.

Keyboards are not a natural way for humans to communicate, nor are using character-driven command sequences. The plain and simple fact is that most of today's applications require us to work in an unintuitive, unnatural manner in order to provide instructions or input to our computer. The use of keyboards and some pointing devices negatively affects our level of productivity, our ability to use our computers optimally, and our desire to learn to use new programs, products, or features.

But what if we could find a way to talk the data into your computer as well as simply ask for some data back? Wouldn't *that* be grand?

How Will the Computer-to-Human Speech Input Problem Be Solved?

Regardless of which off-the-shelf speech solution you purchase, speech recognition products all seem to share the same fundamental issues: They don't have the ability to infer a decision or even to ask for clarification. They lack the *intelligence* to act on the user's behalf or to question the user's meaning. Computers don't understand context. And all too often a human must intervene in the human-to-computer command sequence in order to get the desired result. But this is changing as speech recognition begins to merge with Artificial Intelligence research to create true intelligent machines.

We have seen that there are four types of speech recognition systems: command-and-control, continuous dictation, dialogue systems, and transcription systems. Each of these systems deal with very complex rules when listening to human speech and processing the data received intelligently. Some of these rules include processing syntax and natural language. In order for speech technology to work, computers need to be able to match sounds in their electronic dictionary to alphabetic words. These computers do not need to understand the words dictated, but knowledge of syntax and grammar can aid in producing the right spelling. For instance, when is it appropriate to use "to" versus "too" versus "two"? With respect to natural language, computers need to be able to translate "two cents" into numeric form ($0.02) and understand that you didn't mean "to sense." They need to do so without special instructions by the person dictating. The state of the art for natural language speech recognition currently relies heavily on having the person who is dictating a message or text issue special verbal instructions to the computer to accommodate natural language phrases.

One way to limit the chances of failure is to limit the dictionary of words and vocabulary that a computer needs to process. For instance, if you limit the number of commands and confine the vocabulary to a few words such as "do this" or "do that" an application can easily be designed to handle such tasks. It can listen for certain commands and then look up the appropriate response in its database. This creates the illusion of responding to our requests—but it does not constitute a dialogue with a computer. It is when computers have to deal with very large dictionaries, and even handle words outside their dictionary, that speech recognition starts to decline in effectiveness.

If this is the case—and if command-and-control systems work fairly well—then it is reasonable to expect that the first vestiges of working human-to-computer speech systems will be command-and-control-based. And sure enough, the success of these systems in the market confirms that command-and-control systems work. Companies are buying command-and-control speech recognition systems for customer service applications and phone answering systems with increasing regularity.

So, if command-and-control systems can be shown to work for certain specialized applications, the question then becomes When will command-and-control systems become effective tools for general human-to-computer interfaces? I would argue that the logical place for command-and-control technology to start working its way into mainstream computer applications is as part of the operating system, where it can be used for system management queries and tasks. And guess what? Microsoft is doing just that with the next revision of the Windows operating system.

> In 2001, Microsoft has released its next version of the Windows operating systems (Windows XP). In Windows XP, Microsoft has introduced a "natural interface" to their new operating system, providing users with the ability to integrate "speech, vision, handwriting, and natural-language input via a new 'type-in' box." Using XP, Microsoft claims that users will have a "multimodal user interface" to the underlying operating environment and associated applications.
> Source: http://www.Microsoft.com/enable/products/officexp/features.htm

> IBM, with its market-leading ViaVoice product for speech recognition and continuous dictation, recently announced that it would invest $1 billion in the Linux operating system. With this kind of investment, it is easy to extrapolate that one day Linux will also be voice-enabled.
>
> Source:http://www-4.IBM.com/software/speech/dev/sdk_linux.html

This command-and-control approach to introducing human input to computer systems is a good first step as we look for speech-driven input for our computer systems. However, this approach only gets us part way there. What we really want when interacting with our computers is not only input but also confirmation that our commands have been understood and are being acted upon. We want a dialogue. Command-and-control is only a partial dialogue—we talk to our computers and they respond back with preprogrammed responses. These dialogue systems will go a long way to addressing our user interface issues, but I believe that solid dialogue systems will not be commercially available until the end of 2004 at least. Still, there are constant signs of hope that some technological breakthrough will happen, as evidenced by the following:

> Artificial Intelligence Enterprises (Ai), a speech recognition/Artificial Intelligence company, has written a program that is capable of conversing convincingly with its "carer" (a computer owner/user). Its program, Hal (named after the HAL 9000 of *2001: A Space Odyssey*), has the vocabulary and grasp of language of a 15-month-old child. The company is currently working on expanding this vocabulary to that of a five-year-old. As for the quality of the conversations, transcripts were supplied to independent judges without explanation of what they were. These judges believed that they were reading a write-up of a real conversation.
>
> Source:http://www.transhumanismus.de/SciTech/0104/computer_speak.htm

In the past, the science of conversational computer programs has been based on identifying keywords and then using

CHAPTER 5: SPEECH RECOGNITION AND ARTIFICIAL INTELLIGENCE

statistical techniques to understand the grammar and generate appropriate responses. These programs typically haven't coped very well with very short sentences that do not offer the additional data needed by the computer to fine-tune its guess. The approach used by Ai involves training a computer by inputting stories and questions and answers, from which the computer can learn. The learning algorithms that underpin Hal eventually come to understand which are the appropriate responses.

Will Ai, or some other company, master speech recognition/Artificial Intelligence over the next five years? It is reasonable to expect numerous breakthroughs such as this by 2006, at which time you can expect to fully engage in conversations with "adult" computers.

Other very interesting experimentation in dialogue systems is taking place at the Massachusetts Institute of Technology (MIT) in their Spoken Language Systems Labs. MIT has focused some of its speech recognition efforts on creating dialogue systems that can converse with humans. MIT's approach is to:

1. Convert spoken language to text (for instance, take speech and create a text file).
2. Take that resulting text file and reorient it for information retrieval (in other words, format the text in the form of a character-driven question).
3. Send that now character-oriented text to the appropriate Web source for resolution.
4. Respond in the requestor's natural language using speech synthesis (computer-generated speech from text).

Many examples of this type of dialogue system are available for public access. Go ahead, give one a try:

At the Massachusetts Institute of Technology:

- Dinex is a dialogue system for gaining access to restaurant information (not public yet).
- Jupiter is a dialogue system for gaining access to weather information (1-888-573-TALK).

- Pegasus is a dialogue system for gaining access to airline information (1-877-527-8255).
- Web Galaxy is a dialogue system for performing Web searches (not public yet).
- Wheels is a dialogue system for gaining access to classified automotive advertisements (not public yet).

Source: http://www.mit.edu

Also, SpeechWorks offers the following:

At SpeechWorks:

Many companies provide online or phone-based demonstrations of their products. SpeechWorks, one such company, provides toll-free access (in the United States) to a voice-activated demonstration site that features a speech-driven banking and financial quote system demo (1-888-SAY-DEMO).

Designed to help customers self-service their information needs, SpeechWorks speech recognition solutions let consumers obtain information and complete transactions automatically using voice commands on fixed or wireless phone sets.

SpeechWorks' customers include many of the industry's leading customer service innovators, such as Continental Airlines, E*TRADE, FedEx, Hewlett-Packard, MapQuest.com, McKessonHBOC, and United Airlines. This speech recognition demonstration is an excellent example of a highly accurate command-and-control system.

Source: http://www.speechworks.com

If you did try one of these systems, you will observe that for English language speakers, these systems work quite well. The goal of dialogue systems is to eventually be able to talk to our computers and have our words acted upon and responded to intelligently. Command-and-control systems represent the first step for mainstream consumer access to such technology. You will begin to see them on personal computing devices that will hit the market in 2002; commercial dialogue systems will quite likely arrive in 2005.

The Problems with Speech Recognition to Date

Just to be sure that the picture I've just painted is not too rosy, let me clearly identify several issues that still plague (or look like they will plague) speech recognition technology today. Here are just a few:

- If you purchased early editions of commercial-grade speech recognition products such as those intended to make dictating and word processing easier (also known as continuous dictation products), you found that they missed the mark in ease-of-use and accuracy. Many dictation products are very difficult to use from a navigational perspective. Telling the computer where to make an edit, for instance, still remains cumbersome. It is frequently easier to make the required edits manually. And usage and spelling errors often occur when translating speech to text, despite claims of 95 to 99 percent accuracy.

- You may also have had occasion to work with voice-activated command-and-control systems. For instance, many phone company customers who use long distance phone services interact directly with a computer when placing calling card calls. The computer that answers the phone asks customers if they would like to use a calling card, place a collect call, or be transferred to a human operator. It then proceeds to help complete the transaction. Some of these voice-activated systems work very well—especially if the command set is limited and the choice of options is restricted and contained.

    But some command-and-control systems, such as some implementations of telephone answering/redirection systems, will drive you crazy. These systems will ask you to spell the last name of someone whom you probably have never met using the touchtone keys on your telephone.

What if you don't know the person or misheard the person's last name in the voice mail that he or she left for you? Or, what happens if you mistype the person's name? Some call systems can be very unforgiving. Many leave no way to let you speak to a human operator to take corrective action. On the other hand, some voice-driven systems, such as one I recently used by Thompson Financial, are quite sophisticated. All you need to do is pronounce the name of the person you are trying to reach and voilà, the computer connects you to that person's telephone automatically.
- Other issues that have plagued early releases of speech recognition technologies have included distortion and enrollment. Distortion has to do with noise and other interference from sources within the speaker's immediate environment (for instance, plane noise, car noise, etc.) that gets in the way of the computer's ability to listen to the speaker. Enrollment has to do with the time you have to spend teaching your computer how you speak.

With respect to distortion, if is difficult for humans to control noise in external environments; hence, computer technology needs to improve to adapt to external distortion noise. With respect to enrollment, most people are not willing to spend one, three, or ten hours training their computer to understand their speech patterns. Programs will have to be developed to adapt to speakers more quickly.

The bottom line is that despite shortcomings in programs and logic flow, command-and-control systems work very well if they are performing limited, isolated tasks that make use of a limited dictionary of recognizable speech vocabulary. It is possible for designers to leave "logic rat-holes" that leave users stranded in speech recognition applications. But many of the perceived problems people have with dealing with these systems are not necessarily problems with speech recognition technology, but rather problems with how the program flow, logic, and preprogrammed responses have been written.

Speech Recognition: It's for Real

Having identified these issues, I will, however, no longer agree with critics who contend that speech recognition has a long way to go to become practical for use in business and individual settings. My latest research indicates that for English-based speech recognition systems, command-and-control applications have matured greatly. Dictation systems now offer extremely high degrees of accuracy that approach 99.9 percent accuracy in some cases. Dialogue systems are starting to become solid. And changes in computer hardware combined with advances in speech recognition and Artificial Intelligence software are leading me to conclude that reliable speech recognition interfaces with computers are, despite the claims of some critics, fully achievable today.

How can I justify this position, especially when a lot of people believe that speech recognition is not ready for prime time? Consider the following points:

1. *Computer hardware obstacles have been mitigated—* One of the biggest problems that speech recognition systems experienced in the past was related to PC hardware—specifically CPU processing speed and data storage. Storing large speech files can burn up disk space like there's no tomorrow. Large amounts of storage are now comparatively cheap (a hundred gigabyte hard drive now costs about $350), and CPU speed is about five times faster than that of only two years ago (now in the 2 GHz range). The combination of cheap storage and fast hardware is going to make it far easier for the average user to host, process, and use speech recognition software.

    Also, computer memory is now inexpensive, making

it possible to process speech data in main memory. More main memory means that the data to be processed is moved closer to the processor rather than having to be accessed from disk or from some other input/output device, hence commands and dictation can be more quickly interpreted and displayed or acted upon.

2. *Speech recognition has already made its way into mainstream applications (business opportunities) and will also go mainstream in operating environments—* Speech recognition has already had a enormous effect on customer relationship management software and telephone answering software. Applications such as automated call attendants, voice dialing, dictation, customer service systems, stock quote systems, airline and travel systems, and the like that use speech recognition and Artificial Intelligence technologies are growing like wildfire (see below). And speech recognition will become part-and-parcel of the world's leading desktop computer operating environment (Microsoft's Windows). It is also expected to wend its way into Linux and other operating environments over the next three years.

> Wildfire Communications produces a voice-driven personal assistant that manages communications for mobile workers. "She" takes messages, manages contacts, dials outgoing calls, and sends and receives faxes using intuitive voice commands. The Wildfire personal assistant enhances productivity and efficiency by responding to voice commands to manage mobile communications. Wildfire is offered by Pacific Bell Wireless in the United States, as well as various carriers in France, Italy, and the United Kingdom. Testimonials found on the company's Web site indicate that for some users, business revenues improved by 30 percent because of reductions in administrative overhead associated with call management and the basic fact that Wildfire allows users to concentrate on driving their respective businesses.
>
> Source: http://www.wildfire.com

3. *The promise of modular integration of speech with mainstream applications (Web Services)*—Speech modules have largely been purchased from speech recognition suppliers in order to make this happen. It is only logical that, over time, other mainstream application makers (if it makes sense for their particular applications) will speech-enable their software as a new feature to encourage new sales, as evidenced by this typical scenario:

> Nuance Communications, a maker of speech recognition and voice authentication software, recently signed a deal with Siebel to integrate its speech recognition products with those of Siebel Systems, a leading supplier of business application software, to speech-enable certain Siebel business applications.
>
> The Nuance Communications' deal with Siebel is particularly interesting as it is a clear manifestation of things to come. Siebel and Nuance have teamed together to create a speech-driven interface product that will provide Siebel customers with voice access to time-sensitive customer data (such as sales opportunities, contact information, and the like), as well as to their own personal appointment and calendar schedules—all via the telephone. This deal is one of the first indications that speech recognition is about to become part of the business application mainstream. How long will it be before other industry software giants like SAP, Oracle, and Computer Associates speech-enable their business applications?
>
> Source: http://www.Nuance.com

4. *Mobile and pervasive computing markets are putting strong pressure on developers to create speech recognition-based input solutions. Products are already starting to show up*—The wireless communications market is growing strongly worldwide, and very quickly in the United States (other parts of the world are ahead of the United States in terms of deployed wireless infrastructure and percentage of total population using wireless ser-

vices). In the United States by the end of the first quarter of 2001, there were over 113.4 million wireless users, up from more than 97 million in June of 2000 according to the Cellular Telecommunications and Internet Association. Growth is strong, and is expected to remain strong for several years in the wireless communications industry.

Bearing this growth in mind, IBM is one of a number of companies that has recently introduced speech recognition software that enables mobile device users to query back-end XML (extensible markup language) Internet-based databases using speech. Using this technology, you will be able to access the Internet from anywhere (home, office, airport, café, plane, and even your car). Note that many of the places mentioned do not lend themselves to the use of a keyboard—especially coach class on most major airlines. Hence speech recognition is becoming an important input and output technology for mobile computer users. IBM's move is an important signal that the floodgates for such activities are starting to open.

5. *New dialogue-based developments are encouraging*—Command-and-control systems work marvelously in constrained environments where vocabulary, dictionaries, and responses can be limited. But new systems that enable a dialogue between the user and the computer are now making an appearance, as exemplified here:

California-based One Voice Technologies recently announced the availability of its myIVAN (Intelligent Voice Animated Navigator) product, claiming to offer "the only product of its kind that can provide a voice-activated human interface for the PC and the Internet." The product consists of a state-of-the-art software engine created using *Artificial Intelligence*, an *expert system*, *knowledge bases*, and *natural language processing*. Because of all these technologies, it does more than simply respond to command-and-control phrases. It can actually understand concepts such as the topic, subject, and synonym relationships. It can ask you intelligent questions to help clarify the meaning, and it learns from each interaction.

In initial versions, myIVAN helped Internet users surf the net and manage their PC filing systems using voice command. Ultimately, products such as this could be used to front-end business applications such as customer relationship management or supply chain solutions. Or they could be used to instruct computers to load and run entertainment programs using speech commands rather than keyboard commands.

Source: http://www.onevoicetech.com

6. *Accuracy has improved dramatically over the past two years*—Recently, speech recognition has improved for certain application environments. With accuracy rates that many vendors claim exceed 99 percent, speech recognition is now a viable technology for command-and-control applications as well as for speech dictation. Further, issues such as distortion (noise from diverse surrounding environments) can be overcome, depending on the equipment used and the location of the user.

7. *Enrollment periods are down*—One big impediment to the use of speech technology such as continuous dictation had been that it took a long time to teach your computer how you say things. That timeframe has dropped from four hours to less than two.

8. *The future holds promise of productivity improvements*—Using speech to input data has been shown to increase individual input capabilities by up to a factor of four. An average typist can type between 40 and 80 words per minute. But individuals using speech recognition technology can type (using speech) at 160 words a minute—two to four times faster than using a keyboard. Might speech recognition enable businesses to get twice the work out of existing personnel? It certainly poses interesting questions. Also, *how* much time is lost yearly as computer users search for the proper control character

sequences to execute simple commands? Have you ever been stymied by your inability to find the command or menu item you need to readjust the size of a row or column, or to reformat a document in a particular way? University-level research studies have shown that businesses can expect to realize new efficiencies by enabling computer users to tell their system or application what they are trying to do,rather than trying to figure out where in the drop-down menu the command is to take the desired action—and efficiency frequently translates into additional cost savings.

A shortage of computer-literate and capable white collar information workers has plagued business worldwide for over 25 years. Finding computer/application-trained and literate individuals has always been a challenge. This skills gap is increased from the beginning because those who use computers must be capable of keyboard input (yes, typing). Billions of people on this planet cannot type—but almost everyone on this planet can speak. For businesses, speech recognition technologies hold the promise of helping to overcome one of the biggest impediments to computer use—keyboard input—thereby reducing costs related to training and education.

The International Labour Organisation (ILO) recently reported that it expects the IT skills shortage will triple over the next few years, with 1.6 million jobs around Europe being unfilled by 2002. Further, the ILO is forecasting that 8 percent more IT jobs will be created each year, further exacerbating the IT skills shortage situation.
Source:http://www.ilo.org/

9. *Demand and supply are starting to match up*—This is a typical example of the thirst for speech-oriented technology.

> America Online (AOL) recently introduced its AOLbyPhone service, a new portal that will enable users to leave electronic mail in speech form, as well as have character-driven electronic mail delivered via computer voice. Over 200,000 AOL subscribers signed up for the initial offering of this product.
>
> Source: http://www.wirelessnewsfactor.com/perl/story/5310.html

The maturation of speech technologies combined with evolving business opportunities in hot markets like Customer Relationship Management (CRM) as well as increasing market demand for speech-driven applications and services in mobile environments indicates that the business marketplace as well as the consumer marketplace are ready to make use of speech recognition. The question really is, Is speech recognition technology really ready for the marketplace? All of the above points tend to indicate that it is.

The last thing you'll want to do when visiting virtual reality is to be bolted to a keyboard trying to input directions or to chat with your virtual neighbors. You'll want natural human language command interaction with your computer system, and you'll want a more natural way to navigate and manipulate objects in 3D worlds. The latest advances in speech recognition combined with other technologies such as Artificial Intelligence and expert systems—and the fact that businesses are starting to jump on the speech recognition trend—lead me to conclude that speech recognition technology has finally come of age.

Expected Social Effects of Speech Recognition Technology

If speech recognition technology has truly come of age, it is reasonable to expect certain societal benefits to result from the widespread use of this technology over time. On the individual user side, speech recognition is expected to play an increasingly stronger role in making it possible for handicapped or disabled people to more easily interact with computers. Severely disabled people will soon be able to issue voice commands to their computers to initiate phone calls, take dictation, or even perform robotic tasks—a giant step forward for the disabled and for computing technology.

Speech recognition technologies will make it possible for certain individuals who have resisted computer involvement to at last become involved in new learning, collaborative, social, and entertainment activities. People from all age groups are sometimes computer-resistant. Much of this resistance can be attributed to unfamiliarity with computer systems in general as well as a lack of basic typing skills. Overcoming the keyboard barrier will lead to throngs of new users accessing the Internet for information, education, and entertainment.

Further, speech recognition can be linked to translation services, making it possible for virtual you to interact with people of other cultures—your conversations will be translated automatically and transparently in real time. Imagine speech technology combined with translation technology such that a Chinese-, or Lithuanian-, or Arabic-speaking person could speak to their computers and have their words translated into another language on the fly. Think of the opportunities for better communication, for expanded learning, for better sharing of research, for increased global commerce, and for the breaking down of prejudices. Speech recognition holds great promise for the creation and sharing of new ideas across cultures—ideas that might never have been shared if keyboard input had still remained an obstacle.

An Alternative Approach

Although this chapter has focused on speech recognition and Artificial Intelligence as the up-and-coming replacements for keyboard interfaces to our computers, there are other non-keyboard alternatives in the works. Forthcoming tablet or pad computers present users with a touchscreen and handwriting recognition instead of a mouse and keyboard for navigation and input purposes.

> Frontpath, Inc., recently introduced its ProGear computing device aimed at the hospitality, education, and health-care markets (markets where professionals may need to carry a computer from point to point and may not have a desk or convenient place to input data via keyboard). This computer offers the same amount of computing power as some laptop computers but uses handwriting recognition software for input (as opposed to a keyboard) and uses a touchscreen (as opposed to a mouse) for navigation and manipulation purposes.
> Source: http://www.frontpath.com

Chapter Summary

In Stanley Kubrick's *2001: A Space Odyssey* (filmed over thirty-two years ago), a spaceship commander is seen talking to and reasoning with his computer. This particular computer (HAL) is capable of speech recognition, can act on voice commands, and possesses Artificial Intelligence (so it can reason and make decisions). HAL also understands nuances in voice and actions and is able to respond to subtle clues in inflection. (Unfortunately for the space commander, HAL perceives the commander to be a threat to its own well being and passionlessly ousts the commander into deep space.)

Many people believe that this kind of speech-driven interaction with computers is a long way off. They feel that: 1) computers cannot process the spoken commands they receive with great accuracy; 2) computers cannot accurately transcribe dictation; and 3) human-to-computer speech products are inaccurate and cumbersome.

From my perspective, Kubrick was not far off in his portrayal of a speech-driven human interface to computer systems (just a little off in his timing). This may sound a little far-fetched even in the year 2001, but computers are rapidly approaching the point where we will be able to talk to and even reason with them. In 1997, IBM's Deep Blue, a massively parallel multiprocessor computer, defeated chess champion Gary Kasparov. This demonstrated that computers are capable of abstract thought and reason, a great victory for computer scientists who specialize in Artificial Intelligence. In 1999 and 2000, more and more speech/voice-driven customer interface systems made their appearances in retail, sales, and customer service departments. These electronic operators help route customer phone calls to the proper resource (and in some cases, to route customers to a knowledge database where computers using voice-response are able to assist the customer with his or her problem, issue, or request). Very recently, consumer software debuted that enables users to issue voice commands to their PCs to navigate the Internet. In 2001, commercially available speech recognition software with up to 99.95 percent accuracy have made their appearance in commercial markets, beckoning information workers to move away from keyboard input and into speech-driven command-and-control and dictation technologies.

Two of the four classes of speech recognition are ready for prime time today—and the other two will be ready for reliable commercial use within three years.

1. Contrary to popular belief, some command-and-control systems can deliver 100 percent accuracy today. Note: English-language command-and-control systems are the most accurate—while other languages have some work to do to catch up.
2. The issue with *continuous speech dictation* is not necessarily that computers don't understand our speech—some commercially available products boast 99 percent

accuracy today. The big problem with these systems is the complexity of the editing process. This has slowed down the acceptance of speech technology in the continuous dictation marketplace. Computers have proven that they can understand and transcribe speech accurately—even making adjustments for syntax and natural language considerations. But, from my experience, editing and reformatting documents using voice commands still remains cumbersome. I expect advances in screen manipulation and navigation peripherals to aid in helping to overcome these editing issues.

3. Researchers and scientists have been trying for years to develop *speech dialogue* systems. Recent advances using speech recognition, Artificial Intelligence, and expert systems are showing strong progress in making this type of speech recognition work. Will solid dialogue systems be available within the three-year Sensory Virtual Internet window that I've proposed in this book? I believe that sometime around 2004 we will see the first commercially available, viable dialogue systems make it to market.

4. *Transcription systems* represent the fourth category of speech recognition systems—and thousands of users will testify that transcription technology works well today—especially in environments where a professional, limited vocabulary is used (for instance, in medical or legal environments).

It does not take a researcher long to discover hundreds of programs and projects underway that are developing alternative ways for humans to interact with computers. The Internet is rife with information about human interface projects that examine everything from human interface technologies through the psychological and social effects of human-computer interaction. Hardware and software technology firms in private industry are investing heavily in speech-driven systems augmented by Artificial Intelligence and expert system enhancements. Colleges and universities are hotbeds for user interface intellectual capital. In these environments, you'll find leading-edge human-interface experimentation taking place in areas ranging from biofeedback devices through sensory technologies.

CHAPTER 6

Navigation and Manipulation

Although most of the attention in *human-to-computer* interfaces so far in this book focuses on advances in speech recognition and artificial intelligence, it is important to note that two technologies are only one part of the human-to-computer input equation. Another aspect of how we interface with computers has to do with the spatial relationships the virtual you has with objects and locations as it moves through sensory virtual space. Today our systems are designed to help us move up, down, left, or right on our viewscreens—but in 3D worlds we are also going to have to find natural and intuitive ways to move in, out, and through virtual vistas on the Internet. The devices we currently use to navigate virtual worlds and manipulate objects in 3D space will need to be adapted to deal effectively and intuitively with the concept of depth.

The computer mouse was and is a marvelously innovative device, but it is not ideally suited for grasping virtual objects in virtual space. Furthermore, it may not necessarily be the best way to move through virtual 3D environments. New motion-driven peripheral devices are being developed that will help us navigate more easily through three-dimensional environments. Just as important, other devices are being perfected that will help us manipulate objects found in those environments. This chapter is about these evolving navigational and manipulation devices, which will soon be available for use on the Sensory Virtual Internet.

The State of the Market—Navigation

Today, most of us navigate computer screens with up-and-down, left-and-right arrows, pens, mice or other pointers, joysticks, steering wheels, or gamepads. These devices were originally designed to help us navigate our computer screens using "X" and "Y" axes (e.g., to help us move to the top of a screen, to the bottom of a screen, or to the left or right). As we move into the forthcoming Sensory Virtual Internet, many of today's navigation and manipulation peripherals will prove to be inadequate, clumsy, or cumbersome because they don't provide us with the ability to move easily along "Z" coordinates—depth. This is the dimension we use it to create the illusion of moving forward or backward and how we see things as close or far away (see Figure 6).

For most of us, movement in virtual space is simulated using a mouse or joystick (incidentally, steering wheels and gamepads are variations of these technologies). These devices have certain conceptual limitations when moving along the Z axis in 3D worlds. To emphasize this point, visit some 3D virtual Internet worlds and you will find that moving forward in some 3D worlds means that you need to locate a control panel on your viewscreen and click the forward button, then move your mouse in

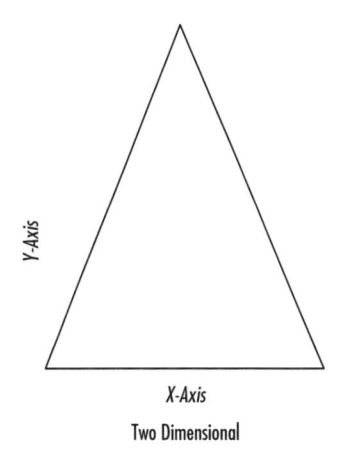

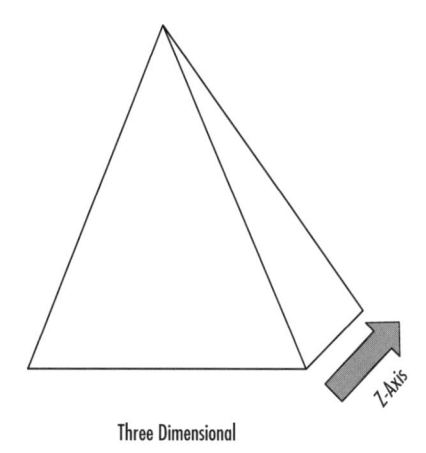

FIGURE 6
X, Y, and Z Axis

an upward motion in order to travel across a virtual landscape. Then, to look up, you'll need to click another control panel button to direct your head to look upward, and again move your mouse in an upward motion to control the upward view. Sounds cumbersome and unnatural, right? It is.

Don't misunderstand—this approach to navigation does work. It's just that this approach is not natural or intuitive. It's contrived, put in place because most users only have access to 2D peripherals. Developers are forced to fit their 3D scenario's interface to 2D peripherals in lieu of using more appropriate 3D peripheral devices designed and optimized for use in 3D landscapes. Perhaps other approaches using other peripherals would be more suited to helping us move more efficiently and naturally in 3D worlds.

There are other technical options on the horizon for more intuitive movement in virtual worlds. One of these, and possibly a more appropriate approach for looking upward when traversing a 3D vista, is a sensor that can detect head or retinal motion instead of requiring hand motions to direct head/vision movement. Headgear devices with these sensors are available today. They are often used by the handicapped. Devices that can track retinal movement are also available, but are extremely expensive. Further, researchers are currently experimenting with body suits that can recreate your torso and limb movements in three-dimensional space. In the not-too-distant future, any or all of these technologies may come into play to help us move in a more natural manner through 3D space.

Personally, I'm very interested in new infrared technologies that can assist in hands-free cursor movement. Eye Control Technologies has several such innovative products in development, such as the ring, the wand, and the dot.

> Eye Control Technologies is in the process of developing its eye Control NaturalPoint track IR cursor control system to assist in hands-free computing. This technology uses infrared signals to enable users to control cursor movements without using their hands from up to 20 feet away. The ring and wand technologies operate as straightforward pointing devices (like a laser pointer that is used by some presenters in business presentations or by some teachers)—except that instead of controlling a beam of light, the ring and wand control cursor movement. The wand is designed to give a user cursor control within 20 feet of the computer being used. The ring is actually worn on the user's index finger and is particularly useful for mobile users who want alternatives to touchpad or trackpoint options on their portables, laptops, or other mobile devices. The dot fits into a category of motion device known as headset controls. A dot user can place the dot on his or her forehead and move the cursor using head movements.
> Source: http://www.eyecontrol.com

State of the Art: Manipulation

Building human interface peripherals to help us control our movements intuitively in a new 3D terrain is one challenge. Another major challenge is how to deal with the manipulation of objects in virtual reality. Current technology involves the use of buttons on a mouse and pointer that when pushed, indicate how a 3D image should be turned on the screen for viewing purposes. If you want a closer look at the object, you push a button to zoom in. If you want to move the object further away, you press a button to zoom out. We have adapted mouse technology to suit both purposes—but are mice truly suited for object manipulation in a 3D world?

The answer: Computer mice are ideally suited for moving up or down, left or right on static screens, but need to be enhanced for other types of movements. For a real-world example, look at how Wacom has combined the use of two input peripherals in some very interesting ways to manipulate objects in 3D space. For instance, Wacom has found a way (using "4D" technology) to not only manipulate an object, but also to actually paint an object in 3D space.

> Washington-based Wacom Technology Co. is in the business of creating specialized peripheral devices and tools. Foremost among its several innovative products are pressure-sensitive graphics tablets, pen tools, electronic erasers, and the Intuos 4D mouse, an easy-to-use mouse with a thumbwheel that gives you the ability to zoom in or out on objects on the fly. Companies such as Microsoft, Logitech, and others have also introduced similar variations on mouse technology for moving through 3D environments.
>
> What is interesting about the 4D mouse is its ability to allow the user additional manipulation capabilities—for instance, the ability to not only grasp an object but also to paint it a different color while holding it in 3D space. Wacom's Dual Track system allows input from *two devices at once.* Thus you can use the Intuos 4D mouse in conjunction with Intuos pressure-sensitive tablets to rotate objects while performing other 3D tasks, such as perhaps painting an object using a pressure-sensitive Intuos pen.
>
> Source:http://www.wacom.com

A more natural approach to manipulate objects in 3D space would involve a user potentially picking up that object (using glove technology) and virtually holding it. The object could be viewed more closely by moving one's hands closer to one's face—or could be pushed further away, again by using hand and arm movements—natural motions and manipulation that mimics how we would examine objects in the real world. Gloves are under development both in university and private business research centers. As with leading-edge advances in navigation peripherals, expect gloves to make their commercial appearance in 3D game environments over the next three years.

An Irony: New Navigation/Manipulation Technologies Are Becoming Available—But the Programming to Capitalize on These Technologies Isn't

From an analytical perspective, the basic hardware needed to simulate motion in 3D environments is advancing nicely. What appears to be missing is the application *code* that will allow these devices to be used effectively for motion in off-the-shelf software.

Consider this, in just about any house in which PC games are played, one is likely to find a joystick or two. And in homes where game players enjoy racing or flying games, PC steering wheels can be found. These devices are well-suited to certain games and are ideal for moving through 3D worlds (for instance, racing steering wheels come with accelerator and brake units designed to simulate real driving controls). How is it that these devices work so well with computer games, while better-suited technologies such as gloves or body suits (which are often more appropriate for such games) have not yet made their appearance? Surely gloves are more natural and intuitive than mice and joysticks for human users who use their hands in real space to pick up and manipulate objects. Shouldn't gloves be hot sellers right now for use in 3D game and virtual world environments? Why aren't they?

Part of the answer seems to lie in how 3D applications are developed. Most games use a mouse as the central input design point. Both joysticks and steering wheels are variations of mouse technology, and therefore 3D games require little additional modification in order to use them. A mouse will move a car or plane left or right on an X left/right axis, just as a joystick or steering wheel will do. By rolling the mouse forward or backward on a desktop (or by stepping on an accelerator or a brake) we can simulate moving along a Z axis. A mouse can even be used to move a car or plane along a Z depth axis. The principles used to program the application to respond to all three devices are essentially the same—so no major modifications are needed to adapt these technologies for use with a wide number of applications.

Such is not the case with glove or body-suit technologies. Gloves, for instance, need to track the movements of five or ten fingers and relay their relative positions and simulate their complex motions in graphical fashion on the display. A body suit has even more movable parts to track. Writing applications that will make use of glove and body-suit technologies is very complex.

Until application programming catches up to navigation/manipulation peripheral development, do not expect gloves or body suits to become mass market items. Perhaps in two to three years the first mass-market gloves will make their market entrance—but this will depend a great deal on the development of applications and games beforehand.

Entertainment and Games: Leading the Change in Navigation and Manipulation

If you want to get a sense of how far mass-market, generally available input devices have advanced, look closely at the entertainment/game marketplace. In games, three-dimensional worlds are all the rage. Game developers understand full well how to build 3D worlds and are happy to take advantage of advances in PC processing power and graphics acceleration to create more realistic 3D experiences. The next frontiers for game makers are 3D world navigation and manipulation.

No matter how enjoyable many gamers find today's 3D gameplay, there are thousands upon thousands of people who have difficulty mastering 3D game controls. Many of today's specialized gamepads are difficult to use, although if a game is fun, gamers will eventually master the complex and unintuitive navigation and manipulation controls. Using a steering wheel or foot pad approaches the real-life driving experience, but somehow using a joystick to run, jump, crawl, and climb does not. The complexity involved in mastering unintuitive navigation and manipulation controls is one of the biggest obstacles preventing gamers from getting the most out of 3D games and computer users from getting the most out of 3D worlds. As new navigation and manipulation devices are being prepared for market, builders of existing mouse products have found a way to add functions to mice that can greatly assist in movement and player control. These programmable mice now enable gamers to issue command functions such as "pick up object" or "move in this direction" rather than having to go through sometimes complex control functions to accomplish the same movement. In this manner, users are able to reduce the complexity of movement in and about virtual, three-dimensional worlds. One example of this new mouse technology is Microsoft's "Sidewinder Strategic Commander."

> Microsoft's Sidewinder Strategic Commander enables game players to move, deploy troops, and issue commands to virtual armies. They can also execute pre-programmed moves faster and more efficiently than traditional mouse and keyboard commands. Users can automatically group units, create buildings, train military forces, and execute up to 72 other commands with the touch of a button.
>
> Source:http://www.microsoft.com/catalog/display.asp?subid=22&site=10516&x=33+y=14

Although initially released for game play, this kind of extended mouse functionality can easily be adapted for use in a variety of 3D world settings. Someday home users looking for increased functionality, maneuverability, and object manipulation capabilities in three-dimensional worlds may use Sidewinder-like devices heavily.

Chapter Summary

The creation of the mouse was a masterful design because it allowed computer users to quickly move around two-dimensional viewscreens. Today some programmers are adapting mouse technology to allow for movement through three-dimensional worlds. Nevertheless, is the computer mouse necessarily the best and only device that we can use to navigate and manipulate 3D objects in the Sensory Virtual Internet worlds of the future? Hardly.

Other screen navigation devices have existed for years. Headgear has helped disabled people make their way around computer screens. Retinal scanners are available that can pick up on eye cues and make appropriate movements. I, personally, am quite excited about interim solutions such as the Eye Contact hands-free infrared devices mentioned earlier in this chapter because these technologies behave like mice (meaning that the programming needed to make them work with off-the-shelf and virtual applications is already available). By combining the dot headgear with glove technology, I could feasibly pick up 3D objects and manipulate them as I move through 3D space with just hand and head motions. These newly evolving peripherals hold the promise of allowing us to move through virtual worlds in a hands-free, natural manner.

The big problem to overcome in terms of adding new navigational and manipulation devices as access points to virtual worlds has to do with programming. Programming for the use of mouse technology (including joysticks, gamepads, and steering wheels) is comparatively straightforward versus programming for finger movements to enable a glove to be used, or body movements to enable head, limb, and torso movement in 3D space. The key question to be asked is, When will programming be available in mainstream applications to enable us to make use of glove and body suit technologies? I would speculate that for gloves, two to three years; for body suits, quite a bit longer.

CHAPTER 7

RECEIVING SENSORY DATA FROM YOUR COMPUTER

In the previous two chapters, I've described how inefficient it is to use keyboards and other navigation and manipulation devices to interact with computers and with one another. Keyboards in particular are unnatural, foreign, and cumbersome. To be used effectively, they require a skill that most people don't have: typing (yes, most of the world cannot type). They require that you be seated or stationary when using them—tethering you to your computer. As an input device, keyboards are just plain difficult to use. But thanks to recent advances in speech recognition and developments in new input devices, I've demonstrated that it is reasonable to expect that keyboards will eventually be completely replaced by speech technology. I've also shown that the ubiquitous mouse will someday be augmented by other input, navigation, and manipulation devices better suited for navigation through 3D environments and for manipulation of objects in 3D worlds.

The next step in improving the human interface with our computers is *outbound from our computers*. Conversing with your computer and manipulating objects in virtual space are both forms of input into your computer. Not only do we need an improved, intuitive, more natural way to input data into computers, we also need more intuitive and sensory-attuned ways to receive output from computers in order to make full use of the Sensory Virtual Internet.

What forms of electronic output are possible from your computer? All forms are possible, each one able to stimulate one or more of your five senses: sight, sound, scent, touch, and taste. This chapter provides the background you'll need to understand how your senses work and how computer technology can be used to stimulate those senses. Subsequent chapters will examine the state of the art of each technology, how these technologies are presently used, and how these technologies will be used in the future to create sensory-enhanced virtual world environments.

What You Need to Know About 3D Visualization

Did you ever wonder how you perceive objects in three dimensions? Consider the following. Three-dimensional vision works on the principle of binocular stereopsis—we use stereovision to perceive depth. Provided that you have no sight disabilities, your two eyes each have a slightly different perspective. One eye perceives an object in one position; the other eye perceives it in a slightly different position. Each eye sends its signals to the brain and the brain interprets those signals to create the perception of depth. Depth is the third dimension.

Try this. Keep your head very still, shut one eye, and look at something close to you. Then close the eye that you have open and open the eye you have closed. Did the object appear closer or seem to move as you shifted from eye to eye? This is because each eye provides your brain with a slightly different image—and that slight difference, when interpreted by the brain, creates the sense of depth.

Now, apply this binocular stereopsis principle to how your computer viewscreen works. How do you create the kind of depth perception that you experience in the real world if your display device (either an LCD panel or a traditional cathode ray tube monitor) can only present flat images and set a fixed distance away? The general answer is that your brain has experience in interpreting visual clues. Based on other data points such as time, motion, lighting, shading, and color hues—your brain can take corrective action that makes it possible for you to perceive and interpret depth—even if you are actually looking at a flat display screen. Now that you know how your body perceives three dimensions, the big question becomes, How can you get your computer to simulate depth?

In the real world, if you are standing still and gazing at a 3D object, lighting, shading, and other clues tell you how far away it is and its depth. If you move forward or backward, your brain has more clues—and comparisons between them—to work with, making your depth perception much more accurate. Now here's the heart of the problem with respect to creating 3D images on a computer: there is no real depth to deal with. Our computer displays are either flat LCD displays or cathode tubes that are one-half inch to eighteen inches deep. You can't look into your monitor or LCD display to see real depth dimension because these devices are not physically deep. Unlike looking through a glass picture window where there truly is depth beyond the pane of glass—there is no real depth behind your viewscreen. To overcome this problem, the challenge that computer graphics artists face is how to mimic the shadows, lighting, relative sizes, and other phenomena that occur in nature to trick our brains into perceiving depth.

How Does a Computer Graphics Artist Paint 3D Graphics on Computer Screens?

In the 1950s, television was introduced. It had the ability to receive broadcast shows (wirelessly) and display those shows on a cathode ray tube or CRT. In order to display images, televisions use a beam of electrons to excite thousands of pixels (small dots) that are shaded in various ways to create the pictures we see on our viewscreens. When viewed together at a fast enough refresh rate, our brains merge these pixels together into a complete image. In order to paint an image on your monitor, your computer must assign color values to each of the millions of pixels that make up your display screen. And as that image changes, your computer must recompute all of the display elements on your screen, reassign values, and make other changes in order to render an image.

Color television added the concept of coloring polygons to achieve various color and shading effects. Monitors also make use of polygons to assign color, to account for shading, to add texture, and so on.

Now extrapolate. For a computer to paint a graphically detailed three-dimensional screen, it needs to be able to compute the location of millions of polygons on a continuous basis—thereby allowing for motion. If you are getting the message that the presentation of 3D graphics is processor-intensive, you are right!

Now consider that pixels are arranged in columns and rows—think of a piece of graph paper. Imagine that your job was to create a round circle on a piece of graph paper—but you were only allowed to do so by filling in boxes on the paper (see Figure 7). You would end up with a jagged set of squares (known as "jaggies") linked together that bore only a vague resemblance to a circle. Apply this concept to a display screen and all of the images you viewed would be squarish or jagged in nature. A per-

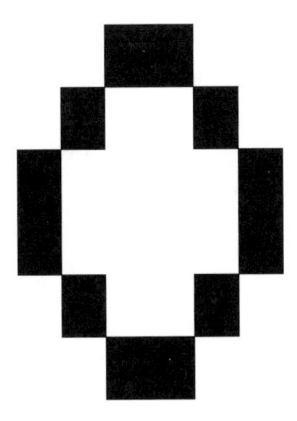

CHAPTER 7: RECEIVING SENSORY DATA FROM YOUR COMPUTER 125

Jaggies

FIGURE 7
A Squarish Circle Illustrates the Need for 3D Aliasing

son represented under such circumstances would likely have squarish shoulders and limbs. Any curves or rounded shapes in the setting would seem jagged in nature. Not only does your computer have to calculate the location of colors within polygons within pixels, it must also make allowance for curves and other shapes that are presented on a row-and-column pixel grid.

In order to simulate curves in alphanumeric characters or vector graphics, computers use a technique called anti-aliasing to blur out the jagged edges of the pixel grid. This technique involves using a series of washed-out colors placed on the edges of a curve. Since pixels are so small, our eyes blend these washed out colors with the darker colors, softening the jagged edges.

Now, take what you've learned about computer graphics— the placement of colors, the manipulation of pixels, the heavy amount of computational work involved—and consider the following: If done correctly, the artist can create an image of an environment that can trick your brain into believing an object on your computer screen has depth. The graphics artist does this by making use of anti-aliasing to create smooth images and by using the right colors, lighting, shadows, and other natural effects. If done correctly, this artificially created scene will be as realistic as looking through a window, including the illusion of distance and depth.

WHAT HAPPENS IF GRAPHICS ARE POORLY DONE?

But, what if graphics are done poorly? If computer graphics are done really badly, they may actually give you feelings of nausea and disorientation, even headaches. This type of reaction is called interface sickness and often results when visual, audio, and other sensory clues do not match or are out of synch—sending confusing signals to the brain that result in a queasy or achy feeling.

When playing or working in some totally immersive simulation environments, some people find that they suffer from one or two forms of this 3D sickness. Whether it be nausea, dizziness, eyestrain, and headaches, these reactions can be caused by badly implemented 3D graphics or, ironically, by a simulated 3D environment being too real (such as the illustrated in the seasickness case described below).

> If a person typically gets seasick in the real world and takes a simulated 3D sail ride over five-foot waves (complete with a motion platform that sways you up and down), it is very likely he or she will also get seasick in a simulated 3D environment. If the simulation is done really well, that person's brain will have trouble distinguishing a real-world situation from the electronically contrived version of the experience.
>
> Basically, if you get seasick in the real world, chances are you will get seasick in a well-designed electronic environment—despite the fact that you are viewing the

waves and feeling the motions electronically. Like me, you would still need a motion sickness pill or patch if you plan to use powerful, realistic sailing simulators.

Another form of simulation sickness can be caused by the failure to deliver a unified, high-fidelity experience. Virtual you could start to feel ill if audio and visual clues are disjointed or out of synch, thereby sending confusing signals to their brains. The primary way for application developers to avoid creating this type of interface sickness is to pay close attention to how the user's brain is being stimulated and avoid overstimulating them. This can be done by properly synchonizing electronic signals or by cutting down on realism effects.

One of the more interesting studies of interface sickness that I came across was conducted by two scientists, Mel Siegel of The Robotics Institute, School of Computer Science, Carnegie Mellon University, and his associate, Shojiro Nagata. Their work, "Just Enough Reality: Comfortable 3D Viewing via Microstereopsis," describes some of the causes of virtual reality sickness (another term for interface sickness). They propose certain work-arounds to help avoid the causes of such sickness.

Siegel and Nagata suggest that we do not have to recreate reality exactly to maximize the benefits of 3D vision in electronic worlds. Rather, they postulate that a gentler stereo approach be used called microstereopsis. This means that the user is able to view 3D images without uncomfortable specialized eyewear, without clue conflicts, and without a locked-in adjustment time to perceive a virtual scene comfortably in full depth. They call for a new class of zoneless autostereoscopic displays.

Should research such as this succeed (and there are dozens of other research projects underway studying the same sort of problems and proposing alternative solutions to stereoscopic sicknesses), the problems that some people experience viewing 3D worlds will gradually be reduced—and high-quality 3D depth perception will become a reality.

Another Point to Consider

Texture, lighting, and shading effects are all tasks that require a great deal of computation. They burn processing power like crazy. Add to this the fact that moving a virtual you through a 3D virtual space creates even more computational overhead (the logistics tracking alone is a potential nightmare). Then multiply this by hundreds, thousands, or potentially millions of avatars visiting the most popular Internet vistas and you'll come to understand the scope of the problem of efficiently delivering Sensory Virtual Internet services to you in the future. The point is that in order to do 3D graphics processing for large populations of users, our back-end computers are going to have to be designed to accommodate heavy number crunching and computation (rather than transaction-oriented) tasks. Meanwhile front-end devices will need to be oriented toward graphics display, audio playback, and the control of other local peripheral devices such as printers, scent systems, touch devices, and the like. This perspective will be explored in depth in Chapter 12.

What You Need to Know About 3D Audio

To mimic real world hearing experiences in our virtual worlds of the future scientists and application developers will need to master the concept of spatial hearing (hearing sounds in the virtual space that surrounds us just as we would hear them in the real world).

The basic concepts of how we process sound are well known. For instance, the way that we hear a sound and know its coming from our right is based upon when sound reaches both of our ears. If a sound reaches our right ear first (and has stronger volume than when it reaches our left ear) we perceive the sound as coming from the right. The elevation of sound (up or down) is detected from spectral changes picked up by our outer ears (or pinnae). The task ahead for scientists and application developers is to find better ways to create realistic sound environments where up, down, left, right, and the range of objects from the listener can be easily simulated in virtual worlds of the future.

The current state of the art in computerized sound is that our computers do an excellent job in delivering stereo sound to computer users—meaning they deliver sound quite accurately to our left and right ears. The challenge ahead lies in completing the spectrum by delivering immersive sound that listeners can discern as coming from above, below, left, right, or from a distance (whether near or far).

Some examples of this sound range element come from Creative Laboratories and from Aureal Software. Along with a Creative Labs Soundblaster card that I recently purchased came software that produces environmental sound effects. For instance, you can create the sound of a basketball player dribbling the ball from far down court to nearby and back again. From Aureal comes software that creates what the company calls a 3D Bee. This virtual bee buzzes around the screen making a humming sound that sounds near as the bee approaches and then far away as the bee flies away on the viewscreen.

To create/simulate surround sound today audiophiles use multiple speakers placed in strategic locations around a room such as in front and to the left and right of a listener, in back and left and right of a listener, with a woofer (for bass tones) speaker placed above or close to the listener. This approach, although somewhat expensive, can today deliver excellent surround sound experiences to listeners today.

The challenge ahead will be to create immersive sound environments that can emulate sound as delivered in various venues such as concert halls, churches, or other metaphorical, virtual places. Certain technologies such as Dolby digital decoding, Dolby Pro Logic, and Dolby 3 allow for this type of immersive experience today—the primary challenge that remains is to encourage application developers to write programs that take advantage of immersive 3D surround sound audio.

What You Need to Know About Scent Technology

The sense of smell (the olfactory sense) is triggered when you pull airborne molecules into your nose. Your olfactory receptors react to these molecules, sending signals to your brain for analysis. A flower releases a chemical that wafts into your nose. This chemical provokes a response in several receptors, all of which send signals to your brain. Just like your visual cortex reconstructs the image on the TV screen, the olfactory region adds these stimuli together into a unified, identifiable smell.

How Do Digital Scent Technologies Work?

Essentially, personal computers and game consoles will be equipped with a peripheral device known as a scent synthesizer. This little box contains a variety of different oils (around 128 at this juncture). When these oils are heated at certain temperatures and in certain combinations, they produce molecules that stimulate designated olfactory receptors. Thus they can reproduce smells such as coffee, candy, leather, or even flowers and perfumes. In concept, the idea is similar to that of a color printer using inks (instead of oils) to produce a broad palette of colors. Only in the case of the scent synthesizer, it is a broad palette of scents. With a printer, when the ink cartridge becomes empty, the cartridge is replaced; the same would be true for the scent synthesizer.

What You Need to Know About Taste Sensation Technology

Smell is closely related to the sense of taste and contributes greatly to the sensation of flavor. Try holding your nose when tasting something and see if it has the same flavor as when you allow complete access to your olfactory receptors. Taste buds also play an important, if not dominant role in our sense of taste—taste buds receive signals that our brains interpret as sweet, salty, bitter, or sour.

The sense of taste (the gustatory sense) is basically comprised of four qualities: saltiness, sourness, sweetness, and bitterness. In order to appreciate the taste of an item truly, we also rely on our sense of smell and of touch—to ascertain the texture (crunchiness, smoothness, etc.).

To date *I am aware of only one line of research in electronic taste technology*—scientists are experimenting with an approach that uses cards with taste imprints printed on them by a printer-like device. These first digital taste devices imprint salt, sour, sweet, and bitter flavors as well as scents on an edible substance (in this case, bland potato paper). They are developing ways to trigger particular tastes in the card electronically. By so doing, these scientists are able to send taste sensations over the Internet.

I am certain that there will be other advances as creative scientists and engineers put together new approaches, but for now the digital taste field is too immature to project future development.

What You Need to Know About Touch (Haptic) Technology

Your sense of touch is also known as your haptic sense. The word "haptic," derived from the Greek word "haptikos," which means "to touch or grasp," thus more than adequately describes the key elements of the sense of touch we are trying to duplicate in our virtual world. We humans want some way to be able to touch objects in virtual worlds to ascertain if they are hard or soft, hot or cold, wet or dry. We also need ways to duplicate many other touch experiences that we feel in the real world when our epidermis touches an object. In addition, we may wish to pick up an object to examine it, or to move it to some other location in the virtual world we are visiting.

Haptic technologies are those that relay the sense of touch (including other sensations such as cold or hot) to the user. The current state of the art in touch technologies are developments for game players in the form of vibrating steering wheels or joysticks, or even haptic-enhanced chairs. You can feel your airplane take a hit from enemy aircraft fire—even feel the jolt as your plane loses maneuverability when its flaps are hit. Or you can almost feel the sway of the high-speed hotrod you're driving as you hit a turn too fast and you head into a skid. But moving beyond this vibration-oriented technology has proven to be quite difficult, primarily because many of the technologies are not yet in place to help the human body feel a virtual hard surface such as cement, or feel the heat of a fire, the wetness of rain, or the slipperiness of oil.

Beyond vibrations and jolts, software and hardware is now available that enables PC users to experience some textures—particularly textures related to on-screen navigation and control. For instance, Immersion Corporation, a maker of touch technologies, has made it possible for PC users to feel the contours of on-screen buttons, pull-down menus, scroll bars, and Web pages as they navigate Windows-based screens or certain touch-enabled Web sites. These touch technologies work by translating digital information into physical sensations. Today, touch-enabled devices such as mice or joysticks use magnetic actuators and sensors built into the device to deliver a resistance sensation called force feedback. These are sensations that we can use with our imaginations and the right visuals to interpret as the feeling of enemy gunfire hitting the fuselage of our planes, or as bumps and potholes on a road, or any of a number of simulated experiences. Touch-sensitive devices can also deliver other forms of feedback including the sensation of liquids, textures, vibrations, and many others. Essentially, provided that you have a device that can relay touch sensations, and as long as the feeling can be translated into a mathematical equation, your computer will be able to convey haptic information to you.

Immersion Corporation develops and markets haptic technologies and products that provide tactile interaction between people and computers. With more than 65 registered patents and 185 more pending, the company is a major force in the haptic market. Although Immersion Corporation does build some of its own products, it also focuses on moving its technologies to market by working with hardware manufacturers, peripheral device developers, and medical simulation product manufacturers to build mice, joysticks, and other computer peripherals. Look closely and you may find Immersion technologies in your force-feedback mice, joysticks, or steering wheels.

Feeling textures is a big step forward in haptic technologies. Immersion Corporation products can help imitate the textures that you see on your screen—doing the computations necessary to mimic the feel and delivering it to your output device. You could move your cursor around the screen and feel the bump as you go over the corner of a window to make it larger, or feel the edge pull back like a rubber band to let you know that you had actually engaged the minimize or maximize feature. You could even feel the small button you may be trying to activate or feel the knob you are trying to turn.

Immersion's testing has shown that adding the sense of touch to computer interaction can improve the time it takes to target objects by as much as 80 percent. This could make shoppers more accurate in finding and selecting merchandise, or workers more efficient in carrying out their job responsibilities. Haptics do not only help complete the human sensory experience, they also contribute to increased enjoyment of games and increased productivity in work environments.

Source: http://www.immersion.com

Simulating real world, real touch, physical sensations such as hot and cold or wet and dry will be extremely difficult for numerous reasons. To experience hot or cold, dozens (if not hundreds) of heat- or cold-generating devices would need to be placed onto some sort of human exoskeleton to mimic real-world heat or cold. If not significantly miniaturized, these devices could prove awkward—unless you're comfortable wearing a refrigerator on your back! The same could hold true for simulating the feeling of wetness (though you may only have to wear a water bottle, not a sink).

It will be quite a long time until we master the delivery of the complete range of human touch experiences over the Internet. A big piece of the problem is how to deliver touch sensory data to our external exoskeleton and epidermis (skin). Will we have to wear body suits? Will we have to sit (or stand) in confined bubbles in order to feel sensations like hot and cold? The question to be tackled is how to deliver a range of touch experiences optimally, such as the slippery feel of oil, a coarse texture, or heat using electronic means. We will gradually tackle this problem, but initial solutions are focused on simple vibrations and textures.

Chapter Summary

Why is sensory output important to us? We learn from stimuli—the stimulation of our senses of sight, sound, touch, scent, and taste. In most cases, we learn better from the stimulation of two modalities (for instance, sight and sound). Actually, though, any combination of the above senses aids our ability to learn more about objects that surround us. Computer sensory output is important because we will need more than sight or sound to understand the environments that we will be visiting when we travel through the 3D virtual worlds of the future.

Sensory output technologies deliver stimuli or information to four of our five senses. Of these five senses, sight and sound technologies are the most mature while taste is by far the least.

In sight technologies, the major effort underway is in 3D visualization. The next chapter will closely examine state-of-the-art 3D visualization devices and their application to business and entertainment markets. Keep in mind how this chapter described how graphic designers build 3D solutions. Lighting, shadowing, anti-aliasing, and a variety of other techniques are used to create electronic environments—essentially tricking the brain into processing images with a simulated perception of depth. If done well, a designer can create a realistic and immersive experience for the visitor to his or her 3D world. If done poorly, the user may experience interface sickness due to overstimulation of the brain. Providing stimuli inconsistent with what the user expects based on previous experiences in real-world situations can also cause these effects.

With respect to sound, the primary effort underway has to do with writing programming that enables sound to be perceived in three dimensions: range (near, far away, and variations in between); up and down; left and right. The big effort ahead in digital technology will be in programming applications with the knowledge of where sound-producing objects are in relation to a virtual visitor, and the capability of producing the right sounds to reflect the changes in distance between the visitor and the object. This will require some fairly complex programming but early versions of such technology have already made it to market.

The sense of smell works by stimulating various olfactory receptors in your nose. Technology is now available that allows users to receive scent data over the Internet through peripheral printer-like devices on their personal computers. The peripheral used to create scents uses a mixture of oils to replicate smells—these oils when mixed, heated, and fanned emit odors ranging from food smells to flowers.

The sense of taste depends heavily on smell to accompany the overall taste experience (which is why certain foods seem to lose their taste when you have a cold—the lack of smell changes the taste experience). Electronic taste technology is the least mature of all sensory technologies. Current research and development efforts are focused on using bland wafers impregnated with tastes such as bitter, sweet, or salty that can be electronically triggered to stimulate your taste buds. These wafers will need to be accompanied by the use of appropriate scent sensations.

Finally, it is important to observe that rendering three-dimensional images is an intensely computational task. The location of millions upon millions of pixels needs to be calculated, as do the colors, shades, lighting, and texture effects directed at polygons within those pixels. Combine this processor-intensive task with the computations necessary for managing our locations and travels through the virtual worlds of the future and you'll start to appreciate my view that much of the computing done to help us move through future virtual worlds will be done on back-end servers. Front-end devices—be they PCs, workstations, handhelds, wearables, or the like—will ultimately become display or play devices that are highly reliant on the back-end processors for applications and services.

With this chapter under your belt for background information, a closer look at the state-of-the-art technology for each of these technologies is warranted. What equipment can be used to deliver 3D visual graphics? What suppliers make scent technology? And how do all of these technologies apply to business or entertainment usage? The next two chapters seek to answer such questions.

CHAPTER 8

3D GRAPHICS

You now have a rudimentary understanding of how 3D graphics are constructed, how they are created, and why 3D sensory output will be important to us as we visit the 3D virtual worlds of the future.

But how are we going to realize this grand vision of the future? Where are the stepping stones that will move us from our current mundane two-dimensional computing world to the vibrant and alive Sensory Virtual Internet of the future?

In order to answer these questions, it would be useful to gain an understanding of how 3D technologies are being used in businesses, in medicine, and by individuals today. We can then build a scenario that shows how 3D technologies will progress in the future. This chapter focuses on the state of the market for today's 3D technologies.

State of the Market: Types of 3D Presentation Displays

The ultimate goal for the 3D virtual reality experience is to create an immersive environment that mimics the real world. To do this, scientists, researchers, and developers need to devise new ways to present data in an efficient yet high-quality manner to virtual 3D viewers. In addition, new display devices will need to be created to help simulate real-world environments.

This section describes four different approaches to presenting 3D visual graphics. They are:

1. Cathode ray tubes (CRTs) as well as liquid crystal displays (LCDs)
2. Head-mounted devices
3. Shutter glasses
4. Projector-based displays

CRTs and LCDs

What's missing now with most of today's display devices is the capability to provide the computer user with depth perception on a standard, commercially available viewscreen. We also need to develop the ability to surround the viewer with a 3D-video experience. For many people, looking at a 3D world through today's computer CRT- or LCD-based monitors does not constitute an immersive experience. Instead the experience is more like looking at a virtual world environment through a window.

Take heart; even the common viewscreen is about to change as new technologies will be introduced over the next several years that will enable computer users to perceive depth. Let's look at the following example.

> In mid-year 2001, New Zealand-based Digital Video Imaging introduced new monitor technology that enables computer users to perceive depth on their computer monitors. The company's "actualdepth" monitors use an LCD that can display images on two physical planes (a

forward plane and a backplane) within the monitor. This technology takes advantage of binocular stereopsis (covered in Chapter 7) to create a depth effect.

Source: http://www.actualdepth.com

Another such effort to bring 3D visual effects to standard viewscreens includes the next example.

> DDD, a Toronto-based developer of 3D TV technology, recently raised $3.2 million through a private equity venture funding to continue its 3D encoding development and marketing efforts. The company's technology digitally encodes and enriches content, making it possible to present three-dimensional images on regular viewscreens. For investors reading this book who are looking to invest in technologies that will become popular as the Sensory Virtual Internet evolves, this may be just the kind of opportunity you are looking for. . . .

Source: www.digiscents.com

Beyond 3D display, you may wish to find computer displays, sound sets, and other technologies that provide more immersive virtual experiences. Other display devices such as head-mounted displays, shutter glasses, and projection-based systems may be more appropriate to your personal taste (and budget).

Head-Mounted Displays

Early research and experimentation in 3D virtual environments has featured the use of head-mounted display (HMD) technologies. These helmet-like devices include 3D viewing glasses, stereo audio, and tracker devices, which together have the ability to create a kind of 3D-in-a-helmet effect. Specialized glasses send separate stereoscopic signals to each eye of the wearer, thus creating a 3D visual effect. Stereo sound is issued to each ear, and depending on the sophistication of the application program, sounds can be made quite lifelike, including Doppler effects as objects approach and recede. In some virtual reality environments, a position tracker mounted in the headgear is used to help the visitor navigate the virtual environment. This pointer reacts to the user's head motions to look up or down, to more closely examine objects, or to move the avatar in a new direction.

> One company that is interesting to watch in the HMD market is i-O Display Systems, LLC. i-O manufactures "personal display devices" and stereoscopic 3D products used for various applications including medicine, business, and entertainment—the company also offers 3D movies that can be viewed using their devices.
> Source: http://www.cyberminduk.com/headsets/iglass_3d.htm

Among i-0's commercially available product offerings are display devices such as shutter glasses (I'll describe these further in the next section) as well as sophisticated HMD devices. By the time this book is published, i-O will have introduced its newest "i-Glasses," an HMD that provides 800 x 600 pixel resolution to the viewer. This is the resolution that most people use when they view applications and data on their personal computer display screens. This means that now commercially available HMDs will have the ability to present data in a similar, high-resolution manner.

By wearing such head-mounted devices, users experience what seems to be a much larger screen. You feel as though the screen is six feet wide. Future improvements will include even greater resolution as these devices further evolve.

Shutter Glasses

A kind of poor man's 3D virtual reality environment can be constructed through the use of commercially available shutter glasses. Generally costing only $50 to $150, shutter glasses work by using stroboscopically alternating frames to each eye. The variance between the flashing images creates the 3D effect—remember our experiment alternating opening and closing each eye? These glasses, in conjunction with a decent four-speaker PC stereo audio system, can go a long way toward creating a semi-realistic, pseudo-virtual reality environment fairly inexpensively. Because they already produce 3D and stereo audio effects, many 3D games can be easily adapted for use in this type of configuration.

A more detailed look at how shutter glasses work shows that shutter glasses use a technique similar to the way that computer monitors and television sets work. Both of these devices create images by putting a picture on a tube or flat panel that is constantly being refreshed. In the case of a computer terminal, images are constantly refreshed at a rate of 60 frames per second or more. A television has a refresh rate of around 30 frames per second. Shutter glasses work in tandem with computer screens to interlace (alternate and align) images, so that while one eye sees an image, the other eye sees only black. The images are then rapidly switched, so that the original eye sees black while the second eye sees an image. This switching on and off of images happens so quickly, that our minds blend the images together into a continuous image. The alternating images are slightly different (this is how our eyes work naturally). The result is that each eye sees the same image with enough additional stereoscopic information for the brain to create a 3D composite.

> Metabyte Inc. has focused on providing consumers with "the best stereovision solution in the world" with its EyeScream LCD shutter glasses, "the best 3D graphics board, and the best driver-level software." These are used to present 3D stereovision for numerous, popular 3D games currently on the market. If the game software is used with the EyeScream shutter glasses, and if it does 3D math properly, it does not have to be modified to use Metabyte's software drivers to deliver exceptional 3D effects. What this means is that many out-of-the-box PC games are already capable of being viewed through shutter glasses, and each of them can deliver impressive 3D effects right now.
> Source: http://www.wicked3D.com

Another supplier of shutter glasses, Elsa (with its 3D Revelator product) also emphasizes the importance of using software drivers to 3D-enable already-existing games. The 3D Revelator uses infrared technology to connect its polarizing shutter glasses to a PC without wires, thereby allowing players a certain amount of freedom of movement when playing 3D games. The Revelator's driver interfaces with Microsoft's DirectX (a computing standard and set of programming interfaces) to help enable 3D application gameplay.

> How does the Elsa 3D Revelator work? The company states that "the software driver aspect of the Revelator consists of a driver that calculates separate on-screen 3D images for the left eye and the right eye. It does this by looking at a game's Z-buffer usage in D3D. If a game doesn't use the Z-buffer (the axis that presents depth information) of 3D, then the 3D Revelator software has nothing to work with and there is no enhanced 3D effect. The images calculated by the Z-buffer are then rendered and displayed on screen on alternating screen refreshes. Frame 1 is for the left eye, frame 2 is for the right, frame 3 left, frame 4 right, and so on. Without the glasses, it looks as if there are two images overlaid upon each other, side by side and slightly offset, which is exactly what is going on.
>
> The Elsa Revelator shows that 3D vision can be attained today—provided that there are pre-existing elements within the application that can be exploited to deliver the 3D presentation.
>
> Source: http://www.elsa.com/international/europe/producte/mmedia/3drevelator.htm

Yet another company, Virtual Research Systems, Inc., produces advanced shutter glasses and is also an interesting study in the head-mounted display marketplace.

> Imagine flying on an airliner or sitting in the back seat of a car watching DVD movies on what appears to be a six-foot screen but in reality is a wearable stereophonic head-

set and viewscreen worn like a pair of goggles on your head. Virtual Research has recently introduced its fifth generation of i-glasses—a head-mounted projector and viewscreen that can display crisp DVD or other computer images on a wearable headset. The i-glasses contain two LCD screens, each with 375 lpi resolution and a 180,000-pixel display. Viewed close to the eyes, these screens create the effect of an 80-inch screen placed 11 feet in front of the user. The company's i-glasses can connect to a Panasonic DVD player to play movies, to portable miniature TVs, or to PCs or laptops. They can also connect to a broad range of other devices (including game consoles such as Nintendo 64 or PlayStation consoles).

Source: http://www.virtualresearch.com

Projector-Based Displays

Shutter glasses come very close to providing the kind of immersive experience that many people are seeking in 3D virtual environments. As a matter of personal preference, I'm very encouraged by some of the technological advances I'm seeing in the area of projector-based displays (also known as LCD projectors).

When using an LCD projector, typically images are projected on a white projection screen or wall in someone's office. These images often appear flat when compared to those on a typical CRT or LCD panel display—leaving a lot to be desired from an immersive perspective.

However, other approaches that use projection technology are evolving. One of the more exciting approaches to providing an enriched, immersive, visual display could be a wide-angle, peripheral-vision hemispheric display system from Elumens Corporation.

> Elumens Corporation is working on a hemispheric display system called VisionStation, which provides an immersive experience for the user seated in front of a

> large, conically shaped display screen. This screen surrounds the viewer with a 180-degree view. Objects on the display seem to move toward or away from the viewer—creating an immersive effect. Other than game-playing, applications for this technology include training simulation, mechanical design, and 3D modeling.
> Source: http://www.elumens.com

Another type of image projection system is underway at Hitachi, one designed to help eliminate the flatness associated with most projector-based systems.

> Hitachi Corporation has an LCD projector that displays computer images on glass. A window or a large pane of glass (to which a thin film is adhered to enhance reflectivity) acts as the projection screen and is capable of showing digital imagery, 3D games, and other applications in large-screen mode. Applications for this technology include store window displays and museum exhibits. Further, this technology could someday be used to allow projections on car windows or in other application environments where people's focus cannot leave the real world, but where computer images may help enhance viewing that world.
> Source:http://www.hitachi.com/icd/

These new solutions from Elumens and Hitachi are very much along the lines of what many consumers will want when they build immersive 3D environments. This projection approach keeps getting better. Try this on for size.

Imagine a stage-like virtual reality environment that can also provide the user with surround video, audio, scent, and touch experiences. Sound farfetched? Metradyne Corporation has already built such a virtual reality environment:

> MechDyne Corporation builds immersive 3D simulation environments primarily for businesses, government, experimental research, and educational purposes. Among its many product offerings is the company's MD CSVR, a

rear- or front-projection display technology designed to provide a wrap-around immersion experience for users. The product can make use of curved screens that are soft, semi-rigid, or rigid. Its optics are folded to reduce overall size of the system's footprint.

Imagine this. MechDyne offers a version of its MD CSVR that is scalable up to a full 360-degree horizontal field of view (FOV) with a 12-foot radius. The radius range (the distance between the user and the screen) can be expanded from 10 feet to as much as 50! The projection technology accommodates geometrical corrections in order to present an accurate 3D environment. The system also has options that allow for tracking, video, fiber/copper matrix switching, teleconferencing, audio, and a customizable user interface. It even allows for linkage to motion bases, so people can move physically through immersive environments.

Note that systems like MechDyne's can cost far less than $100,000—an entry-level system can cost $30,000 to $40,000. In order to get a completely immersive experience today, be prepared to pay handsomely. Over time, costs for these types of displays will decline.

Source: http://www.mechdyne.com

The issues facing this kind of technology approach to building immersive 3D environments are related to expense and programming. Creating a true immersive experience is costly. Hundreds of thousands of dollars can be spent to build a totally immersive environment. Then once that environment is created, where do you get the software to take advantage of the sense-around sensory virtual features of this environment? Though not affordable by everyone, this immersive experience is the direction that our Sensory Virtual Internet is moving toward. The technology exists today to allow for such experiences—what's missing is applications that exploit this kind of completely immersive environment and an affordable cost model that can make this kind of sensory-rich experience available to middle and low income Internet users.

Other Interesting 3D Display Efforts

Finally, note that over the next few years, low-cost high-definition TV will make its way into the consumer marketplace. Experiments conducted by the High Definition Systems Program of the Advanced Research Projects Agency's Electronic Systems Technology Office have shown that it is possible to create high-definition stereoscopic imagery on these HDTVs by using one high-resolution color camera and two low-resolution monochrome cameras. Perhaps someday soon even our television sets will also provide high-resolution 3D imagery.

How Is the Market Using 3D Technology Today?

3D technology is already in heavy use in four market sectors: engineering, creative content development, electronic games, and healthcare. They use 3D technology to create object models that aid in visualizing products in three dimensions, in creating special effects for the movies, in providing exciting 3D game experiences, and for diagnosis, teaching, and research purposes in the healthcare field. More specifically, engineers are using 3D technologies to collaborate on complex design and modeling projects. Gamers are starting to participate in 3D multiplayer games on the Web. Medical personnel are making use of 3D technologies for diagnostic and consultative purposes; while the entertainment industry uses 3D to build creative content and special effects.

The reason that 3D is used so successfully in engineering and medical environments is largely due to due to the availability of high-speed networks—either private intranets or extranets that allow business partners to participate in collaborative/consulting exercises. As for the success of 3D in Hollywood, 3D content creation does not rely heavily on the use of networks, but rather on powerful, self-contained graphics and number-crunching computers that can generate 3D visual effects for movies and other forms of entertainment. In the case of multiplayer games, 3D games are being used successfully despite the fact that gamers are generally using 56 Kb or less Internet connections to engage in gameplay (gamers get reasonable graphics quality due to the use of sophisticated file compression techniques and because the size of game files are not as huge as most medical image or engineering files).

In the past, consumers and retailers have resisted the use of 3D technology on the World Wide Web because of the length of time it took to download 3D graphics and imagery. But this is about to change in the near future as the availability of high-speed networks combined with more optimized compression technologies will soon enable the general Web populace (even those with low-speed interconnections) to more quickly access 3D images. Also expect that initially people will use 3D technologies to view products or to play games, but gradually people will start using 3D images of themselves as they collaborate, conduct commerce, or socialize in 3D virtual worlds.

Business, Entertainment, and Healthcare Uses of 3D Technology

For over 25 years, businesses have been making use of 3D design and modeling applications to help visualize products in the design cycle or for hundreds of other visual/conceptual uses. For instance, it is used to project and model behavior, to visualize marketing trends over time, to map a projected weather pattern, and to study the human genome.

Hollywood and the entertainment industry have been making heavy use of 3D technologies for years to create realistic spatial effects in movies. Aliens, spaceship battles, dinosaurs, and other special effects are often modeled and generated using 3D technologies.

The games industry has greatly advanced the science of 3D presentation by adding shadowing, lighting, and reflective effects to objects in the game environment. These games use 3D rendering engines to provide semirealistic 3D effects on computer monitors, TV sets, or flat-panel displays.

The healthcare industry has been using 3D technologies to assist in diagnosis and especially in radiology through the use of computerized axial tomography (CAT) scans. 3D simulations are used to train doctors and medical personnel and to assist in medical research such as the study of the human genome.

Let's take a closer look at how each market segment uses 3D technology today.

How Business Uses 3D Technology Today

Business typically uses 3D technology for two purposes: visualization (for modeling and retailing purposes) and collaboration.

Visualization: 3D Modeling

Typical use of 3D technologies is for visualization and modeling purposes. For instance, a computer model can be used to determine if all the doors in a new car design open and close properly or if they will be obstructed in any way. It can also help in ascertaining if a driver's seat leaves enough foot and leg clearance room for a rear passenger. Using 3D graphics combined with computer modeling technologies allows companies to produce product designs that can be visualized and tested before entering a modeling/prototyping stage. Prototyping can cost hundreds of thousands or even millions of dollars. Modeling reduces this financial exposure while at the same time reducing development time and time to market.

Another use for 3D technologies in business includes simulation visualization. In weather forecasting, for instance, computers crunch simulated model after simulated model to show meteorologists possible weather patterns. Remember, we learn better when we have access to multiple modes of input. Visual computer simulations give us a better conceptual understanding of a forthcoming weather pattern than a simple verbal radio report.

Other uses of 3D technologies include oil and resource exploration, visualization using sophisticated decision support and data modeling tools to project marketing trends, and for scientific research purposes (such as seismic analysis).

> Using sophisticated seismic analysis tools that also feature the use of 3D visualization technologies, researchers, and scientists have discovered that the ground near the highly populated Southern California city of Los Angeles (more specifically, a large area in the San Gabriel Valley) consists of a basin of soft sediment that is about three miles deep. This is almost one and a half times deeper than previously estimated.

This example serves to illustrate that 3D technologies can be used for far more than creating virtual venues or game playing. Geographers, planetary ecologists, and geologists have used 3D visualization techniques to better understand the geographical make up of the earth, to assist in oil exploration, and for a number of other important commercial uses.

From a business perspective, the benefits of 3D graphing and modeling are generally related to efficiency. In the product design and development world, 3D computer design and engineering can shave weeks, months, or years off the development process.

For almost 30 years, most business 3D usage has centered around Computer-Aided Design and Computer-Aided Manufacturing (CAD/CAM) applications. These products help design parts (ranging from small widgets through massive airplane or car parts. Computer-Aided Engineering (CAE) uses 2D and 3D models heavily throughout the design process.

The bottom line is that business and academia have been making successful use of 3D technologies for years for product development, market analysis, research and analysis, and exploratory purposes.

Visualization: Retailing

It is interesting to note that to date, 3D technology has not met with great success on the Internet with retailers or marketers. There are a few good reasons why 3D technologies have not taken off.

1. The primary reason is because consumers and information seekers are not willing to invest the time necessary to wait for complex 3D images to download. Most retail buyers are not shopping from work, but rather from their home—environments that frequently have connection speeds to the Internet of less than 56Kbps. Simply stated, by an overwhelming majority Internet users prefer faster downloads to fancy graphics. People are just plain unwilling to wait for long downloads of graphical data.
2. Many Internet retailers are aware that users won't wait for lengthy downloads and are shying away from using 3D or multimedia presentations to display and market products. Ironically, most of these retailers know that 3D presentation of goods and services greatly increases the stickiness of a given site. They also know that there is a direct correlation between capturing a customer's attention and the making of a sale.

Until 3D graphics compression gets radically better (such that 3D images can be downloaded more quickly), or until consumers upgrade the speed of their communications lines, the retail use of 3D display technologies will be slow in coming.

Still, there are many sites that have successfully experimented with 3D Web technology and are currently reaping the rewards of using new 3D display technologies to market their goods. Lexus, Macy's, Timex, and Tyrwhitt are but a few of the hundreds of sites that you can visit to find 3D-displayed merchandise. Several of these sites have seen tangible business benefits in implementing 3D product views, despite consumer resistance to long download times. Charles Tyrwhitt Shirts is a good example of a small business that is using 3D technology to grow and reap additional revenue.

> Charles Tyrwhitt Shirts (*www.tyrwhitt.co.uk*), a mail-order shirt company, received an E-nitiative of the Year business award from the UK publication *Real Business* and the Confederation of British Industry (CBI). The company received the award in recognition of its successful deployment of an advanced, interactive 3D Web site based upon Computer Associate's Jasmineii eBusiness platform.
>
> Charles Tyrwhitt Shirts was one of the first apparel companies to recognize that customers might want a better view of the items they are looking to purchase. Although many buyers are currently comfortable with a two-dimensional view of the products they buy, most would admit that having a more information-rich 3D view is more desirable than a 2D view. Tyrwhitt provided such information-rich 3D views of its products. By so doing, the company has been able to increase sales by 7 percent in December 1999 to 21 percent in November 2000. Customers have been coming to the site, staying longer, and purchasing products more often than before.
> Source: www.tyrwhitt.co.uk

In the past, consumers and retailers have resisted the use of 3D technology on the World Wide Web, but this is about to change in the near future. You can expect the availability of high-speed networks combined with more optimized compression technologies to soon enable the general Web populace (even those with low speed interconnections) to more quickly access 3D images. Also expect that initially people will use 3D technologies to view products or to play games, but gradually people will start using

3D images of themselves as they collaborate, conduct commerce, or socialize in 3D virtual worlds.

Collaboration

Over the past two years, product design and development has focused on improving 3D content delivery and *collaboration* between builders of finished products and members of their supply chain such as parts suppliers. One recent development is that 3D modeling technology is being used with greater frequency in conjunction with collaboration software to allow engineers, designers, and business partners to work cooperatively together over the Internet to build new products.

> A recent Ford Motor Company experiment embodied the benefits of effectively using 3D technologies combined with collaboration software to reduce product costs while at the same time reducing product time to market. In the business world, mechanical and electrical engineers have been using 3D modeling for over 25 years to build prototypes of products—especially in the airline and auto industries. Ford recently completed the design of a new car, the Mondeo, in 16 months. This process typically takes 40 to 48 months (see Chapter 15 for further details).

It is important to note that business partners are often geographically dispersed, yet the collaborative software and the Internet can bring them together to work on joint projects while 3D technologies enable cooperating parties to visualize new product designs and models. The combination of collaborative software with 3D visualization technology and a new technology called colocation software (software that enables parties to see and hear each other while using collaboration software) will all combine to create realistic 3D just-like-being-there environments of the future.

In commerce environments, 3D visualization, collaborative, and colocation software will also be used by buyers and sellers to conduct transactions where the seller will display and sell items using 3D technology and the buyer will view and examine items in 3D mode.

For businesses that use 3D technology today, the next frontier will be the integration of 3D technology with other sensory technologies (such as voice, scent, and touch), in order to further facilitate Internet-based product collaboration. Businesses now save billions of dollars annually using 3D visualization technologies. Imagine how much more could be saved if businesses could find streamlined ways to work with their supply chain partners to prototype and build new products in virtual space. *The next big wave for 3D in business will come when businesses adopt speech and voice technologies to augment existing visualization technologies—and combine these sensory technologies to collaborate better and reduce product development cycles.*

How the Entertainment Industry Uses 3D Technologies Today

The entertainment industry uses 3D technologies today in two ways: to develop digital content and special effects (fancy, eye-popping visual effects for movies), and to create videogames.

The Cinematic Use of 3D Technologies

Movies such as *Ants*, *Casper*, and *Toy Story* are all examples of how Hollywood is making use of 3D computer graphics to provide enhanced 3D viewing for theater audiences. Other creative artists use 3D digital content creation technologies to produce special effects (such as a plane, train, or automobile crashing, a building exploding, or a spaceship disintegrating). Like big business, the movie industry has found that using 3D technologies can reduce costs and cut down on time to market. Special effects that could take months to create using traditional methods can be created almost automatically with the use of modern 3D content creation technologies.

The Use of 3D Technologies in Games

Sony, Nintendo, and others make game consoles—dedicated hardware created only for the purpose of running advanced 3D games. A computer purist might argue that a discussion about these game consoles doesn't really belong in this book. However, due to the great degree of hardware optimization built into these boxes to handle 3D presentation graphics, and the fact that many consoles are just now becoming Internet-enabled, I would argue that the humble game console might just become the chosen device by many consumers who wish to participate on the Sensory Virtual Internet of the future. I make this statement because I believe that game consoles will have distinct advantages over PCs for the next three years—perhaps longer. Hence, this section takes a close look at what's happening in the game console marketplace, the ramifications of the recent consolidations in the industry, and the effects of advances in graphics handling on that marketplace.

The Games Industry

The games industry (not to be confused with the gaming industry, which means gambling) is a $13 billion industry worldwide. In the United States alone, video game hardware and software sales will exceed $6 billion in 2001. Today, computer games (including games that run on game consoles) are one of the fastest growing segments of the software industry.

The game console market is dominated by Sony, but Sony's PlayStation lead is constantly being challenged. Competitors include the Nintendo 64 and the soon-to-be-released Nintendo Dolphin system and Microsoft's new Xbox game technology (due year-end 2001). This industry has come a long way from 2D video game originals like Pong and Pacman, or later-generation games such as 16-bit Super Mario Brothers and the rest of the early Atari, Sony, Nintendo, and Sega stables. Today's games are visually exciting and highly representative of where the general-purpose computer market is heading from a 3D-visualization perspective. They display depth, shadowing effects, lighting effects, and other special effects that make computer screens and television sets come alive with vivid 3D imagery. The virtual you can race cars on imaginary racetracks or through city streets; take off in flight simulators and fly over the countryside; establish ancient empires; initiate trade with your friends and neighbors; build cities using 3D geographic information systems to construct roads, install water, gas, and plumbing lines, and to architect buildings; or shoot your way through maze-like environments and rack up points and kills.

Game Consoles Have Strong Advantages Over PC Architectures

If you've ever played Kong, Super Mario, Super Smash Brothers, Zelda, James Bond in Goldeneye, or any of a number of videogames, chances are that you didn't know or didn't care that you were using a very powerful, dedicated computer and related peripherals—far more powerful than most PCs in both presentation and display graphics perspective and sheer computing power. In fact, Sony's PlayStation 2 qualifies as a supercomputer—it even ran into export issues in Japan because of this. These super-powerful game consoles use their power to display depth, light and shadow, and other special effects that make computer screens and television sets come alive with vivid 3D imagery. The sheer power of these dedicated controllers gives gamers audio and visual experiences that mimic real-life 3D environments.

I would argue that the best consumer graphics to date are found on dedicated game controllers. A game console's graphics are generally better than a PC's due to the console's superior graphics processing power and the powerful proprietary graphics processing units used by game consoles that eclipse anything available on today's PC. Game consoles can process graphics more quickly than PCs—thus providing superior graphics, better screen flow, less choppiness, greater focus and detail, and the like.

Another advantage that game consoles have over PCs is the ability to process 128-bit data streams. These data streams describe how an image is to be portrayed. Most personal computers can process only 32 bits of data at a time. But game consoles can process four times as much information in the same time frame, thus rendering superior imagery. In short, game consoles have better system bus design, memory access, and superior processing capabilities than PCs currently have.

> When Bill Gates of Microsoft introduced the prototype of the company's forthcoming Xbox game console, he said: "I'm talking about an extended PC—a PC that talks to the TV set-top box, talks to the music player devices, [and] coordinates with other PCs." He added, "with its breakthrough technology and incredible graphics capabilities, Xbox will set the standard in gaming for years to come."
>
> The Xbox features four game controller ports and a DVD player. Most likely it will allow players to connect voice-activated headsets. When released (late 2001) Xbox is expected to feature a 600 MHz CPU, a 300 MHz custom-built graphics processor, 64 Mb of main memory, a 4x DVD, an 8 Gb hard disk, and 64 audio channels. In addition, Microsoft has enlisted close to 200 software companies around the world to create Xbox games for the launch.
>
> Source: http://www.2ndf.net/news/business/97886587217422.php

What Mr. Gates stated belies what is really happening. The Xbox is the harbinger of the next-generation home entertainment system to come: an Internet-based 3D graphics system that will run games, play music CDs, present DVD movies, and have other consumer electronics features—but will also connect to the Internet, essentially becoming a super-powerful Internet 3D graphics receiver and a potential rival to the personal computer. It is only a matter of time until PCs look more like game consoles and game consoles look more like Internet-enabled PCs.

PCs Versus Game Consoles

The downside of dedicated game consoles is that they:

- Are generally not multifunctional. A PC can be used to run spreadsheets, do word processing, play games, edit digital content, and do thousands of other things.
- Are usually not upgradeable. Adding memory, more advanced graphics processing cards, new sound gear, or new peripherals is generally not an option. For instance, 70 million people own Sony's first-generation PlayStation. But in order to take advantage of the features of the new PlayStation 2 and gain access to the latest graphics, Internet access, DVD, and other consumer electronics features, current PlayStation owners will be forced to completely replace their existing consoles. On the positive side, many of the games that run on the first-generation PlayStation console will also run on PlayStation 2, meaning that the user's investment in potentially hundreds of dollars of PlayStation games will be protected.
- Are limited by the number of games that are written for that particular game console. Games written to exploit the power of one game console (such as Sony's PlayStation 2) will not work on another dedicated, proprietary console (such as Nintendo 64) unless rewritten for Nintendo's architecture and vice versa. PC games, on the other hand, are written to be played on any PC (with certain minimum requirements such as the PC must meet prescribed CPU speed levels and have certain graphics card capabilities).
- Are usually not able to connect to the Internet.

Each architecture has its plusses and minuses. However, the differences in terms of game quality are starting to fade. PC architectures are ahead in multifunctional capabilities and Internet play. Dedicated controllers are currently ahead in graphical display capability and raw processing power. But expect the situation to change over the next few years:

> An interesting PC/console hybrid is starting to be developed: the dedicated Internet PC. This is a low-cost, Internet-enabled PC that ultimately will someday integrate the game consoles' powerful graphics. Soon this new device will start to encroach on dedicated controller markets, especially as some of the complex applications and graphics processing starts to be run on back-end computers. If the technologies are otherwise equal, a betting man might opt for multifunctionality over a dedicated approach.

Can dedicated controllers stay in this game? The dedicated devices can only win this game by staying ahead of the 3D game curve by providing more powerful processing, better graphics display, and the latest and greatest games. However, Internet-connected PCs will soon be able to take advantage of online servers for additional processing power and for compressing highly sophisticated computer graphics. PCs are already eroding the consoles' graphics advantage. Furthermore, it is not likely that consoles will continue to have the latest and greatest games, given that far fewer games are being developed for the dedicated controller market than are being developed for PCs.

Can consoles stay ahead of PCs? Looking at the technology horizon it appears that consoles will continue to lead PCs for at least the next three years in terms of graphics processing. Consoles are becoming Internet-enabled, which means they will pose a significant threat to PCs if they become more multifunctional (or are able to emulate PCs in order to take advantage of new, highly graphical applications that run on back-end processors on the Internet).

Still, I can easily envision a scenario where the game console becomes the primary Internet access device for the Sensory Virtual Internet of the future.

> nVidia's forthcoming NV20 chip will be used in the soon-to-be-released Microsoft Xbox. This chip's graphics processing unit, the XGPU, is based on the same chip technology used in nVidia PC GPUs. It will perform considerably faster than PC versions because it will have a direct channel to the Xbox CPU rather than having to use the slower Advanced Graphics Port (AGP) video bus, which most PCs use. The XGPU and CPU can pass information back and forth and make use of the same high-speed memory with no PC bus architecture slow-down of the data transfer in the middle. The XGPU will be able to process 125 million polygons per second, while NVidia's current GeForce 2 Ultra can at present process around only 31 million polygons per second.
>
> How does the XGPU do this? The CPU and XGPU share 64 Mb of 200 MHz double-data rate (DDR) memory. This type of memory is twice as fast as memory used in most PCs today. With no bus between the graphics chip and CPU, it is reasonable to expect performance well beyond the capabilities of the PC.
>
> Source: http://www.xboxweb.com/news/0201/030.html

Expect that for the near term (at least the next three years), game consoles will lead PCs in terms of graphics processing capability.

How the Healthcare Industry Uses 3D Technologies Today

X-rays began to be used as a routine diagnostic tool in the 1920s. Today, doctors and healthcare professionals still rely heavily on 2D data from X-rays to diagnose and evaluate patient problems. However, because X-rays produce only a two-dimensional view of a patient's anatomy and physiology, patients with ailments need to turn in various directions to give doctors the X-ray pictures they need to fully assess a broken bone or diagnose some other disorder.

It wasn't until 1972 that doctors were able to get a 3D view of the human body using a process called Computerized Axial Tomography (CAT) scan. The CAT scan produces computer-generated cross-sectional views of the body. CAT scan equipment is very expensive and the procedure is not needed for all patients, hence it is still relatively uncommon to use CAT scans as a diagnostic tool. Still, it is important to note that such 3D technology is available and in use in the healthcare field, helping to diagnose disorders and leading the way to corrective action.

In addition to CAT scans, 3D is used to create simulations and training experiences for medical personnel. For instance, one can practice removing a virtual appendix before actually performing such an operation on a human being. Medical students can practice hundreds of simulated medical procedures, helping to increase their familiarity with the human body without risking any patients. Someday, this kind of simulated training will be commonplace on the Sensory Virtual Internet.

Some of the most interesting use of 3D technology in the healthcare field is centered around medical research. Researchers can zoom in on three-dimensional images of viruses or use three-dimensional models to gain an understanding of the chromosomal make-up of a sequence of cells. Being able to view objects in 3D rather than 2D enables medical researchers to understand the size, position, color, texture, and other visual aspects more quickly and in a more meaningful manner. Perhaps this will lead more quickly to scientific observations and discoveries.

> Panasonic is helping to reinvent the healthcare industry with "tele-homecare" technology. The company's home unit acts as a patient terminal, a Doctor Terminal or Nursing Station is used by the healthcare professional and an "activeServer" coordinates between the two.
>
> Voice instructions walk the patient through tests

just like an in-person physical examination, including taking blood pressure, listening to the chest with a stethoscope, taking the temperature, monitoring heartbeat with an electrocardiograph, monitoring blood-oxygen saturation and blood sugar with sensors, and so on.

Source: http://www.panasonic.com/telecare

Chapter Summary

Significant improvements in the way that our computers can present 3D graphical data are underway. New technologies are evolving that will allow our computer viewscreens to present us with the perception of depth so that we can actually see images in three dimensions. Improvements in display technologies are also taking place with advances in LCD technology, headmount displays, shutter glasses, and other forms of graphics presentation devices well underway. Advances in these types of displays will greatly enrich our Internet 3D experiences of the future.

A close examination of how 3D visualization technology is being used today shows that for the most part 3D technology is used for visualization or collaborative purposes. Examples include business conceptualization and visualization (where 3D is used for activities such as modeling and design); healthcare (where 3D is used for diagnosis and training); and entertainment (where 3D is used for movie production and games).

The hot growth areas for 3D technologies can be found in retailing and in entertainment such as 3D games because with the greater availability of high-speed interconnection to the Internet for home users the use of 3D is increasing. Capitalizing on better network performance, Internet retail sites are now evolving that will allow buyers to more closely examine virtual merchandise from all angles—examining virtually the articles they are considering purchasing.

In game environments, 3D technologies are driving the creation of new peripheral display devices designed to provide players with a richer, immersive experiences (see Chapter 7 for more details). But games—or more precisely, game consoles—are the real bellwether to watch when following the 3D consumer products marketplace. Game consoles have been, and will continue to be, the leaders in terms of graphics processing and display capabilities. If you want to see how good PC graphics are going to get, examine game console graphics. PC graphics generally lag game console graphics by about a year.

All told, advances in 3D graphics display presentation devices combined with consumer and business demand for 3D visualization, collaborative, and entertainment products are likely to spur a boon in demand for new graphics presentation video cards, entertainment consoles, and programs that can capitalize on these advancing technologies.

CHAPTER 9
Sound, Scent, Touch, and Taste

Much of the action in sensory development to date has taken place in 3D visual presentation. However, there are new developments in audio technologies that bear close examination as well. New scent and touch technology products are available for consumers to purchase. Taste technology is also starting to evolve. This chapter examines the state of the art in all four of these technologies.

The State of the Art in Audio Systems

To me, the state of the audio marketplace has not changed tremendously over the past few years. Microphones are still used for analog input and new digital sound systems, headsets, advanced digital devices, and CD and DVD players have all come to market—each focused on recording sound on various media or replaying it for particular audiences.

Still, changes that have occurred or are occurring include:

1. The media that is used to record audio data. Over the past 20 years, we've moved from reel-to-reel tape, to cassette tape, to CD-ROM, to DVD.
2. The format and compression technique used to record audio data digitally. The latest hot format is MPEG-3, commonly known as MP3.
3. The quality of the codecs (coders/decoders) used to compress and uncompress digital sound.
4. Advances in spatial hearing (creating sound cues that increase or decrease in intensity as objects come near or move off into the distance; as well as interpreting direction such as up/down or left/right). One of the best research sites I've found on this topic can be found at *http://phosphoric.cpic.ucdavis.edu.*

The Need to Manage the Size of Sound Files

The nagging problem with sound technology is not the quality of the sound but the size of the files that are used to reproduce it. There is a big difference in file space needed to record a sound in 8-bit mono mode versus 16-bit stereo mode. Sixteen-bit stereo sound files can be two to three times larger than 8-bit monaural files. Essentially, digital audio boils down to this: If you are willing to accept lower-quality sound, then your file size will be smaller. Smaller file size means that the file can be transmitted over the Internet more quickly—but if you require high-quality sound, expect longer downloads (even with compression techniques such as MP3).

This problem with the size of sound files manifests itself in several places on the Internet today:

- Graphics-intensive games may clog Internet network lines (especially if the line speed is less than 56 Kb) but adding sound to these files is a sure way to inhibit game performance.
- For some businesses that are looking to run voice and data over the same network, the size of sound files becomes an issue if the enterprise's network does not have enough capacity to handle large files, such as high-quality sound files. This situation becomes particularly acute at peak network and telephone usage times—between 9:00 a.m. and 5:00 p.m. in most businesses.
- If you have tried to use the Internet to make free phone calls, you will have noticed that these large voice files sent over the Internet at peak usage times frequently results in voice lag, throwing the natural timing of conversation between a speaker and a receiver out of synch. Also, when combining voice and video simultaneously over low-speed lines, you will often experience less-than-satisfactory video and audio fidelity. Both of these issues can be attributed to the size of the sound files as well as the visual graphics files.

The good news on this front is that developers are getting far more sophisticated in creating compression algorithms that will allow high-quality voice to travel over the Internet without chewing up a lot of bandwidth.

3D Sound

It is fair to expect better sound quality and better compression algorithms over time—with major near term advances taking place in spatial hearing. From a sensory virtual perspective, observers need to watch how program developers use sound. If you've ever played a flight simulator combat game, you'll have noticed that as planes come near you, their sound increases and as planes pass by and move away, the sound replicates the real-world Doppler effects and changes frequency and volume. Writing this kind of auditory complexity into software can be difficult. Providing this kind of auditory landscape for hundreds or thousands of avatars in virtual space could prove to be a gargantuan effort. It will be interesting to watch how virtual space developers tackle this task.

The State of the Art in Haptic Systems

The state of the art today in commercial haptic systems is manifested in force-feedback technologies—devices that vibrate or shake as a game player rounds a corner in his or her racecar, or takes enemy gunfire in an action game.

One of the big problems that researchers face in the haptic interface area is trying simulate real-world tactile experiences such as hardness. Current research indicates that motors or electromagnetic forces would have to be used to deliver the tactile sensation that would force our hands to repel along a given surface. Dozens of small motors would have to be fashioned and controlled by a touch-replicating computer. The microtechnology necessary to accomplish this feat is not yet generally available, and building a repeller device of some sort today would prove to be prohibitively expensive for mass market use.

Another area of haptic research currently underway is the development of body suits (a form of reusable exoskeleton that can reproduce a multitude of touch sensations). The current issues with this type of technology include delivering sensations such as hot and cold, hardness, stickiness, smoothness, and other touch sensations that we experience in the real world. In part, these issues need to be resolved by advances in touch and haptic microtechnolgy hardware development—but as is typical in the delivery of other sensory information, software will also have to be developed to deliver touch sensations to body suit users.

Programming to deliver touch sensations can be expected to be a huge hurdle to overcome. Computers will have to understand logistical data, such as where the avatar is and what is around them in a virtual environment that may have to be duplicated from a tactile perspective. The haptic programs will also have to synchronize with other audio and visual programs to deliver realistic effects. Of all the technologies described in this book, haptic technology may be the hardest to implement. Still, the first peripherals in the form of force feedback systems have been well received in the marketplace—it is reasonable to expect that as other new devices (and related programs) come to market, users (especially gamers) will be anxious to try them out.

THE STATE OF THE ART IN DIGITAL SCENT TECHNOLOGY

Digitized scent is created by mixing a variety of distinct oils in a variety of combinations to mimic scents such as chocolate, or flowers, or baked goods. There are very few vendors currently in this market (the vendors are discussed in the next section), but initial demands for their products have been encouraging.

As usual, the game sector leads the market in demand for new sensory technologies on the consumer side of the market. Games continually push the envelope in terms of 3D graphics display, spatial hearing-oriented sound, and touch (with haptic mice, joysticks, steering wheels, and other peripherals). This is also the case with digital scent. Many game players are anxious to have access to smell sensations when playing action, strategy, and other games. On the commercial side, demand for scent technologies have largely been seen in the food business.

Scent technologies are expected to make many game environments far more realistic. Imagine being in a 3D world. You're wearing 3D shutter glasses to provide 3D depth to your game simulation. You are surrounded by a four-speaker Dolby sound system so that virtual planes or cars that zoom past you sound realistic. You're able to smell the burning rubber or gasoline at the motorbike race track, or the aroma of popcorn at the ballpark, or get a subtle whiff of new car smell as you prepare to drive your virtual rented car through the streets of London. Expect this kind of experience to be delivered in self-contained game environments (such as on PCs and game consoles) and to become commonplace in Internet game environments and retail settings later on.

Beyond the 3D/virtual reality game market, scent technology is expected to play a huge role over time in Internet retailing. Imagine being able to walk through a virtual mall and smell the scents coming from a bakery or a candy store, or being able to smell the scent of a bottle of perfume before you purchase. Scent technology provides a way for retailers to differentiate their products as well as a way for consumers to better understand products before purchasing. This will go a long way towards eliminating costs related to returning, refunding, and restocking items that may have been purchased blindly over the Internet. The name of the game in sensory technologies is additional information. Scent technology is becoming one more critical and crucial piece of the puzzle that will enable the Sensory Virtual Internet to become a reality.

Who Are the Leading Market Players?

Producing digital scents is a new field in computer sensory technology. There are relatively few players involved in building digital scent technologies, and as of yet, very few applications available that can take advantage of such technology.

On the game console side of the game business, Nintendo has already announced its plans for the addition of a digital scent peripheral for Nintendo 64. Other console makers such as Sony, Sega, and Microsoft (with its Xbox) are expected to follow suit in short order. On the PC side of the game business, there are few competitors at this point. Digiscents is evolving as the market leader, but another company, Trisenx, is currently making headway by claiming to offer technology that can dispense digital scent as well as taste sensations. For $270, you can purchase a Trisenx device that emits scents such as that of chocolate chip cookies. The Trisenx software used to load the device with scents and run it is free.

> One of the early market innovators is a company by the name of DigiScents, a privately held corporation founded in February 1999 by Dexster Smith and Joel Bellenson and located in Oakland, California.
> DigiScents makes a computer peripheral device, iSmell, which emits various fragrances and scents; ScentTracker, an authoring tool for the creation of scent scores for movies, musical compositions, and interactive games; ScentPlayer, for playing scented media such as videos, music, or even scented greeting cards; ScentMixer, a tool to help developers create scents; and ScentStream, a scent environment designed to send scent signals to music listeners and movie viewers over the Internet. The basis for building scent software resides in the company's ScentWare development environment. ScentWare is a developer toolkit that provides the fundamental programming environment that enables developers to add smells to interactive games, applications, and Web sites.
> It should be noted that DigiScents pioneered the Internet's first scented Web site (at *www.snortal.com*). Snortal will eventually provide users with access to scented movies, aromas to accompany specific music, scent-enhanced e-commerce buying and selling, scented 3D interactive games, and scent enhancements to online advertising. Today, visitors to Snortal can create scented e-mail using their own custom scents.
>
> Source: www.snortal.com

Trisenx is another provider of sensory-enhanced Internet experiences. Trisenx focuses on developing technology that renders smell and taste simulations over the Internet. In addition, other players and contributors to the development of digital scent technologies include the following companies and organizations:

- The Association for Chemoreception Sciences
- The Fragrance Foundation
- The Florida State University Sensory Research Institute
- Leffingwell & Associates
- Monell Chemical Senses Center
- Pacific Northwest Laboratory
- Perfumer & Flavorist magazine
- The Howard Hughes Medical Institute
  Spray Technology

Taste Technology

Digital taste is all about delivering sensations such as saltiness, bitterness, sweetness, and the like to some receiving device that can reproduce the appropriate sensation on some physical receiver such as a liquid solution, a paste solution, a gel solution, or a bland cracker-like substance. The challenge in delivering such sensations are three-fold: 1) the receiver needs to physically resemble in texture the original substance that the sender is trying to replicate (such as a smooth, waxy texture for the delivery of a chocolate sensation); 2) some way must be found to adjust the temperature of the digital taste substance received; and 3) taste relies heavily on the sense of smell to augment the olfactory experience (meaning that taste and scent technologies need to be integrated in order to deliver a realistic taste sensation).

The current state of the art involves using bland potato-based cards with taste imprints printed on them constitute some of the first digital taste experiments. This approach is capable of delivering the salty, sweet, or other taste sensations that we seek, but much work needs to be done to resolve texture-, temperature-, and scent-related issues before this technology can make a substantial market impact.

There will assuredly be other advances, but for now the digital taste field is too immature to project future development.

Chapter Summary

This chapter examined audio, scent, and touch sensory feedback from computer systems. Digitized sound has become a somewhat mature technology. The really interesting 3D audio developments that are now taking place have to do with the concept of spatial hearing that replicates sound direction in 3D worlds by computing how objects such as cars, planes, or trains can approach and depart from the virtual listener as if they were approaching or departing in the real world. The primary issue with delivering sound over the sensory virtual Internet is that depending on the sound quality, sound files can be extremely large. Sending voice-quality mono sound does not stress most storage or network subsystems, but sending CD-quality 32-bit stereoscopic sound can be a huge drain on network and communications resources.

On the touch (haptic) front, several new products arrived on the market last year that provide touch-and-feel sensations to users—primarily users of games. Force-feedback mice, steering wheels, and joysticks are but a few examples. In the future, expect chairs, gloves, and body suits to become available, all featuring touch/feel technologies that will emulate real-world tactile sensations such as softness, coarseness, oiliness or slickness, dryness, heat and cold.

Scent technologies remain the brunt of many jokes—but scent technologies are real and will play an important role in the 3D virtual worlds of the future. Expect smell sensations to permeate virtual malls as you pass by bakeries, candy stores, and the like. Expect the smell of burning rubber as you nail the accelerator on your virtual BMW and begin to race.

Taste technology is a relatively immature technology at this juncture. The most salient point with taste technology is that taste must be accompanied by scent sensations in order to deliver a realistic digital experience to a virtual user of such technology. Additionally, ways to accommodate texture and temperature must be developed in order to ensure commercial viability of taste products. Of all of the sensory experiences covered in this book, taste technology will be the hardest to master.

Even though there have been strong advances in the development of new haptic and scent peripherals, there has been a paucity of new applications made available to capitalize on the availability of these new sensory technologies. The encouraging news is that game console makers and computer game makers are now showing signs of willingness to incorporate these technologies into the games that they sell. If game companies can make an impact with scent, touch, and taste technologies, it won't be long until commercial interests use these technologies for delivering sensory experiences over the Internet.

Part IV: Infrastructure

Now that you know how speech recognition and new navigational and manipulation devices will be used to input commands and sensory data in the future and how computer systems will output that data using new 3D display technologies, improved audio delivery systems, haptic devices, and scent peripherals, the next natural step in building your understanding of the Sensory Virtual Internet is to show you how sensory-rich data will be delivered to thousands, potentially millions of virtual yous in virtual worlds on the Internet.

The issue on the table is that sensory-enriched data files can be extremely large. In general, the more realistic the sensory experience, the larger the file. The challenge that lies ahead is to find ways to efficiently process sensory data and ways to efficiently transmit these large files. This involves taking a closer look.

Processing Large Amounts of Sensory Data

We need to examine how our computers are designed, built, and deployed.

1. Users of the Sensory Virtual Internet will get access to high-speed networks. Low-speed networks—speeds of 56 Kb or less—will never be able to deliver high-quality, immersive, sensory-enriched 3D video, 3D audio, scent, touch, and taste experiences. So to maximize the Sensory Virtual Internet experience, high-speed networking is a requirement.

2. Front-end receiving/capture devices (such as workstations, PCs, laptops, etc.) need to be redesigned to better accommodate the reception, processing, and sending of sensory-rich data streams. The computing and graphics proccessing power will need to be optimized in

order to be able to capture, display, and present sensory-rich visual, audio, scent, touch, and taste data.
3. Back-end servers need to embrace the concepts of grid and peer-to-peer distributed computing in order to handle the increased sensory processing workload of the future.
4. Algorithms for compression and decompression of files will have to be improved continuously in order to allow for the efficient transmission of large data files, such as streaming media and those needed in a virtual world that contains sensory information.

The Primary High-Speed Networking Issues

There are two networking issues that must be overcome in order for people to gain access to rich, immersive, Sensory Virtual Internet experiences: *access* and *cost*.

1. The biggest issue that most people face with high-speed networking is how to gain access from their home or work environments to the high-speed backbone of the Internet. In major urban areas throughout the world, high-speed access is generally available using broadband wired connections such as DSL (explained in greater depth in Chapter 10) or cable modem connections. For suburban or rural areas, high-speed wireless connections such as satellites, fixed wireless technologies, or other approaches are sometimes available.

    The primary issues with DSL wired access have to do with the proximity of the business or individual to switching equipment and the quality of the telephone line. If the user is too far from a phone company's telephone switch, DSL won't work well. Phone companies and DSL independents have had a great deal of difficulty providing consistent, high-quality service. Providers of DSL services have received scores of complaints about sporadic quality

of service and poor customer service. There is little that can be done about the line-quality issue short of rewiring and putting a switch closer to the prospective DSL user, but readers should consider that there are plenty of other alternative options to DSL for high-speed Internet connections.
2. The other major issue with high-speed networking has to do with cost. At the time work started on this book, the typical cost in the United States for high-speed Internet access was around $49 per month. It was generally believed that this cost would head downward over time as competition increased and as larger volumes of users signed on for high-speed services. Instead, due to numerous failures of high-speed Internet service providers, restructuring of the industry, as well as increased pressure for profits, the remaining high-speed Internet access suppliers have started to charge premium prices for high-speed service. High-speed Internet connection prices are heading upward to the $59 per month price range instead of downward.

Fortunately, the argument that prices will come down over time is still valid for two reasons: 1) In the wired broadband space, cable suppliers are competing very strongly with phone-based DSL providers. This competition will eventually result in costs being lowered as these companies try to build market share. 2) Eventually, high-speed network suppliers will be forced to lower costs in order to appeal to the vast majority of middle- and low-income households worldwide.

> This upward pricing trend is truly disturbing. It is serving to create a digital divide between those wealthy households and businesses that can afford such price increases and those that cannot. From a socioeconomic perspective, providing one class of people with access to faster, better, and richer services while setting the cost beyond

the means of the majority of middle income and poor households is probably not a good idea. It deepens the cultural and economic opportunity gaps between economic classes.

Ironically, the country that helped level the playing field among rich and poor classes—France—is also becoming involved in leveling the Internet playing socio-economic playing field. According to a June 2001 Reuters article, France is considering introducing a "nation-wide broadband Net"—allowing a large portion the country's constituents to gain access to high-speed Internet services by 2005.

Apparently the French Government has concluded that relying on the private sector alone will not bring high-speed Internet services to all Frenchmen—especially those in rural areas (areas that are uneconomical for most private sector communications companies to service). The French government is considering providing over $1 billion in loans to encourage the public sector to make high-speed access more broadly available at an affordable price—and could spend over $4 billion on other infrastructure and incentive improvements to foster the growth of high-speed Internet connections in France.

Source: http://www.reuters.com

Front-End Modifications

The primary changes that need to take place on PCs and other personal computing devices have to do with "headroom" (processing power) for processing large, complex sensory files (especially 3D graphics); the integration of new peripherals for navigation, manipulation, and the integration of scent and touch sensations.

Now that PC processing power is approaching 2 GHz, today's PCs have plenty of local processing power for handling streaming media and combined audio/video files. But note, for the most part today's sensory data streams are primitive. They offer limited 3D sight and sound experiences and very limited touch experiences (generally confined to vibrating mouse peripherals, joysticks, or steering wheels). Soon they will have to process scent or taste sensations. As more sophisticated sensory information is captured and sent between PCs and server environments, it is reasonable to expect that PCs (and like devices) will require 5 GHz, 10 GHz, or even faster processors in order to handle very complex graphics and sensory data streams.

Raw CPU processing power is only part of the story. PCs now make use of very powerful graphics processing units in order to process highly detailed 3D graphics data streams. In fact, some of today's PC game cards can process 800 million pixel locations per second—finally enabling PCs to approach the quality of 3D graphics that exist in many of today's game consoles from companies like Sony or Nintendo. Changes need to continually take place in PC and like device graphics processing in order to position these devices for handling very complex and large 3D graphical data over time.

One of the topics we will be discussing in this part is the change taking place in PC architecture, such as graphics handling, bus architecture, processing architecture, and other subsystems.

Back-End Modifications

Today's back-end systems are primarily focussed on handling the transactions of e-commerce. In the future, these systems used in virtual worlds will need to be redesigned to focus on computational processing tasks. For those who claim that back-end systems cannot handle the computationally intensive workload demanded by the processing of complex 3D graphics and visuals as well as other sensory data, I will say that the return of peer-to-peer computing and the advent of a new grid architecture for building switched networks of processors, storage subsystems, and communications devices known as Infiniband will more than mitigate alleged processing overhead shortcomings.

What This Part Is About

The way that your computer systems are *designed, configured, and networked* will have a huge effect on the quality of sensory data that you can receive and process. This part closely examines these three aspects of computer infrastructure.

- Chapter 10 describes the numerous options available for high-speed Internet access.
- Chapter 11 follows the improvements on the computer "front end" (workstations, PCs, laptops, etc.) that are taking place to facilitate the capture as well as the reception of sensory-rich data. This chapter pays particular attention to PC hardware and graphics display improvements that can be expected to significantly improve the ability of front-end devices to handle rich sensory data.
- Chapter 12 examines the improvements taking place at the computer back end (mainframes and servers) that will allow these machines to handle ever-more-complex computational tasts. This chapter pays particular attention to peer-to-peer computing architecture and Infiniband— elements of a sophisticated way of networking computer communications networks, storage peripherals, and distributed processing power now becoming known as grid computing.
- Chapter 13 examines certain techniques that are used to help process, compress, deliver, decompress, and play or display sensory data transmitted over the Internet. For instance we will look at the use of browsers to present graphical data and new compression/decompression techniques.

The bottom line is that this part is about the infrastructure changes that need to take place in order for computers to provide individuals with rich sensory experiences and about the changes needed in back-end supporting computers to enable those computers to support very large populations of virtual Internet users.

What I Hope You'll Learn in This Part

Changes to PC architecture combined with changes to back-end server architecture and configuration (specifically the use of peer-to-peer computing and Infiniband architecture) will combine to enable the processing and presentation of huge sensory data files. What I hope you'll learn is that:

- There are several different approaches that you can use to obtain high-speed network access today—and that new advances are taking place (especially in the area of wireless networking) that will provide an even wider range of choices for high-speed network access in the future.
- New architectures are evolving for personal computers that will enable them to process very complex sensory data files more efficiently. It is important that you understand these forthcoming architectural improvements because improvements in graphics subsystems, bus architecture, and the like will greatly influence how well your computing devices can process rich sensory data files.
- Back-end server environments will need to change in order to accommodate the processing of rich sensory and logistical information that pertains to virtual yous in virtual environments. Most of today's back-end servers are transaction-oriented. They focus on completing financial or other types of transactional tasks. But tomorrow's back-end servers will have to be designed to handle data that will help avatars move through a myriad of virtual environments and provide them with the ability to pick up and examine virtual objects in those environments. I'd like you to become familiar with terms such as Infiniband and architectures such as peer-to-peer processing in order to better understand how back-end servers will

process and present complex sensory data streams in the future.
- Compression and decompression techniques will play an important role in the presentation of sensory data to personal computers and other devices in the future. I'd like you to understand what compression and decompression are and how these techniques can be used to streamline the presentation of sensory data to personal computers and other devices in the future.

CHAPTER 10

Networking: Overcoming the Biggest Obstacle to Realizing the Sensory Virtual Internet

Picture this:

The Harbor Hills: Ultimate Bandwidth, Incredible Beauty

"If you were driving up the Pacific coast, to your right just after you've crossed into Oregon, you'd see some high rolling hills. These are the Harbor Hills. They rise from near sea level to over 1400 feet... At their foot is a narrow bench, site of the famous (locally at least) Harbor lily fields, source of most of the world's lily and hydrangea stock. Beyond is the Pacific. To the northwest is the Chetco River and the Port of Brookings/Harbor. To the south are the Winchuck River, the Smith River, Pelican Bay and, beyond, the arc of Crescent City...

"We're developing a master plan for the hills that is based on the work of the revered architect Bernard Maybeck. To see a current draft of the master plan and work focused on the Harbor Hills by two University of Oregon School of Architecture classes [visit *OregonCoast.net*]..."
Source: OregonCoast.net

Now here's the best part.

"The Harbor Hills will have the world's most extreme Internet access, with as much as 1.8 Gbps (gigabit per second) [as an upgrade] to each home, using fiber-optic-to-the-home (FTTH) technology."
Source: OregonCoast.net. Reprinted by permission of Harbor Hills.

I want to live here (or someplace just like it)....

This chapter focuses on the state of the art in high-speed network technology for the home. It examines why ultimately you will need to obtain high-speed network services. It defines various networking terms. In addition, it describes your options, based on your location, for obtaining high-speed networking services. Finally, it discusses future high-speed networking directions, including fiber-to-the-home (FTTH), power line networking, and future directions in high-speed wireless communications.

Is High-Speed Networking in Your Near-Term Future?

Do you want to participate to the fullest extent in the next-generation Sensory Virtual Internet? Would you like to use videophone services that allow you to see the person with whom you are conversing from the comfort of your own home? Or how would you like access to v-mail messages instead of dry, lifeless, character-driven e-mail? Would you like to participate in a learning experience, attend a live concert, or go shopping without having to physically go to a school, concert hall, or mall?

Would you like to have on-demand access to shows and movies? Would you be pleased if you could approach a kiosk in a store or at an airport and ask for (not by typing, just speaking) a product or ask for directions and have the computer respond back to you in a verbal and possibly graphical form? Would you like to meet with your fellow workers or friends and be able to work collaboratively or chat in Sensory Virtual Internet space?

It is possible to perform every single one of these activities today using first-generation sensory applications such as videophone services (from companies such as Visitalk, Microsoft, and others); e-learning applications (from companies such as Centra or Learning Tree); virtual world applications (such as those at Active Worlds or Cybertown); or specific e-tailing applications that run at various retailer Web sites (such as Lexus, Macy's, Timex, etc.).

However, if you want to take advantage fully of the next wave of user interface and sensory technologies, and if you want to avoid the World Wide Wait as you upload and download data, *you will have to have high-speed Internet access*. Without high-speed Internet service, you will more than likely suffer through poor and choppy audio and visual presentations when downloading sophisticated 3D images and imagery, endure seemingly interminable data uploads, and experience lots of arms-folded time as you wait for multimedia documents and movies to display and run. In other words, *if you really want to enjoy the forthcoming sensory-enriched world of the Sensory Virtual Internet to its fullest measure, you will need to have access to high-speed networking.*

Why You Will Need High-Speed Internet Service

The reason that high-speed networks will be crucial and indispensable to Internet users in the future is simple: *sensory-rich data files consisting of graphical, audio, haptic, and digital scent data are very large*. Without a fast Internet connection between a user and back-end Internet server, the network congestion that will result from the sending and receiving of large data files will choke your computer's ability to display/stream 3D visual effects, to deliver complex and high-quality audio files, and to deliver coordinated touch and scent experiences.

Files enriched using the sensory technologies (as described in the previous two chapters) are usually around a few megabytes to hundreds of megabytes in size. Compare this to the size of two-dimensional word processing, electronic mail, or HTML files, which are often only a few hundred or thousand bytes in size. These large, sensory-enriched data files—affectionately termed BLOBs (short for *B*inary *L*arge *OB*jects)—contain the information needed by receiving devices to present 3D graphics, CD-quality audio, and touch and scent sensations to Internet users. In order for receiving devices to display, play, and transmit sensory experiences, they need to be able to receive and process these large blobs of data quickly and efficiently. Further, the data we receive must be presented without break-ups in video transmission or lag time in synchronization of speech, touch, and scent presentation to the user. Otherwise we humans will have trouble processing out-of-synch sensory data, and we will just plain reject sensory technologies and opt for slow-speed, low-sensory, 2D experiences.

It is therefore critical to have access to high-speed networking in order to experience satisfactory system/application performance levels and acceptable, coordinated sensory experiences as we enter Sensory Virtual Internet worlds. If our systems cannot send and receive large blocks of data and rapidly process and present that data in a synchronized form, users will reject Sensory Virtual Internet technologies and continue to gravitate toward 2D graphics presentations of the old-world, static Internet.

Toward Understanding High-Speed Networking Terminology

In order to gain an appreciation of how high-speed networking operates and why you need it to participate to the fullest extent on the Sensory Virtual Internet, a short high-speed networking tutorial may be in order:

High-Speed Networking: The Basics

High-speed networking can be defined as anything over 100 megabytes per second (Mbps). Using this definition, all home-based and business-based modems using a 56 Kb or slower connection to the Internet do not qualify as high-speed connections.

There are three terms that are very important to any discussion about high-speed networking: bandwidth, latency, and broadband. Bandwidth and latency deal with the quality of networking service that is ultimately delivered to you. Broadband is a type of data transmission.

- *Bandwidth*—Bandwidth has to do with the amount of data that can be transmitted in a fixed amount of time. Think of bandwidth as the total capacity of a pipe. If you've got a big pipe and you want to send a small object through that pipe, chances are that it will get through quickly if the inside of the pipe is unobstructed. If other large objects are in the way, your small object may not get through expeditiously. Accordingly, if a network connection is clogged with large blobs of information, the available bandwidth (the amount of room in the pipe) is likely to be low and the resulting time needed to send your data quite long because the available bandwidth is being taken up by those large files. This concept is important because Internet network bandwidth varies greatly based upon the number of users currently making use of

the network pipe, the type and size of the data files being sent, and other variables. For instance, just because your modem is capable of 56,000 bytes per second doesn't mean the network is willing to yield such performance to you. Obstructed bandwidth may greatly reduce the amount of data you can send or receive at any given time.
- *Latency*—Latency has to do with the amount of time one system component waits to send or receive data from another component. In other words, it's a measure of time—more precisely, wasted time. Your network connection may have plenty of bandwidth, but your computer may be underpowered and therefore only able to deliver information slowly. Although the total experience may have been exacerbated by a slow component, the network bandwidth was not the culprit for poor performance. This concept is important because high-speed networking relies not only on bandwidth but also on the components needed to send and receive information through the data pipeline. Very simply stated, if you have plenty of bandwidth available (i.e., if your network is fast) and yet you are still getting poor performance, it is probably lag time as the network waits for slow systems to respond. This lag time is called latency.
- *Broadband*—Broadband is a broadcast method that allows multiple signals to be sent over a single transmission medium (e.g., wire or fiber-optic lines). Other broadcast methods are important, such as wireless, satellite, and infrared, but wired broadband service (such as Digital Subscriber Loop [DSL] or cable connection) offers the highest bandwidth, and is therefore worthy of special attention (DSL and cable are covered in great detail in this chapter). It is also important to know that although a networking line may be capable of providing up to 2.5 million bits per second, bandwidth utilization constraints on the public Internet will often substantially reduce the

maximum bandwidth available. For instance, if you are using a cable modem and several thousand of your fellow cable modem users are all logged on at the same time, you will effectively be sharing the available cable bandwidth with other users, thereby greatly reducing the amount of total bandwidth available to you.

Figure 8 illustrates the concepts of bandwidth, latency, and broadband.

Network Connection

BLOB BLOB BLOB BLOB   Bandwidth

Your Object

Latency—you may have plenty of bandwidth available to send and receive data, but you may lose time retrieving, processing, or storing data. This loss of time is referred to as "latency".

Broadband—a type of transmission method

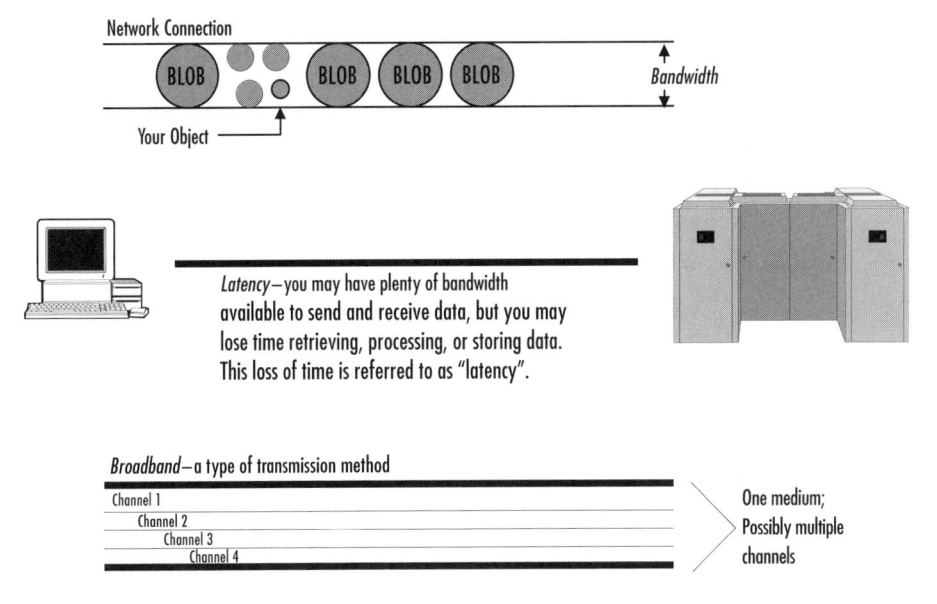

| Channel 1 |
| Channel 2 |
| Channel 3 |
| Channel 4 |

One medium; Possibly multiple channels

FIGURE 8
Bandwidth, Latency, and Broadband

High-Speed Technologies— Your Options

Now that you understand key high-speed networking terms, it is now appropriate to explain the types of networks that you may be able to choose from to access such services:

- *Wire-Based Broadband Interconnect*: The leading wire-based broadband interconnect technologies are variants

of Digital Subscriber Loop (DSL) and cable modem connections (through your local cable provider).
- *Satellite connection*: Satellite communications are broadband but wireless connections. Satellite connections can be made from anywhere, as long as you have clear line-of-sight access to a broadcasting/receiving satellite. This makes satellite services especially important in suburban or rural areas where high-speed telephone switching offices are few and far between.
- *Wireless LAN*: Wireless LANs (also including Fixed Wireless) are yet another type of broadband connection. Wireless LAN technologies offer high-speed connections to the Internet from fixed points along a broadband network. In other words, fiber-optic or copper lines provide a backbone network that terminates at a wireless, high-speed hub. If you are located in close proximity to that hub, you will be able to take advantage of high-speed wireless LAN services.
- *Standard modem over twisted pair*: Despite the fact that standard modems do not really provide high-speed access to the Internet today, standard modems will continue to be heavily used for connection to the Internet. For this reason, a discussion of future modem technology is included in this chapter.

Note: Wireless communications such as the type used by mobile phones, PDAs, etc., are not discussed heavily in this chapter. At present, wireless speeds (with the exception of wireless LANs) are far below those of even standard modem connections—generally in the 9.6 Kbps to 19.2 Kbps range from suppliers such as AT&T Verizon (with its 19.2 Kbps CDPD service) or from Sprint (with its 14.4 Kbps IS-95 CDMA service). Worthy of note is that the Sprint product can deliver speeds of 40–50 Kbps when using the company's Bluekite compression algorithms. This wireless picture will change substantially over the next three years as better compression methods are used (Sprint is working on delivering a 144 Kbps solution in the near term), and as third-generation (3G) wireless solutions come to market with Internet connection speeds in the 2 Mbps range. Right now, wireless communication speed is not even close to being considered high-speed; hence it is not covered in depth in this book.

The above-mentioned technologies are general technical approaches to gaining high-speed access to the Internet. Within many of these categories there are subcategories and various options that you can choose from in order to obtain high-speed network services. In general, your decision will be made on the basis of cost, where you are located, and what amount of line speed you are willing to accept.

Standard Telephone Modems: The Future Is Murky

Even though standard modems do not qualify as high-speed Internet connection devices, I feel compelled to comment on them given the fact that they will constitute the most popular means of connecting to the Internet over the next five years. There are several different types of modems on the market today including standard modems that can run over twisted-pair wiring, cable modems, ISDN modems, DSL modems, and more.

Standard, telephone-based modems usually perform in the 28.8 to 56 Kbps range and are by far the most popular means for consumers to connect to the Internet today. These devices are fairly easy to install (provided that your computer system has the right modem drivers). Once the modem has been physically installed, you can simply plug the modem into an existing telephone jack, connect to an Internet Service Provider (ISP), and you're off to the (Internet) races in no time.

Over the past 20 years, standard modems have continuously improved in speed and performance, while prices have declined steeply. First-generation, 300 bits-per-second modems were first made commercially available in the late 1970s. They cost around $300. Today's most popular telephone-based modems are now capable of sending and receiving up to 56,000 bits per second (56 Kbps) and can cost as little as $20!

As for the recent advances in dial-up modem technology, the following example serves to illustrate that advances in speed and accuracy are taking place largely due to advances in the ability to compress/decompress information being sent.

> In January, 2001, Zoom Telephonics, Inc., began high-volume shipment of V.92 modems—modems capable of uploading 48,000 bits per second (as opposed to 33,600 bits per second on many of today's V.90-based 56 Kb modems).

To achieve this significant increase in speed, Zoom's new modems make use of both the V.92 modem standard and the related V.44 compression standard for transferring data. Zoom's implementation of V.92, known as QuickConnect, also significantly reduces call setup time. Further, this new modem lets users receive a voice call while online (users put their data sessions on hold during the voice call, and, when finished, resume their online session). To take advantage of V.92 services, phone users must have call waiting—and their Internet Service Providers (ISPs) must offer V.92 data transfer support. It can take some ISPs six months or more to release such support. Note in this example that the new standard modem speed delivered through the V.92 specification is still less than half what I consider to be a high-speed Internet interconnection.

Despite this, the important point to consider is that for at least the next five years, standard modems will remain a popular, if not the most popular, way for most people to access the Internet. The reasons:

- Standard modems are easy to install.
- Most computer users already have access to a telephone in their place of residence (so users do not have to rely

on a high-speed service supplier to make a high-speed set-up service call).
- High-speed Internet service using cable or DSL-based technologies can cost over $50 per month, while standard modems using existing phone lines represent no additional cost to the consumer if used for local calls.

Because most Internet users will continue to gravitate toward standard modems as their Internet connection option over the next five years, most users will not be able to take full advantage of the additional sensory cues delivered on the Sensory Virtual Internet. (I hope this book will convince readers to make the switch to high-speed interconnection.)

Given the fact that most Internet users will continue to access the Internet using standard modems, and also given the fact that compression techniques will play a huge role in the sending and receiving of sensory data to standard modem users, it is important to understand the role that data compression techniques will play on the Sensory Virtual Internet of the future. A discussion regarding how data compression techniques will rapidly deliver compressed data efficiently to users of low-speed modems is contained in the Infrastructure section of this book.

Broadband Technologies— A Closer Look

In the short and long term, the most popular technology choices for high-speed Internet services will be based on wired and satellite broadband technologies. To review, broadband is a method for transmitting multiple signals over a single medium— fiber, copper wire, or wireless transmission, for example. In urban areas, there is generally greater access to a variety of broadband services, and accordingly, considerable overlap in types of broadband services available to the home high-speed networking buyer. Cable, DSL, and ISDN are but a few of the broadband choices available in most urban areas. In suburban and rural areas, other technologies such as satellite-based broadband services and in some cases fixed wireless services play a bigger role as viable options.

In terms of marketshare, the number of broadband Internet subscribers worldwide will exceed 15 million users at the end of 2001. This number is expected to double to 30 million users by the year 2004, according to a recent study conducted by the Multimedia Research Group (MRG). In the United States, the Federal Communications Commission (FCC) tracks the deployment of broadband technology within its domestic borders and publishes its findings biyearly. The site *http://www.fcc.gov/Bureaus/Common_Carrier/News_Releases/2001/nrcc0133.html* contains the latest report information. The FCC's most recent finding based on data gathered throughout 2000 and early 2001 indicates that:

- The number of homes and businesses using high-speed broadband connections increased by 158 percent in the year 2000 to a total of 7.1 million users.
- Of this 7.1 million users an astounding 5.2 million new users have deployed high-speed connections in small businesses or residences.
- High-speed DSL (ADSL) connections accounted for 2 million of the total new users.
- High-speed coaxial cable systems accounted for 3.6 million of the total new users.
- Satellite and fixed wireless technologies grew from 50,000 users in December 1999 to 112,000 users in December 2000.

In short, DSL and cable solutions grew strongly in the United States, while satellite and fixed wireless options also started to gain marketshare.

One big question regarding these figures is—with the major slowdown in the U.S. economy in 2001—will broadband continue to experience such strong growth? Initial indications are that DSL broadband growth has been flat but that cable subscriptions have been growing steadily. The next round of government-sponsored FCC broadband survey results needed to answer this question will not be available until the final quarter of the year 2001. Contrary to speculation that high-speed growth will be flat in 2001, private report sources such as one issued by the National Cable & Telecommunications Association (NTCA) reported that cable subscriptions grew to 70,000 new subscribers a week through the second quarter of 2001, bringing the total number of U.S. high-speed cable connections to 5.5 million users. This report indicates solid growth in the number of high-speed cable modem interconnects to the Internet.

Which Are the Most Common Broadband Technologies?

The wired broadband technologies that most prospective high-speed network buyers are likely to consider for high-speed networking service are Asymmetric Digital Subscriber Loop (ADSL), and cable access. The wireless options that most people will consider are satellite and wireless broadband LAN (the 802.11b specification) connections. In the future, fiber-to-the-home (FTTH), wiring plant, and infrared broadband technologies will also become viable, affordable options.

What Are xDSL, ADSL, SDSL, HDSL, VDSL, ADSLLite, G.Lite, and UADSL?

Digital Subscriber Loop (DSL) is a family of products designed to use existing telephone twisted-pair wiring (the kind found in most home telephone lines) to provide high-speed access to the Internet. Essentially, this technology uses existing telephone lines to connect users to a phone company switching office, where the phone company routes voice calls over the existing public telephone network and routes data through an Internet Service Provider to the Internet at very high speeds.

The *x* in *x*DSL refers to any of a number of variants of DSL technology. The various members of the DSL family include:

- Asymmetric Digital Subscriber Link (ADSL)—Provides data download rates at speeds up to 8 Mbps and data upload rates up to 640 Kbps.
- Symmetric Digital Subscriber Link (SDSL)—Provides data download rates at speeds up to 2.3 Mbps and data upload rates up to 2.3 Mbps.
- High-Bit Rate Digital Subscriber Link (HDSL and HDSL2)—Provides data download rates at speeds up to 1.54 Mbps and data upload rates up to 1.54 Mbps.
- Very-High Bit Rate Digital Subscriber Link (VDSL)—Provides data download rates at such astonishing speeds as 51 Mbps and data upload rates up to 51 Mbps.
- Light Versions of the ADSL Standard (ADSL*Lite*, G.Lite, or UADSL)—The U in UADSL stands for universal. This technology provides data download rates at speeds up to 1.5 Mbps and data upload rates up to 384 Kbps.
- Super High-Density DSL (SHDSL)—Though still on the drawing board, expect that over the next three years this new, higher-speed version of DSL to become available. SHDSL is expected to be capable of speeds of 2.3 Mbps over standard twisted pair wiring.

Most home users and small businesses are offered ADSL or ADSL*Lite* services by Incumbent Local Exchange Carriers (ILECs) (your phone company). Independent competitors to these phone companies are called Competitive Local Exchange Carriers (CLECs).

ADSL

ADSL allows for the simultaneous use of *normal telephone services and high-speed data networking* services both on the same line. By using different frequencies over plain-old-telephone service (POTS) lines, ADSL is able to split the signals used for voice and for data. Telephones use a frequency range up to 4 kHz, while data is transmitted in ranges from 40 kHz to as high as 2 MHz, depending on line quality. The specification for this technology allows for data transfer up to a theoretical maximum of up to 7 Mbps, but in the United States ADSL is limited by Federal Communications Commission regulations to a maximum of 1.5 Mbps.

From a design and implementation perspective, ADSL assumes that most Internet users download and look at more information than they upload, hence ADSL divides the data frequencies that a line can carry in favor of downloading. The net effect created is that for most users connection *from* the Internet for browsing and other purposes can be three to four times faster than the connection *to* the Internet (upstream feeds generally range from 64 kb to 640 kb per second).

ADSL is a distance-sensitive technology. You must be within 18,000 feet (5,460 meters) of a phone company's switch architecture to access ADSL service. Though many ADSL providers restrict the maximum allowable distance significantly more to ensure that customers get reasonable line speed and quality of service, which can vary between 64 and 640 Kbps.

It is important to note that ADSL service is becoming popular in countries with established and mature wiring that is well dispersed on a geographical basis to serve those countries' populations (countries such as the United States, Canada, and those throughout Europe). In many parts of the world, physical telephone wiring is not available to large parts of the population. Hence satellite and other wireless solutions offer more promising growth in underdeveloped countries.

Probably the most important element concerning ADSL and its relation to the Sensory Virtual Internet is that it is downstream-bandwidth optimized. This means that ADSL lines are designed to be able to deliver large files to your computer, such as the video, audio, haptic, scent, and 3D image files we have been discussing.

How is ADSL used today? ADSL is used for fast access to the Internet primarily for the purpose of viewing and downloading files. Telecommuters make use of ADSL lines to access and run business applications from their home environments. Doctors make use of ADSL to download complex images such as X-ray photographs. Consumers are just starting to use ADSL for home entertainment purposes.

> Last year, British Telecommunications (BT) began to offer HomeChoice to their customers. This is a television-on-demand service that runs over ADSL lines. This video service, regulated by BT partner Ofcom, constitutes one of the first large-scale video-on-demand service that is being delivered to large populations of users over ordinary telephone lines.
>
> Since the beginning of the project, BT's rollout of ADSL has run into a number of technical and administrative issues, including problems relating to video service outages during times of peak telephone usage, and phone company infrastructure issues related to who to call when such service suddenly drops out. Do you call the service provider division within BT or the ADSL division within the same company?
>
> A lesson to be learned from this first big test of ADSL is that despite the readiness of ADSL technology, applications, and service infrastructure need to be in place for it to be successfully deployed. Otherwise, the phone company and its service providers will risk customer dissatisfaction, which will likely retard their efforts to promote such applications to an even broader base of consumers in the future.

What About SDSL and All of the Other xDSLs?

Single-Line, or Synchronous, Digital Subscriber Line (SDSL) splits a DSL line equally so that businesses can send data streams up to 1.5 Mbps in each direction equally. SDSL is more often found within business or enterprise environments, where sending data bidirectionally is a requirement. *SDSL is optimized for data traffic and does not support voice through the plain-old telephone service.*

The remaining *x*DSLs are designed to provide specialized services for businesses and powerful high-speed links for telecommunications providers. These DSLs are particularly important to providers of back-end Internet infrastructure services and large businesses and less relevant to home consumers.

HIGH-SPEED CABLE INTERNET ACCESS

Over the past few years, cable providers have been rushing to upgrade their physical wiring plant to include high-quality coaxial and fiber-optic cable and upgrading their switching infrastructure to accommodate high-speed Internet usage and digital cable broadcasts. Furthermore, these efforts have been rewarded. According to a recent National Cable & Telecommunications Association (NTCA) report (described earlier in this chapter), the total number of U.S. high-speed cable connections now reaches 5.5 million users.

The cable industry is expected to sustain strong growth over the next few years. Boston-based Yankee Group projects that the number of U.S. households subscribing to digital cable services will reach 27 million by 2005. That's a ten-fold growth factor over the next four years! The driving forces for such strong growth include the availability of new services such as video-on-demand and interactive TV.

Note, however, these driving factors for growth in the cable industry are entertainment-centric. They are not necessarily related to Internet usage. Digital cable is being marketed to the cream-of-the-crop affluent households. These are the same target households for ADSL Internet service provider. These households are willing to pay for more programming. Because there is a relationship between affluence and educational level, many of these households have been Internet educated, have the desire for high-speed network access, and are willing to pay for it.

From a Sensory Virtual Internet perspective, the real question is what percentage of households that install digital cable are likely to use that cable for high-speed Internet access? According to a recent Yankee Group report, *one-third of all cable customers will not sign up for digital cable Internet services*. Of the remaining 66 percent, most estimates project that *far fewer than half will sign up for digital cable modem services*. This means that according to the Yankee Group by the year 2005, when 27 million households will be using digital cable services, less than nine million will be using cable modems for Internet access. To me this seems counter-intuitive: If the pathway to deliver high-speed Internet services to 27 million homes exists—and if the economic factor of $50 per month can be reduced—I personally believe that the number of cable Internet subscribers will be significantly higher.

Why Has Cable Been So Successful to Date?

Some of the primary reasons for the strong market affirmation of cable broadband services have to do with: 1) the ready availability of service in many locales; and 2) the ease of ordering and installation. These are also the reasons that many researchers are projecting the use of cable modems for broadband Internet access in the United States to soar so rapidly by 2005.

Many cable providers got very aggressive early on in providing high-speed cable-based network services to their customers—particularly those in densely populated areas. These cable companies rushed to upgrade their systems, wiring plants, and switching architectures so that many customers could easily connect to cable systems for high-speed network services. Further, cable providers hurriedly rushed to find ways to make installation easier and less expensive (using a technician for cable modem installations costs upwards of $300 per visit). Recently, cable suppliers have started to allow their customers to purchase and install cable modem themselves—reducing installation costs on behalf of the cable supplier (costs that would eventually have to be recovered) as well as providing convenience for high-speed cable network users.

Horror stories abound about businesses and individual consumers having problems obtaining DSL service from phone companies, as do stories about poor account service. It is well known that many phone companies have been less than responsive in providing DSL services to the general population, have been slow to upgrade their network infrastructure, and have spent a lot of time fending off challenges by competitor CLECs (like Covad and others) rather than focusing on customer service. This CLEC challenge was created when the U.S. Congress mandated that communications carriers (phone companies) share access to their central offices with outside providers of DSL services—thereby creating a competitive scenario in the DSL services arena. In the United Kingdom, numerous DSL Local Exchange Carriers (DLECs) such as Atlantic Telecom, Easynet, Iomart, Oncue Telecommunications, and Versapoint, complained that phone company stalling techniques were so effective that it could take up to 30 years to get on an equivalent footing with British Telecom in the DSL/high-speed networking space.

Meanwhile, CLECs and DLECs are making inroads by providing phone company customers—both consumers and businesses—with better service and administration of customer accounts. Still, independent providers of DSL services have had troubles of their own on financial as well as services fronts. Some DSL firms—most notably Covad Communications and PSINet—have laid off (made redundant) staff members and scaled back service expansion in order to deal with problems resulting from high operational overhead costs.

To help correct customer service installation issues, large DSL suppliers are also starting to allow self-installation of DSL modems available from retail stores. Verizon Communications and SBC Communications are two DSL suppliers that now make DSL modems available through consumer outlets.

In balance, there are technical reasons for the problems that traditional phone companies have experienced servicing their customer bases. Significant upgrades of telephone systems have had to take place to allow for high-speed DSL service offerings. And DSL is not available to everyone given its distance limitations. (DSL service depends on how far you are away from the phone company's central office and the quality of your local loop line.) And phone companies have had to set up a support infrastructure specifically for DSL technologies, whereas the incremental effort for cable providers to support cable modems has been fairly minimal. Still, it is easy to argue that stumbling and bumbling by phone companies has been a major impediment to the delivery of DSL services to the general populace.

The Satellite Broadband Option

Why would you buy a satellite service for high-speed access? Essentially, satellites can go where other wired broadband solutions cannot. Satellites conquer the last-mile problem because satellites do not have to be near a phone switching center or wireless station to provide high-speed service.

At present, the satellite market is intriguing. It has experienced solid growth recently as a result of advances in upload and download speeds and more reliable quality of service. From a market size perspective, forecasts from Pioneer Consulting project that the satellite industry could become a $20 billion industry by the year 2005. In 2001, various research firms predict that satellite high-speed networking services will finally start to catch up to wired cable and DSL service in terms of speed. By 2003, some forecasts indicate that satellite high-speed network users should number almost two million, as contrasted with almost six million DSL users and almost seven million cable modem users.

According to U.S. government studies, the U.S. Digital Broadcast Satellite (DBS) industry grew by 30 percent in 2000, from 10.1 million homes in 1999 to 13 million homes at the end of 2000. As a percentage of the total broadband market, DBS systems now account for 15 percent of all multichannel subscribers. Still, by contrast, homes with cable services now number over 67.7 million—DBS represents about 20 percent of this market share.

The major Digital Satellite Network (DSN) suppliers include Tachyon.net from Tachyon; SpaceWay from Hughes Electronics; Astrolink from Lockheed-Martin; products from Gilat-to-Home, a subsidiary of Gilat Satellite Networks; and StarBand from broadcaster Echostar. Stakes just to get into this game are high, which may account for why there are so few players. A satellite in geostationary orbit can cost between $160 million and $240 million to build and at least $100 million to launch.

Note that America Online, the leading Internet Service Provider in the United States, has partnered with Hughes Networks to enable its customers to obtain high-speed, satellite-based broadband Internet services. These services could be available as early as 2003 and could reach a 400 Kbps download rate! Considering that DSL has a speed limit of 52 Mbps, satellite service is well on the way to surpassing DSL service transfer rates.

DBS satellite network services have been available for several years but the high-speed network element worked only in one direction—high-speed downloads. In the past, commercial satellite systems could only upload data at rates of 56 Kbps or less. But recently this scenario changed. Download speeds have reached the 400 Kbps range while uploads are now reaching 128 Kbps (with optional 256 Kbps service also now available).

> In December, 2000, Hughes Network Systems, a leading provider of satellite-based broadband services, announced the first shipment of its fourth-generation

DirecPC satellite system featuring *two-way* high speed Internet access. The new two-way DirecPC system allows users to bypass a dial-up connection, allowing always on high-speed Internet connection. The new system offers upload speeds of 128 Kbps, optionally 256 Kpbs, and allows data to be downloaded at rates of up to 400 Kbps. Pricing is competitive to other available broadband services.

By 2003, DirecTV will shift from its DirecPC telephone-return system to a Ka-band satellite system called Spaceway—potentially offering 400 Mbps download speeds and 16 Mbps upload speeds.

Source: http://www.hughes.com

Prices for satellite broadband are generally comparable to DSL services.

Wireless LAN/Fixed Wireless

Wireless local area networks have been around for decades. As it pertains to consumers, the issue with Wireless Local Area Network (WLAN) technology—also known as fixed wireless—has to do with how to bring these services the last mile from the telephone company switch to the consumer's home office or home entertainment center. Initially using radio frequencies for data transfer, these LANs can now also use infrared transmission. One of the first prototypes for Ethernet—the world's most dominant wired LAN standard—was Alohanet, a wireless LAN.

To date, WLAN technology has been proprietary in nature for the most part. However, in 2000, the 802.11b standard was formalized, providing a basis for interoperability between vendors and between WLAN products. This move should help ignite the WLAN market (a market that did almost $1 billion in 2000). Helping to improve product interoperability usually results in increased demand, which ultimately drives lower costs. According to a report from the U.K. research firm ARC Group called "Broadband Access: Opportunities in Fixed Wireless

Worldwide," the fixed wireless access market will be more than $41 billion in five years. This report also observes that the fixed wireless access market will rapidly expand beyond the United States and Europe to reach all regions of the world. The report forecasts that by 2005, Europe will account for around $11 billion in WLAN revenue, followed by the United States at approximately $9 billion. The rest of the world will purchase around $22 billion worth of WLAN services that year alone.

Wireless LAN technology has made inroads already in the healthcare and higher education fields. It is used by mobile medical personnel moving from room to room providing patient care and on business and college campuses, where it allows mobile users to compute and access files from anywhere within range of a wireless receiver.

Wireless LANs also have applicability in metropolitan and urban business settings where they can help different buildings gain high-speed access to each other rather than having to deal with expensive building rewiring. Costs to lay fiber cable can be exorbitant. Costs are estimated.

$25,000 per mile	Cost to lay fiber-optic cable in the U.S.
$3 million per mile	Cost to lay fiber-optic cable in New York City
$2,000 per square mile	Cost for wireless broadband

Further savings can be found within the enterprise by reducing wiring costs at the department level. This is because WLAN technology means that offices no longer need to be physically wired (which is labor intensive) to allow employees to connect to application, file, and print services.

The new WLAN technologies have serious repercussions for home office users and telecommuters because these technologies allow connection rates of 11 Mbps from the home (as opposed to dial-up connections in the 56 Kbps range), providing almost-there office-like connection speed for remote office workers and telecommuters. (This should tempt standard modem users to enter the high-speed networking world.)

Many countries of the world are ideally positioned to use WLAN technology because these countries—in areas such as the Far East, Africa, the Middle East, and South America—have country-wide fiber- and wire-based backbone infrastructures in place but lack the infrastructure for universal delivery over the last mile to the home. This probably prevents delivery of telephone voice service—and certainly data delivery—to many homes. To compensate, many of these homes in recent years have adopted wireless phone service. These same homes are good prospects to adopt WLAN solutions as they become available.

Another wireless technology, Bluetooth, potentially overlaps with the 802.11 standard. It uses the same radio frequency range and allows for wireless devices to be connected in the home. For instance, PCs would be able to instantly recognize and use peripherals such as printers without having to use expensive cable connections. However, Bluetooth only works within a 300-foot range while WLAN 802.11b allows for wireless connection over distances of up to 35 miles. Bluetooth is seen by many analysts as a Personal Area Network (PAN) solution and not necessarily as a business solution.

At the start of 2003, when so-called third generation wireless services arrive, wireless cellular connection speed in the United States could increase to as high as 144 Kbps. This is almost triple what most desktop users experience from their homes today.

Some wireless standards may offer speeds up to 2 Mbps indoors and up to 385 Kbps outdoors (using GSM w-CDMA, wideband TDMA, or CDMA2000 3X protocols), though 144 Kbps seems a safer bet at this juncture. Note that all of these speeds are tremendously faster than today's best speed of a mere 9.6 Kbps. These increases in speed indicate how quickly the wireless industry is responding to the need for high-speed mobile wireless access.

Today, over 90 percent of wireless LAN applications are found in business, healthcare, or campus environments, where wireless devices are ultimately linked to an Ethernet LAN wired backbone. Wireless devices talk to a receiver that acts as an access point, allowing wireless devices to bridge into existing Ethernet LANs.

In home environments, WLANs are generally not linked to an existing Ethernet environment but instead are used to enable PCs to transfer files or to share peripherals such as storage and print devices. However, this home scenario is changing and is starting to mirror the business WLAN scenario. Only home users are now starting to use wireless connections to the telephone system in order to gain access to high-speed networking services.

Figure 9 shows the general idea behind WLAN services for home users.

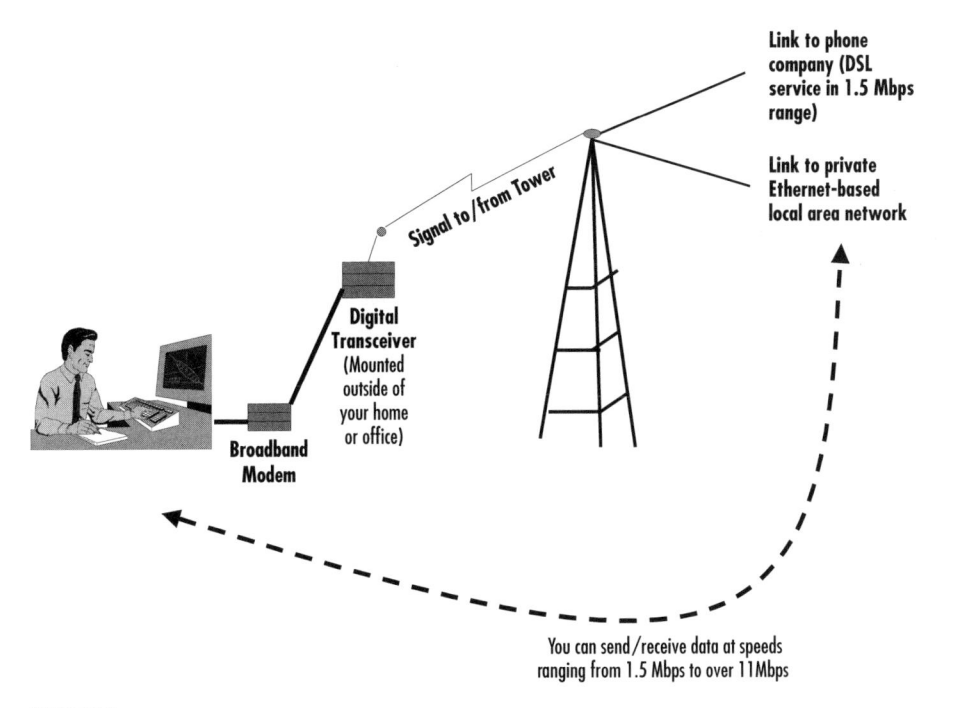

FIGURE 9
How You Can Use a Wireless LAN for High-Speed Access

208 VISUALIZE THIS

At home, users who desire high-speed Internet access need to install a wireless LAN adapter (a PCMCIA card in mobile computers or a PCI or EISA adapter card in a desktop computer) or use an integrated wireless device within a hand-held computer. These WLAN adapters use an antenna to reach an access point (a receiver)—usually located on a tower several miles away. The access point connects to a wired network—this can be a private Ethernet-based network (to take advantage of file transfer speeds in the 11 Mbps range) or the phone company's DSL services (in the 1.5 Mbps range). These would otherwise not be available to the home user due to the DSL range limitation of two miles. The access point receives, buffers, and transmits data between the Wireless LAN and the wired network infrastructure.

> Sprint Corporation is one of a number of suppliers of Wireless LAN broadband connection services. The company's Broadband Direct uses a stationary digital transceiver mounted outside of a home or business to send and receive radio transmissions to a tower located with 35 miles. The radio transmission tower can provide a high-speed link to the Internet, thereby providing users in metropolitan areas, including suburban and rural areas, with access to broadband services that they may not have been able to receive from wired broadband suppliers.

Because WLAN technology makes use of radio frequencies, the Federal Communications Commission restricts and monitors the number of U.S. suppliers allowed to offer these products and services. Companies licensed to deliver broadband Internet access via fixed wireless technology include:

- 360 Networks
- Adaptive Broadband Corporation
- Advanced Radio Telecomm
- ADC Telecommunications
- Advanced Radio Telecom

- AT&T
- Cisco
- Clearwire.com
- DMC Stratex
- Fuzion
- Gigabit Wireless
- Global Crossing
- Hybrid Networks
- Intel
- MCI WorldCom
- Level 3 Communications
- NextLink
- Nokia
- Nucentrix Broadband Services
- Quest
- Sprint
- Terabeam
- Teligent
- Williams Communications
- Winstar
- Vyyo

Wireless PANs: BlueTooth

Much heralded in the press as a low cost, Wireless LAN solution that will enable devices in home offices or business environments to connect and share information and peripherals, Bluetooth technology is really a Wireless Personal Area Networking (WPAN) scheme that is best used for device and peripheral interoperability. This technology is designed to provide a 1 Mbps, small form-factor, low-cost wireless solution between mobile phones, mobile computers, other portable handheld devices, printers, and a wide range of peripheral devices—as well as to provide connectivity to the Internet. Its general transmission range is about 30 feet.

The primary differences between Bluetooth technology and Wireless LAN 802.11b technology are that 802.11b allows data to be transmitted about 100 times as far and 15 times as fast as Bluetooth, while Bluetooth uses far less battery power. Wireless LAN technologies are more appropriate for desktops, mobile PCs, and for use by various devices in large campus environments while Bluetooth is better for mobile phones, hand-helds, palms, and other small computing devices.

Market penetration estimates for Bluetooth technology are glorious. For instance, a recent Merrill Lynch estimate predicts Bluetooth sales will reach $4.3 billion by 2005 (not bad considering that it has not made much of an impact as we enter 2002). Shipments of products using Bluetooth technologies should start to ramp upward by the middle of 2002 as the Bluetooth standard for interoperability becomes formalized, chip costs decrease, and software matures.

Powerlines

If you decide to wait out the broadband DSL, satellite, cable battles for a few years, you may find that the electrical lines you currently have running to your house may also be capable of providing you with access to high-speed Internet services.

Today, most users are connecting to the Internet using dial-up modems that perform in the 56 Kbps speed range. The Internet backbone that wires cities and countries together can transfer data today in the 10 Gbps range (and technologies to increase this to around 40 Gbps are not far away). Powerlines can be linked to these high-speed Internet backbones at speeds of up to 10 Mbps—thus providing a clear alternative to ADSL service (currently at 8 Mbps) and to cable and satellite approaches.

> Shortly after Germany's megagiant Siemens Corporation put its plans for powerline Internet services on hold, Germany's top power supplier, RWE, announced that to-

gether with Swiss partner Ascom they plan to offer commercial technology for high-speed Internet access via electricity cables. This new broadband-like service promises to be cheaper than telephone- and cable-based high-speed Internet connections. From a performance perspective, this technology could potentially provide users with download speeds up to 250 Mbps (significantly faster than traditional modem and ISDN connections).
Source: http://www.markt_aktuell.de/ak/mk/news/703700_20010220_100417.html

Meanwhile, Hewlett-Packard and RCA/Thompson announced a collaborative effort manifest in their System-Link Powerline Home Network kit—a powerline network that uses existing AC power outlets in the home to create a subchannel for the transfer of data from one end of a home to another area. This product in effect is a local area network based on powerline technology. It is reasonable to extrapolate that someday this technology could be bridged to an external Internet environment.
Source: http://library.northernlight.com/FB20010419780000154.html?=0&SC=0#doc

In the United States, prototype powerline modems should start to penetrate broadband markets in 2004, and deployment should commence in 2005—provided the service providers can surmount certain legislative hurdles.

Fiber-to-the-Home (FTTH)

In a perfect world, we'd all have access to fiber-optic connections to the Internet from home. Fiber-optic technology would give us the fastest possible connection to the Internet by essentially providing a dedicated link—an information super-superhighway—from our homes to a high-speed Internet backbone (which, by the way, also happens to be built on fiber-optic technology).

File transfer speeds that can be attained on fiber-optic links are incredible. Nippon Electric Corporation recently announced that it has successfully transmitted data at 6.4 Terabits per second—a terabit is one million megabits. They used fiber-optic C- and L-bands to send 40 Gbps by 160 wavelengths over a distance of more than 180 kilometers using a technique called Dense Wavelength Division Multiplexing. But don't expect this type of service to your home. Your Internet carriers will use this kind of backbone technology to handle the millions upon millions of data packets sent by the virtual yous of the future.

On the more practical side, testing of fiber-to-the-home connections is already underway in Atlanta, with 160 Mbps speeds being delivered to selected home sites. This service allows for DVD-quality streaming media reception (in the 5 to 10 Mbps range) as well as for HDTV reception (in the 17 Mbps range)—leaving plenty of bandwidth (a total of 160 Mbps is available) for Internet and data transfer applications.

Atlanta testing aside, you may be able to attain FTTH service today depending on where you are located. It is reasonable to expect to achieve over 1 gigabit per second Internet access speed today if you are rich enough to afford a dedicated fiber-optic connection—and close enough to a switching office to obtain such service.

> One company, Usen Corporation, now offers 100 Mbps FTTH service in Japan for a subscriber fee of approximately 4,900 yen per month (around U.S. $40 per month) for those fortunate enough to be located near a fiber-optic backbone. It will be interesting to see if Usen can recruit enough subscribers to sustain its low-cost high-speed cost structure.
> Source: http://www.usen.com

For your information, standards bodies are working on finalizing specifications for 10 Gbps Ethernets—primarily to be used by businesses in metropolitan area networks. These are intra-company networks characterized by short distances between access points and the need to transfer very large files. The 10 Gbps Ethernet (10 GbE) standard should be completed in

2002—paving the way for new high-speed networks at least at the metropolitan area network level. Ultimately, Ethernet products developed for business have a way of finding their way down to the home over time, as prices for these technologies decrease due to volume purchasing.

> A recent advance in fiber-optic technology has made it possible for data carriers to send digital information over long distances without the use of optical-to-electrical regenerators. These regenerators have been used to boost the optical signal of digital data transmitted over long distances. With new technology from Corvis Corporation, digital signals have now been sent 6,400 kilometers at a speed of 10 Gbps without having to use a regenerator along the way.
> Source: http://www.corvis.com

The ramifications of this technology definitely have implications in shorter-distance LAN and metropolitan area networking. There are even bigger implications in terms of lowering costs and making high-speed service more available. By eliminating regenerators, the equipment costs to send data are reduced. Also, by eliminating regenerators, the number of optical channels a single circuit can carry can be increased, thus making more service available over the same physical fiber wiring plant.

Commentary

Unlike most industry analysts, I do not believe that the consumer market is going to rush as rapidly as many analysts project into adopting broadband network service over the next two years. I believe this primarily because compelling applications have not arrived to entice most users to do so. Observe that:

- In today's world, many people are content using character-driven interfaces as their primary means of access to 2D, static data over the Internet. They can read newspaper reports, search and locate data, send and receive electronic mail, and play games such as Scrabble or Wheel-of-Fortune quite contentedly using simple character-oriented screens over low-speed (less that 56 Kbps) network connections—and that's all that they want to do. These people will not embrace change in the near term—and will, quite likely, not adopt change in the long term.

- Some argue that video-on-demand will change this situation—but without greater integration of PCs with television technologies or broader, cheaper access to such service, I highly doubt that video-on-demand will create a wholesale move by consumers to purchase high-speed networking technologies.
- Notice that there is currently a glut of broadband capacity worldwide—largely found in urban areas. For those unlucky many who find themselves in rural, inner-city, or certain suburban settings, broadband is not—nor will it soon be—an option for gaining high-speed access to the Internet. Without greater accessibility—and without better service delivery by suppliers of broadband technologies—consumers will be unable to capitalize on broadband technology.

According to the market research firm IDC, by 2003 only one-third of all Internet residential users (approximately 65 million users in the U.S. at that juncture) will have access to broadband services. This projection amounts to less than one-third of the projected U.S. population in 2003. This means that in two years, most U.S. households will still not be able to get broadband services—even if they desperately need them, want them, and can pay for them.

Chapter Summary

Simply stated, to participate in a three-dimensional computing world where you will both send and receive sensory data on a regular basis, you are going to need network speed that is higher than the speed found on most home computers today (which is typically in the 28.8 to 56 Kbps range). If you intend to take advantage of new, more powerful 3D applications, collaborative applications, video-on-demand, and other bandwidth-intensive applications, transmission speeds in at least the range of 1.5 Mbps will be required.

Your options for obtaining high-speed network connections to the Internet are many. High-speed wired connections include DSL, ISDN, and cable modem access—and someday may include fiber-to-the-home (FTTH) and electrical powerline connections. Wireless high-speed connections include satellite and fixed wireless solutions—and third generation (3G) wireless connection in the 2 Mbps range are coming in the not-too-distant future.

The high-speed option that you choose is highly dependent on what high-speed services you have access to. In urban and suburban areas, depending on how close your home or business is situated to a phone company switch, DSL options may be your best choice. Or your existing cable TV line may also accommodate high-speed Internet connection. Or you may be located in close proximity to a WLAN station. Or you may have a clear line of sight to a satellite service. Regardless of which approach you choose, you're going to need high-speed networking to participate in the Sensory Virtual Internet.

CHAPTER 11

PERSONAL COMPUTING DEVICES

As we venture toward sensory-rich virtual worlds, the capture, transmission, reception, and playback of sensory data will place new demands on our computing devices. Our computers will need to capture and process large blocks of sight, sound, touch, scent, and taste data instantaneously in order to provide us with the most realistic experiences.

To accommodate the processing of large blocks of sensory data, a complete redesign of the personal computer is under way. Some of the major advances in PC design include the advent of 64-bit processing (which will enable the CPU to process more data more rapidly), great improvements in graphics processing capabilities using specially designed graphics processing units, and a complete redesign of the PC bus architecture to a switched architecture (discussed later in this chapter).

This chapter focuses on the forthcoming design changes that will make our personal computers better able to capture, process, display, send, and receive complex sensory data files. It is intended to help you understand which computer design elements are important if you plan on participating in sensory-rich electronic worlds of the future.

Stationary versus Mobile/Portable Devices

As you are undoubtedly aware, there are dozens of different kinds of computers, including mainframes, minicomputers, desktop PCs, workstations, laptops, hand-helds, Palms, wearables, embedded systems, and more. There are computers primarily used for personal computing tasks (word processing, spreadsheets, etc.), those dedicated to the playing of audio files (MP3 players), those dedicated to playing games (game consoles), those optimized for multimedia presentations, and so forth. Even your mobile phone (if you own one—as 700 million people do) is a computer.

Stationary computers are the computers that you use from a fixed position. These computers are most often found connected to a local area network or connected to the Internet through a modem from a home. These computers are the ones that get the latest-greatest hardware and software enhancements— mobile/portable devices need to wait until stationary computer enhancements are miniaturized in order to catch up in terms of power and in order to accommodate new hardware features and functionality. This phenomena is most evident in graphics processing where stationary graphics cards are generally one-third faster than graphics processors on mobile devices—and it usually takes six to twelve months for a mobile device to catch up. By then, the stationary device has set a new performance threshold.

In addition, mobile and portable computers are usually slower than stationary computers from a communications/networking perspective. Most mobile devices often rely on slow speed connections to the Internet (today's wireless speed is generally between 9.6 Kbps and 19.2 Kbps) or phone line connections at 56 Kbps or less.

Given these shortcomings, stationary computers are the ones that you will most likely use to receive the highest quality sensory input, and they are also likely to be the ones you will use to present (play, display, or produce) the highest quality sensory output. It just so happens that these are the computers that are undergoing the most redevelopment in the industry as current architectures are adapted to handle (in varying degrees of quality) sensory-rich data streams.

The State of the Market: Stationary Devices

Workstations and PCs are stationary devices, but some laptops and portables are now also considered stationary when used in a docked mode at home and at work. This section takes a closer look at each type of stationary device, providing commentary on the current state of the art for each as well as projected future directions.

On the UNIX Workstation Front

Over the past 15 years, UNIX workstations have been the market-preferred platform for creating high-performance, high-resolution graphics. Before UNIX, proprietary systems from IBM, ComputerVision, Apollo, Silicon Graphics, and other companies dominated the graphics scene, particularly in CAD/CAM environments. In the future, Linux-based computers are expected to challenge UNIX workstations from a high-powered graphics processing point of view. Today, high-end

UNIX workstations render higher-quality graphics in the industry with greater resolution and more realistic colors, lighting, shadows, and anti-aliased curves than even the most powerful PC-based systems.

Typically, high-end UNIX workstations have highly optimized graphics subsystems and very powerful, specialized graphics microprocessors, called graphics processing units or GPUs. The most popular UNIX workstations also make use of microprocessors that are 64-bit-enabled. (What this means is that Sun's SPARC and IBM's PowerPC chips can process 64 bits of information at a time as opposed to Intel CPUs, which are only capable of 32 bits at this time. This ability to process more data gives these workstations a distinct processing advantage over consumer Intel-based PCs.) These specialized processors combined with other system components and overall architectural design such as the amount of memory available or the system bus architecture all work together to deliver extremely high-quality, on-screen 3D depth effects.

The following is a typical example of the types of features and power offered by a UNIX workstation—in this case, IBM's Model 170 UNIX workstation:

Excerpted from IBM's Web site:

Somers, NY, December 19, 2000—IBM today announced the world's fastest UNIX-based computing workstation, offering nearly two times the performance of similarly configured new UltraSparc-III based servers from Sun Microsystems.

The IBM Model 170 UNIX workstation uses copper-fueled microprocessors and the latest GXT6000P 3D graphics accelerator from IBM to provide unprecedented levels of performance for companies designing products such as airplanes and automobiles.... With state-of-the-art, copper microprocessors, the Model 170 outperforms comparable Sun, HP and SGI UNIX systems in key benchmarks including SPECviewperf OpenGL industry standardized performance measurements. OpenGL is the underlying graphics library in most 3D graphics visualization and design applications.

The POWER GXT6000P graphics accelerator brings a new class of function and performance to UNIX workstations to meet those needs with room to spare. It was designed to take on large MCAD models, complex simulations, and the challenges of visualization that are often encountered in the most demanding applications.

Advanced 3D Features:
- Advanced hardware geometry acceleration supported in hardware
- Up to 108 MB of texture memory
- Gamma-corrected anti-aliased lines
- Dual textures, 3D textures, and texture color tables
- Linear, bilinear, and trilinear texture filtering
- Hardware occlusion culling
- Gouraud shading, depth cueing/fog, transparency
- Four hardware color maps
- Supports screen resolution up to 1920 x 1200 at 76 Hz
- *Double-buffered stereo viewing in a window (up to 1280 x 1024)*
- DDC2B support, ISO 9241 compliant
- P-buffer support

Entry price for the Model 170 is $10,495. Orders for the GXT6000P began shipping in mid-December 2000. The high-function, high-performance 3D UNIX workstation with graphics accelerator is available at less than $30,000.

Source: http://www-1.IBM.com/servers/eservers/pseries/news/pressreleases/2001/Dec/3dgraphics.html Advanced 3d Features

It is highly unlikely that a typical consumer reading this book is going to invest $30,000 simply to see 3D graphics images at home or in school. Further, the lion's share of 3D-enabled consumer applications run on Microsoft Windows, not on UNIX. Still, it is relevant to note that UNIX workstations are usually where consumers should look if they wish to get an advance glimpse of what's coming down the pike in terms of 3D imaging technology. UNIX 3D technology advancements almost always find their way into PC architectures over time.

Although UNIX workstations continually lead the market in terms of graphics performance and the richness of their graphics display, Linux (an open-source, UNIX-like operating system) is slowly beginning to challenge UNIX in the high-end graphics-processing marketplace. Meanwhile, powerful personal or professional PC workstations (PWSs) form the high end of the market while basic, low-end Internet-enabled personal computers (such as the Apple iMac and Compaq's Ipaq) are example of low-end personal computers that can display 2D and rudimentary 3D graphics.

PC Graphics Processing

In 1996, I started writing about the demise of the low-end UNIX workstation market as personal computers became capable of processing 3D graphics. At that time, personal computers had managed to exceed a CPU speed of 100 MHz. When these consumer PCs were combined with a commercial graphics card, they could display passable 3D graphics. The terms used to describe these specialized, 3D graphics-enabled and graphics-optimized personal computers were personal workstations or professional workstations (depending on the maker's preference).

PCs today can do a pretty incredible job at processing 3D graphics. This is again thanks to increases in raw processing speed (at this time PCs can process at up to speeds of 1.7 GHz), faster system buses, and the development of specialized graphics controllers from companies such as nVidia and ATI.

The PC graphics controller market bears closer examination as consolidation takes place and two companies emerge as the primary makers of graphics GPUs for the PC industry. At present, both nVidia and ATI are vying for market leadership in the

PC graphics industry while a third manufacturer, 3Dfx, was recently acquired by nVidia when it ran into financial difficulties. (These troubles were the result of 3Dfx's decision to become the sole source and distribution channel for its GPU and card.) Both suppliers have strong graphics controller market entries—but nVidia currently has the strongest PC graphics controller with its GeForce 3. This controller has the ability to process 800 billion pixels per second and a fill rate of 800 million pixels per second—giving PC buyers the ability to process extremely realistic 3D graphics. Note that we still need PC software that can exploit the graphics processing capability of this controller; as is often the case it takes time for software developers to build software that can exploit the power of the new hardware.

Raw CPU power also contributes to graphics performance. Fast GPUs supported by fast CPUs even further improve our ability to view 3D graphics. The PC graphics performance situation is only going to get stronger as new graphics controllers combine with Intel's line of 64-bit processors that will find their way into PC architecture over the next few years. The combination of super-fast graphics processing units and the new 64-bit RISC architecture will go a long way toward enabling PCs to catch up to UNIX workstations in terms of overall graphics performance.

A Closer Look at 64-Bit Computing

One of the big shifts in consumer PC graphics systems forthcoming involves the use of a 64-bit chipset known as IA-64. Current Intel chips can process instructions 32 bits at a time, which has the effect of limiting how much data can be put into and out of main memory. Thirty-two-bit systems can only process up to 4 Gb of data in main memory, while initial 64-bit systems will allow 16 to 32 Gbs in main memory—and have theoretical limits in Petabytes.

Sixty-four-bit processors handle instructions 64 bits at a time as opposed to the 32-bit rate of the current Windows operating systems. By having the ability to process instructions in bigger chunks, the amount of data placed in memory can be greatly expanded beyond the current limit of four megabytes. By placing that amount of data in memory (which is faster to access than disk) the whole job of processing information is greatly accelerated. The closer the data is to the CPU, the faster the CPU can process that data. And the more data that can be put in main memory, the faster a system can process it. The bottom line is that as 64-bit Intel systems arrive on the market, you can expect a huge increase in performance in graphics handling and graphics processing.

Ultimately, the advantage of 64-bit addressing is that it allows for the placement of a lot of data in main memory instead of having to retrieve that data via an SCSI or fiber connection from a storage peripheral, meaning that the CPU can read memory-resident data more quickly. As a result, some applications will see a *hundredfold performance improvement* when implemented in a 64-bit mode. This is a huge increase for the next generation of consumer PCs. (See Figure 10 for an illustration of the ramifications of 64-bit computing.)

Intel's IA-64 architecture will be the first consumer PC 64-bit chip in the market in 2001. Be aware that UNIX workstations running microprocessors such as the UltraSPARC, and Apple Computer's PowerPC, have offered 64-bit computing for years. Also be aware that AMD, Intel's primary competitor, is expected to offer a 64-bit chipset within the next two years. And finally, it is reasonable to expect that chipsets will reach 128-bit speeds by 2006.

PC Bus Architecture Changes

Your PC has a "bus" architecture, which is simply a pipe or pathway between the CPU, the GPU, memory, storage, network-

32-BIT SYSTEM

32-bit = up to 4GBs of data in main memory

Data is accessed using a slower-than-internal-bus connection such as SCSI or Fiber

More data resides on disk; slower response...

64-BIT SYSTEM

64-bit = 16 to 32 GB of data in main memory (with theoretical limits in the Petabytes)

Less data is needs to be accessed using slower-than-internal-busconnections such as SCSI or Fiber because more data is placed in main memory

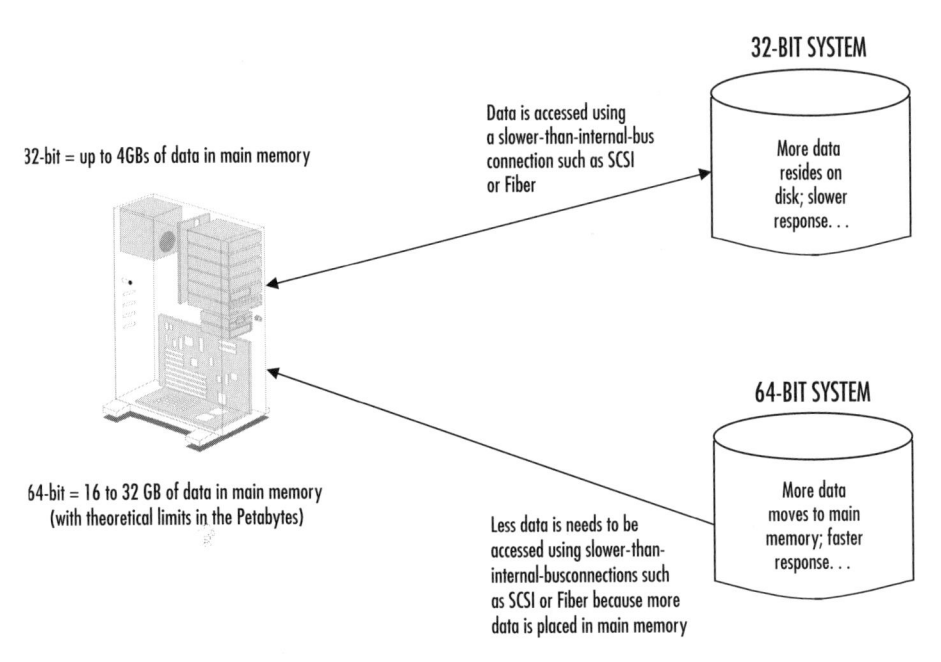

More data moves to main memory; faster response...

FIGURE 10
The Ramifications of 64-Bit Computing

ing, and other I/O connections. It is through this pipeline that data is sent and received. Before 2000, bus speeds on most PCs ranged from 100, 133, and 200 Mbps. The year 2000 saw the bus speed move up to 400 Mbps on the standard consumer PC. PCs of the future will require far faster speeds for complex graphics and sensory data processing.

The PC architecture of the future will be switch-based, where PC components can call other system components over very high speed connections to move data around, as illustrated in Figure 11. This calling approach is significantly different than today's approach where all PC components make calls over the same link—the PC bus. Switching enables components to talk to each other without having to share space on a common bus architecture—thus resulting in higher-speed communication between components and therefore better performance for users.

226 VISUALIZE THIS

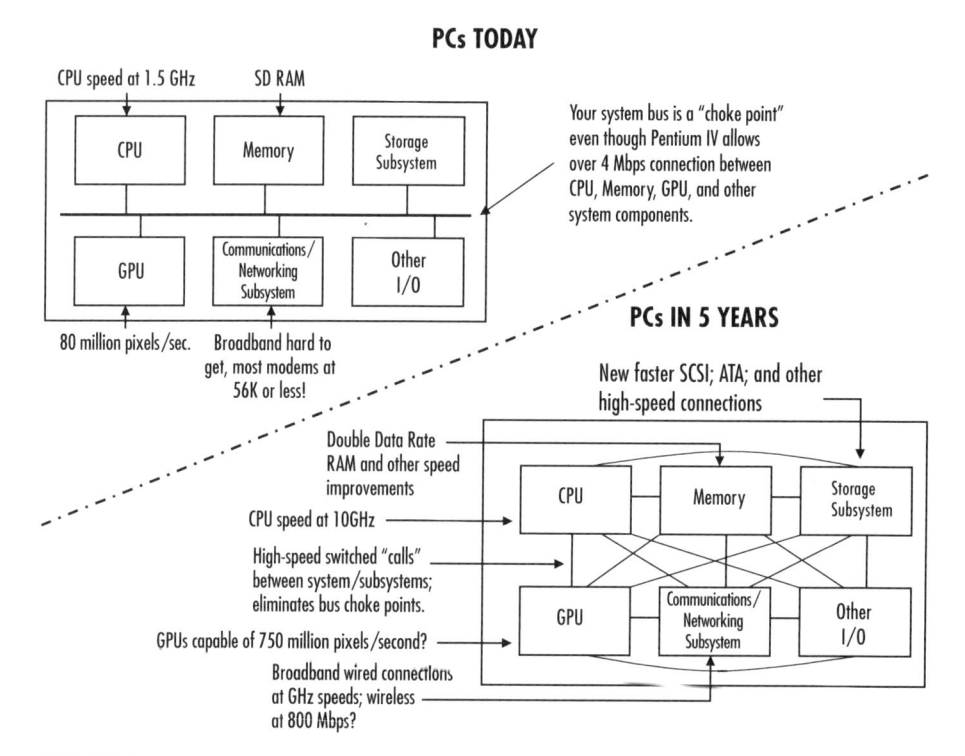

PCs TODAY

- CPU speed at 1.5 GHz
- SD RAM
- CPU
- Memory
- Storage Subsystem
- GPU
- Communications/Networking Subsystem
- Other I/O
- 80 million pixels/sec.
- Broadband hard to get, most modems at 56K or less!

Your system bus is a "choke point" even though Pentium IV allows over 4 Mbps connection between CPU, Memory, GPU, and other system components.

PCs IN 5 YEARS

- Double Data Rate RAM and other speed improvements
- CPU speed at 10GHz
- High-speed switched "calls" between system/subsystems; eliminates bus choke points.
- GPUs capable of 750 million pixels/second?
- Broadband wired connections at GHz speeds; wireless at 800 Mbps?
- New faster SCSI; ATA; and other high-speed connections
- CPU
- Memory
- Storage Subsystem
- GPU
- Communications/Networking Subsystem
- Other I/O

FIGURE 11
Your PC Today and Tommorrow

STORAGE ACCESS WILL BE FASTER

Connections to local storage peripherals will include ATA and SCSI connections. Over the next five years, the speeds of these input/output connections could triple or quadruple.

It is also important to note that disk access speeds are also going to improve in the future, which will allow CPUs and GPUs faster access to data stored on disk. One company, Broadcom Corporation, announced its acquisition of ServerWorks Corporation in order to provide IT departments with super-fast access to data stored on disk. Broadcom and ServerWorks were jointly developing server/storage network products aimed at providing CPUs and memory subsystems with access to high-speed data transfer from disks. Over the next few years, expect data transfer speeds from disk to hit the 10 Gbps range (at least triple today's best access speed).

A Closer Look: Forthcoming PC Architectural Improvements

Let's take a closer look at forthcoming changes to PC CPU, GPU, and bus architecture. The three "throttles" for optimizing PC performance are:

1. The speed of the CPU
2. The speed of the GPU
3. The speed of the system bus

Futhermore, a possible fourth throttle that may influence PC performance is the instruction set used to enable applications to use the CPU most effectively. By improving and streamlining the instructions used by programs to take advantage of graphics subsystems—instruction sets such as AMD's 3Dnow and Intel's Streaming SIMD Extensions—graphics processing performance can be further increased.

Forthcoming Improvements in CPU Performance

Today's PC CPU battles are largely being fought between Intel and Advanced Micro Devices—with each company issuing chips using excellent technologies that constantly leapfrog each other in terms of performance. The recently released Intel Pentium 4 has a 42-million-transistor integrated circuit and boasts processing speed greater than 1.7 GHz. And in the future, the current PC power roadmap indicates that desktop computers should be capable of running 400 million transistors at 10 GHz (almost ten times the speed of today's fastest CPU) by the year 2006!

Intel is currently pinning its hopes on a process known as Extreme Ultraviolet (EUV) lithography. It is based on optics technologies developed for the Hubble telescope as well as laser technologies that resulted from the U.S. "Star Wars" defense initiative research. EUV lithography is similar to taking a picture and then superimposing that picture on silicon. In a fabrication plant, chipmakers use a specialized photolithography device to print an image of a series of circuits on a silicon wafer. The picture is then developed and certain materials are then removed or deposited, layer by layer, to build a chip. The process is similar to taking a photograph and then airbrushing and retouching the picture for the best results. By using this process, it is feasible that PC chip developers will double performance every year for the next several years.

Still, other CPU technologies may play a role in improving desktop performance and, certainly, mobile computing performance. At the high end, IBM's recently patented silicon-on-insulator (SOI) technology may help to increase desktop PC performance, although this technology has so far been targeted at only high-end servers. IBM's latest microprocessor technology, CMOS 9S, connects a very powerful copper-based chip with SOI to allow fully functional mainstream microprocessors (as opposed to specially developed microprocessors) to run on mobile devices, while at the same time using less power. CMOS 9S will initially run on high-end IBM Internet eServers that will be made available in 2001, but will quickly move to premium-priced wireless devices and networking products shortly thereafter.

As other scientific advances take place, as-yet-unidentified technologies may also appear to further brighten the PC performance picture in the not-so-distant future.

Forthcoming Improvements in GPU Performance

On the GPU side, today's PC graphics cards are doubling in performance every six months. As I have said, one of the today's hottest PC cards, the nVidia GeForce3, processes 800 billion pixels per second. This high level of performance rivals Sony's highly successful PlayStation 2 (a game controller with outstanding computer graphics) and is starting to rival the performance of some high-end UNIX workstations.

Forthcoming Improvements in PC Bus Performance

One of the choke points in personal computer graphics handling has been the PC *bus architecture*. A bus is like a pipe that links processors to main memory and I/O systems such as printers, hard drives, and modems. A big pipe enables the GPU and CPU to share data and handle graphics more efficiently. Until recently, PCs using a PCI bus could only handle 100 MHz on the front side, and many new PCs still being offered on the market only offer 133 MHz bus speed.

The key point to consider about bus architectures is that all of the data being processed needs to pass between various components like the CPU, GPU, and storage subsystem through one, common pipe. As we move to the Sensory Virtual Internet world, we will need our computers to pass huge files between processing components within our PCs—and a single connection point like a bus has the potential to create bottlenecks in processing.

However, the good news is that PC architecture is starting to undergo significant change as new, faster bus architectures arrive. An Intel-sanctioned 400-MHz front-side bus has arrived with the Pentium 4 microprocessor. Over time, advanced switching, such as that used in large server environments and in some UNIX workstations, will make its way to PC architecture. Currently, Intel is planning such a switched architecture with a memory controller hub architecture that will speed up processing between Advanced Graphics Port (AGP) subsystems, Universal Serial Bus (USB), I/O subsystems, memory, and the CPU. In the short term, however, expect faster bus architectures to help alleviate PC CPU, GPU, and I/O data sharing performance constraint issues.

Finally, it should be noted that Intel has introduced extensions to its Pentium 4 line of processors known as Streaming SIMD Extensions 2 (SSE2), which provide 144 new instructions that help speed up video, multimedia, and 3D performance while also assisting in imaging and encryption handling. Combinations of improvements in hardware at the GPU and CPU levels, bus speed, and systems instruction sets will all help to make PCs far faster than what we see today on the market. In addition, Intel plans to greatly increase the speed of its Advanced Graphics Port (AGP) interface (a fast graphics connection to the central processing unit) when it releases its next series of beyond AGP4X extensions, which should result in significantly faster graphics processing (on the order of two or three times faster than today's AGP speed).

Note that Intel is not the sole driver of change to consumer PC architecture. For instance, Advanced Micro Devices (AMD) has been extremely active in driving CPU performance, constantly leapfrogging Intel for PC performance leadership. In addition, AMD is also highly active in building advanced PC bus architectures. Of particular interest is their new HyperTransport bus.

> In January, 2001 at the Platform Conference in San Jose, CA, AMD announced that 10 leading suppliers of graphics technologies (including graphics leader nVidia Corp) had licensed AMD's Lightning Data Transport (LDT)—subsequently renamed HyperTransport—(a new PC systems bus architecture) for use with their respective technologies. This announcement was followed by announcements that Broadcom, ATI Technologies, and others had agreed to use the new bus architecture.
> In February, AMD decided to freely license HyperTransport technology to the industry—seeking to gain widespread industry support and adoption for its new, fast bus architecture. If successful, HyperTransport could eventually replace the Peripheral Component Interconnect (PCI) bus that has become standard in PCs and many server environments. With bus speed expected

to eventually reach the 6.4 Gbps range (versus the 266 Mbps PCI bus found on most motherboards today), the AMD implementation will be almost 24 times as fast as the current PCI bus architecture. Note: not all suppliers of HyperTransport peripherals will make use of the full 6.4 Gbps—primarily because HyperTransport uses separate inbound and outbound paths. Alpha Processor Inc., for instance, will only make use of 1 GB in each direction (to/from the CPU) in its first implementations.

By licensing AMD's HyperTransport, nVidia was essentially signaling to the world that its intent is to make its GPUs very compatible with AMD's Athlon CPUs and potentially optimize its products for use with Athlon.

In short, bigger pipes between GPUs and CPUs combined with faster GPUs and CPUs will yield greatly improved PC graphics performance in the very near future.

Source: http://www.amd.com/news/prodpr/21083.html

State of the Art: Portable/Laptop Computers

With respect to graphics performance, the big problem with portables and laptop computers to date has been that the integration of 3D graphics has largely been proprietary in nature. In an effort to minimize the size of a portable, computer makers have have had to build their own implementations of 3D graphics onto their respective systems boards. As a result, portables and laptops have not been able to capitalize on powerful, mass-market controllers like the GeForce 3, and have instead lagged stationary computers in terms of graphics processing capability. Due to shortcomings in graphics memory and GPU processing power as well as a slow bus architecture portables have consistently lagged behind PC desktops by a significant margin in terms of graphics performance and graphics handling.

Over the past year, however, commodity graphics controller makers like nVidia have turned their focus toward making commodity products specifically designed for mobile and portable devices. For instance, nVidia is in the process of releasing graphics controllers designed to render 3D on portable computers that will improve a portable's graphics handling capability by a factor of ten. These controllers will narrow the large graphics processing gap between desktops and portable computers—but it should be noted that laptops and portables will consistently lag stationary devices in the ability to process 3D graphics for at least the next three years.

In addition to lagging stationary devices in graphics performance, mobile computers generally trail desktops slightly in the availability of the highest speed CPUs—primarily because the processors used in mobile computing devices have to be designed to meet lower power consumption needs. It is reasonable to expect the CPU power gap to shrink as Intel starts using its new EUV photolithography process to shrink the transistor gate length from 130 nm (nanometers) to 30 nm (sorry for the tech talk), enabling Intel to dramatically scale processor MHz frequency upward while decreasing operational voltage to less than one volt. What this means is that Intel will be able to increase processor speed and potentially deliver these high-speed processors on mobile devices at the same time that they are delivered on desktop PCs. It also means the company will be able to substantially lower the electrical power demands of these microprocessors. Ultimately, the deployment of this technology should make it possible to close the CPU performance gap between stationary and mobile computing devices.

Chapter Summary

This is an important chapter in terms of foreseeing the arrival of the new Sensory Virtual Internet. Very significant changes are under way, particularly in PC systems architecture. These changes signal that PCs are being designed to better capture, transmit, receive, display and/or play 3D graphics, thus greatly enriching our visual experiences on the Sensory Virtual Internet.

Note that a complete redesign of the PC bus architecture is taking place. Graphics handling is being streamlined. New superpowerful graphics processors are being brought to market. Intel and AMD are developing new multimedia and graphics extensions that will improve PC graphics processing even further. Also, Intel's 64-bit microprocessors will over the next two years make their way into PC architecture—resulting in great improvements in overall processing power. You may be tempted by the current bargains to be found in the PC market today, such as Gigahertz-plus computers with a fair amount of memory and storage in the near-$1000 price range. You'll need to keep some of these changes and their ramifications in mind as you purchase your next-generation personal computer.

Soon desktops, hand-helds, Palms, wearables, laptops and other Internet-enabled mobile computing devices will be used by all of us to access the Sensory Virtual Internet. Each device will offer capture, transmission, and playback at varying levels. Stationary devices, such as workstations and PCs, will continue to be among the most powerful Sensory Virtual Internet devices for the presentation of graphics, sound, and other sensory experiences. Mobile devices will either be optimized to handle one of the sensory experiences extremely well (for instance, playing digital audio), but will more than likely be comparatively less able to deliver multi-sensory experiences at a quality level equivalent to a personal computer or workstation.

When you put together all of the changes taking place on stationary and edge-of-network devices—and you consider how the Sensory Virtual Internet could be set up to capitalize on these changes—you will most likely come to the conclusion that the new architectural changes under way will create radically-different-from-today graphics processing systems with plenty of ability to process the rich sensory data streams that we can expect to receive as we participate in virtual worlds on the Sensory Virtual Internet.

CHAPTER 12

Back-End Peer-to-Peer/ Grid Systems

☐ kay, just suppose that we manage to overcome various human interface, network speed, and personal computing device limitations over the next few years. We are still going to be faced with the issue that providing 3D rich visual, sound, scent, touch, and taste experiences will require a vast amount of processing power—both on front-end PCs as well as on back-end servers. In addition to processing graphical and sound data, we will need even more computational support to allow the virtual you to navigate and move through virtual vistas and to handle and manipulate objects in those worlds.

To handle vast amounts of data, computer systems will need to be able to use sophisticated algorithms to compress audio, video, and other sensory data streams and send these streams over the Internet to potentially millions of individuals using avatars to interact in Sensory Virtual Internet communities. Receiving systems, such as the next-generation PCs discussed in the previous chapter, will then need to be optimized to decompress and display/play/present such information.

Further, it is important to note that the type of processor workload for moving through virtual vistas is different than the type of processor workload experienced today by most business systems. Instead of processing hundreds and thousands of *transactions* (in a bank these would be credits and debits), the Sensory Virtual Internet will require that hundreds and thousands of *computations* be made to depict movement or for object manipulation. This type of processor workload is likely to require that companies that provide virtual environments reorient their computer systems to allow for both transaction and computational processing.

This chapter focuses on the changes that need to take place on the computing back-end to allow for vastly improved computational processing on virtual reality servers.

The Sensory Virtual Internet Requires a Shift from Transaction-Oriented Processing to Computation-Oriented Processing

Previous chapters described the complexity involved in creating 3D images and rendering 3D environments. Now consider having to do so for hundreds or thousands or millions of users who are moving through virtual 3D spaces. Each avatar will be located at different points within a 3D virtual vista. Some avatars will be shopping, while others may be chatting with other members of a virtual community. Not only are the computing and 3D display activities computationally challenging, but the logistics of keeping track of virtual visitors and the applications that they are running (such as chat or collaborative software) are also extremely complex and will require a tremendous amount of computing power. In other words, to handle very large populations of virtual visitors, today's processing power will need to be vastly increased, meaning a new way for computers to work together to handle these complex computations has to be devised.

In this new model of virtual world computing, back-end systems will need to be able to perform billions of calculations, and IT managers will need to find a way to link their back-end systems with tens, hundreds, or possibly thousands of other computers to share the heavily computational 3D virtual workload.

At first glance, the use of supercomputers could be viewed as ideal for handling this type of workload. Supercomputers are very powerful computing complexes that have been optimized for number-crunching and modeling tasks and can almost effortlessly handle the task of computing and displaying 3D images for hundreds if not thousands of simultaneous users. But supercomputers can cost tens to hundreds of millions of dollars to build and operate. And costs in this range present a huge barrier to entry for companies that would choose to venture into creating 3D virtual worlds and space.

Another way to approach handling the processor load for virtual reality is to find a way to *distribute* the huge graphics-processing load across multiple computers. This means having each computer take responsibility for some amount of processing and then having each one coordinate the results of these computations with a controlling computer or series of computers. The basic concept behind this mode of computing is known as *distributed computing*. The specific task of processing data across multiple distributed computers is known as "workload balancing."

Peer-to-peer computing is a version of distributed computing. It describes a computing configuration that will allow us to gain access to a vast amount of processing power. In the future, it may be the most effective way to deliver sensory data to millions of virtual visitors. Peer-to-peer computing is expected to make it possible for builders of virtual worlds and services to gain access to the heavy computational power that they need to support thousands or hundreds of thousands of avatars in virtual settings such as malls, universities, business offices, conventions, and the like. So let's take a closer look at the peer-to-peer computing model.

Peer-to-Peer Computing

Peer-to-peer computing is a term that has been with us since the 1970s but has recently come back in vogue to describe workload sharing across multiple distributed computers. This type of computing allows multiple computers to be linked together as if they were one in order to share files or to tackle very large computing tasks.

The big change between the 1970s version of peer-to-peer computing and the 2000+ version is that large numbers of computers owned by various people and organizations are being loosely coupled together. (In the 1970s version, peer systems were usually 10 or fewer computers all within the confines of an enterprise's computing complex.) Today's peer-to-peer computers are "network aware" and can find and use available processing power from any of a number of other computers that they have authorization to use. In this manner, today's peer-to-peer network can make use of the processing power of hundreds or thousands of other computers to perform complex data processing—essentially using the power of multiple distributed computers to create one large virtual computer capable of handling complex computational tasks.

Examples of Peer-to-Peer Virtual Supercomputers

The best-known example of today's version of peer-to-peer processing is a project known as SETI@home. The Search for

Extra-Terrestrial Intelligence makes use of hundreds of thousands (and by some estimates up to 2 million) computers worldwide to analyze extraterrestrial radio signals in the hopes of discovering extraterrestrial life. Computer users who support the SETI project load a program on their computers that downloads data collected by the Arecibo Radio Observatory in Puerto Rico. When these computers are not needed for other tasks, they perform mathematical analysis of the signals and forward the results back to the laboratory.

SETI@home essentially bands computer systems together in a fabric, a loosely connected networked environment. As a result, from a performance perspective, the SETI@home computers combine to run at over 15 teraflops (15 trillion floating point calculations per second) at a total implementation and management cost of about $500,000. Contrast this with the world's most powerful supercomputer (manufactured by IBM), which runs at a speed of 12 teraflops and cost over $100 million to build. The SETI@home project serves as a proof point that virtual peer-to-peer processing has the potential to be used to achieve the processing power required to support a highly computational environment (such as the forthcoming Sensory Virtual Internet) in a flexible manner and at low cost.

What is extremely important to note about this example is that the SETI@home application is a screen saver. It only activates at slack times when the owner isn't using the computer. In other words, the SETI@home network makes use of computing power that is just lying about idle! Whether this approach will be mimicked by commercial projects as we move to heavily computational 3D Virtual environments remains to be seen. But SETI@home proves the concept that peer-to-peer computing can work on a grand scale.

Another SETI-like example of using distributed processors to provide supercomputer-like capabilities is the approach that HotBot uses for searching the Web. HotBot is a search engine developed collaboratively by Inktomi Corporation and Hot-Wired, Inc. that makes use of many workstations in parallel to search and index Web pages instead of using supercomputers or a farm of clustered minicomputers. HotBot's Network of Workstations (NOW) is one of the early examples of the use of the peer-to-peer computing model for a commercial application.

The SETI@home example cited earlier is only one example of peer-to-peer being used for scientific research purposes. A number of other organizations are collaborating to help build PC supercomputer networks. These organizations are involved in causes ranging from discovering new drugs to combat AIDS and other diseases to analyzing the human genome. These efforts involve providing free software to volunteer PC users who offer their spare computing power to analyze data and send the results back to a central computing source. Entropia Inc., for instance, helps scientists search for new drugs to fight AIDS. In order to make money in the process, Entropia sells some of the donated computing power to pharmaceutical companies that would otherwise rent a supercomputer.

Now that these volunteers have proved the virtual supercomputer concept, certain commercial ventures are looking to find ways to capitalize on the peer-to-peer method of computing. Companies such as Porviro and Centrate are aggressively embarking on programs designed to remarket their company's raw computing power to other companies that need access to supercomputer-like processing. DataSynapse is another such company.

> One commercial approach to creating a virtual supercomputer network can be found at DataSynapse.com. In this case, computer owners are directly rewarded for their participation in creating a peer-to-peer environment with potential contest winnings and "Internet bucks." Following the precedent set by the SETI@home project, DataSynapse.com has made it known that it

wishes to rent time from PC users whose PCs are connected to broadband networks in order to run a few thousand extremely complex mathematical calculations. In exchange, the company offers participants who choose to allow access to their personal computers the chance to win a Palm Pilot or even a Porsche. And to further sweeten the pot, DataSynapse.com offers participants "flooz," Internet money that can be redeemed for gifts or donated to charity.

DataSynapse.com is looking for clients that have calculations that can take as long as 70 hours if done in house. They offer to spread the processing load around to a few thousand PCs, which could result in 70 hours worth of calculations being performed in as little as 30 minutes.

Source: http://www.Datasynapse.com

Another approach for commercially harnessing available raw computing power can be found at the headquarters of Internet Service Provider Juno. In a move to improve its financial condition, Juno decided to change its Internet service from that of a "free Internet" service provider with much of the operational revenue underwritten by advertisers to a service that includes free Internet services provided that Juno subscribers leave their computers on to perform computational work when idle. In this manner, Juno is looking to augment its financial bottom line and make itself more solidly profitable by selling the computing power it gleans from its subscriber base to organizations or companies that need such services.

On January 18, 2000, Juno made clear its intention to require subscribers to allow it to download "computational software" to their computers, thus creating an instant peer-to-peer virtual supercomputer network from its existing subscriber base of 14.2 million users. By some estimates, if all of the raw power in its user base could be harnessed, the proposed Juno Virtual Supercomputer Network could break the petahertz barrier with a hypothetical effective processor speed in the order of a billion megahertz!

"In connection with downloading and running the Computational Software," the Juno contract reads, "Juno may require you to leave your computer turned on at all times, and may replace the screen saver software that runs on your computer while the computer is turned on but you are not using it. The screen saver software installed by Juno, which may display advertisements or images chosen by Juno, is an integral part of the Computational Software and you agree not to take any action to disable or interfere with the operation of either the screen saver software or any other component of the Computational Software."

The company further states that "Juno agrees that it shall exercise such right only to the extent necessary" and that "you [the subscriber] shall be responsible for any costs and expenses (including without limitation any applicable telephone charges) resulting from the foregoing."

The Juno proposition is interesting. You could continue to get free Internet service in exchange for providing access to your computer at times when it is not being used.

Source:http://dl.www.Juno.com

The Juno proposal is an interesting example of how a peer-to-peer virtual supercomputer environment could be created. But what happens under the hood or behind the scenes of this proposal? How does Juno intend to protect the privacy of individuals who commit to this proposed service agreement? How can Juno assure its users that they are protected against viruses and other damaging influences? How will Juno effectively manage this network? The Juno idea highlights what is possible using a peer-to-peer networking approach, but it also makes obvious certain areas of concern with regard to peer-to-peer computing, specifically system security, personal privacy, and system management.

It is also worthy of note that ISPs such as Juno face another hurdle. Most subscribers use dial-up connections to access their ISPs and dial-up connections do not fit the "always-on" criteria needed to ensure that workload can be assigned, processed, and returned to a central source. Many users of ISPs have only one phone line and thus would be loathe to forfeit the right to make personal telephone calls just to gain access to free Internet services or Internet reward dollars. Users of DSL, cable, or ISDN technologies would not have this problem because their Internet service is always on and they have simultaneous use of their telephone for voice calls.

Peer-to-Peer Tomorrow

The future of peer-to-peer computing hinges on finding available CPU processing power for heavy computational work. There are billions upon billions of computer processing cycles wasted every day throughout the world as businesses close for the night or as users shut down their dial-up sessions with their individual Internet service providers.

In the case of large multinational organizations, the capture and use of available CPU cycles will be more straightforward than it will be for small- or mid-sized domestic enterprises. For large multinationals, the effort to find available computing power may be as simple as using systems and network management products as well as workload management products to locate and exploit existing computing power within the organization. But for smaller companies, finding available computing cycles may involve the need to structure agreements with owners of computer equipment who are external to the organization in order to gain access to those computers when they are idle. And it is reasonable to expect that many organizations will not be willing to share unused computing cycles due to the security risks.

How Big Business Will Use Peer-to-Peer Networking to Increase Processing Power and Resource Utilization Efficiency

The creation of the virtual supercomputer networks discussed in this chapter foreshadows how big business will apply peer-to-peer processing to better utilize existing computer cycles and peripherals, especially storage devices.

Tools exist today that can enable businesses to build internal, peer-to-peer networked environments by balancing workload across multiple processors. Workload-balancing utilities can be found in UNIX and Windows operating systems. Database suppliers such as Oracle provide tools and products that allow for workload balancing and database synchronization. Napster, an infamous provider of access to MP3 audio on the Internet, has made use of open program-to-program standards to provide Napster users with access to music. What is often overlooked in the great Napster debate is that Napster does not itself host any of the audio files. They only provide a conduit between their customers for sharing these files, which is the definition of peer-to-peer computing. Other companies such as Gnutella and FreeNet also make use of the same fundamental peer-to-peer computing concept.

So if the technology is widely available, why haven't more businesses taken advantage of peer-to-peer computing as a means to better utilize computer power they already own and reduce investment in new computers? The answer is simple. Because the process of setting up a peer-to-peer network, securing that network, establishing permissions, and a host of other administrative obstacles get in the way. Using today's technologies, it is simply too time-consuming, too labor-intensive, and too expensive to build, manage, and secure large-scale peer-to-peer networks.

Intel's Evolving "InfiniBand" Standard

All of this is about to change, however. Over the next few years, as Intel rolls out its InfiniBand architecture, an architecture that allows superfast switching and workload-balancing between computers and peripherals. Although I would say that it is too early to call InfiniBand a standard, I believe it soon will be because

1. There is clearly demand for virtual supercomputer services. Giganet currently provides such services. Although the subject of a recent takeover, Giganet continues to have solid sales.
2. This demand for peer-to-peer computing is expected to increase as we enter the computationally intensive Sensory Virtual Internet age.
3. Intel is building a new architecture—NetBurst—into its Pentium 4 chips that will allow PCs to better handle the computationally intensive work that peer-to-peer computing demands—and NetBurst will help drive demand for back-end peer-to-peer processing.
4. Intel also has a huge vested interest in the success of peer-to-peer networking beyond the PC. It sees the future as network devices, networked servers, and shared storage. Intel is investing heavily in what it hopes to be the emerging, industry-standard fabric. It foresees this fabric simplifying communication between multiple, disparate systems, improving system interoperability between dissimilar system environments, increasing overall system performance and reliability, allowing for greater cohesion of networks, computers, and storage, and enabling greater scalabilty than ever before. That fabric is InfiniBand. Incidentally, this evolving standard has backing from IBM and other major computer makers.

What is "InfiniBand"?

InfiniBand may well become the architectural and product standard for building peer-to-peer—or an even newer term, "grid"—networks.

Allow me to explain. In 1998 and 1999, major system vendors set out to define a common standard for handling communications and networking I/O. They sought a more streamlined and efficient method than a bus architecture. One industry group, the Next Generation IO, was backed by Intel, Dell, and Sun; while another, the FutureIO group, was backed by IBM, Compaq, and Hewlett-Packard. In 1999 and 2000, these two groups resolved their differences, choosing to combine their efforts in the search for one new standard. This standard was initially called System I/O but is now named InfiniBand.

Intel, Hewlett-Packard, Compaq, IBM, Microsoft, Sun Microsystems, and Dell—have now chosen to focus on "developing a new common I/O specification to deliver a channel-based, switched fabric technology that the entire industry can adopt." The group of seven initial founding companies is know as the InfiniBand Trade Association. They have been joined by, at current count, 140 other companies that wish to help build a common, high-speed switch architecture.

Switch-Fabric Architecture

For computers to deliver increased performance, CPUs need to go faster and faster and data needs to be delivered rapidly to these increasingly more powerful central processing units. There are a number of methods for increasing data flow to a CPU while ensuring that the data kept in memory or on disk remains coherent and whole, but the bottom line idea is to get data to a processor for rapid processing.

Bearing this in mind, on low-end systems, data is delivered through what is called a "bus" architecture. Current PCs and servers have buses that run in the 100 to 133 MHz range. The new Pentium 4s from Intel will accept bus speeds around 400 MHz. But in the Sensory Virtual Internet future, back-end systems will need to be made capable of sending data back and forth to memory, to disk, and to communications subsystems in the gigahertz, not megahertz, range. Megahertz may be fine for receiving devices such as PCs and mobile computers. But to process huge volumes of computational data, much faster data delivery mechanisms will have to be created.

Today's PCs and most low-end and midrange servers use a shared bus configuration. A switch-fabric architecture decouples I/O operations from memory by using channel-based point-to-point connections. By streamlining the communication and data delivery between various system, memory, and I/O subsystems, InfiniBand promises to simplify computer-to-computer communications, computer-to-remote-storage, and computer-to-network-devices. By so doing, data flow within a computer and to other computers will improve and more processing will take place more quickly. The InfiniBand fabric will better balance workload by spreading processing across multiple computers transparently. It will also better utilize the network to share data access networked storage (volume management). In some respects, it is like a high-speed dedicated phone line that can be used by CPUs to call memory, by memory to call disk, or by I/O storage subsystems to call other I/O storage subsystems to deliver data and information rapidly rather than being choked by a systems bus. See Figure 12 for an illustration of this concept.

InfiniBand products have already hit the market. They include a high-speed Host Channel Adapter; an InfiniBand switch, which connects servers to remote storage and to network devices such as hubs, bridges, and routers; and an InfiniBand Target Channel Adapter, which provides attachment between storage and networked devices within an InfiniBand fabric.

Bus Architecture
All components try to share data across a common highway, a system bus

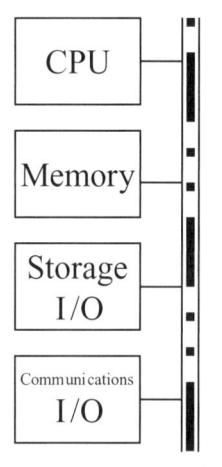

```
CPU
Memory
Storage I/O
Communications I/O
```

Data traffic-jams can take place as all resource share the same highway

Switched Architecture
All components can make phone calls at channel connected speeds to other system components, eliminating contention and roadblocks common on a system bus

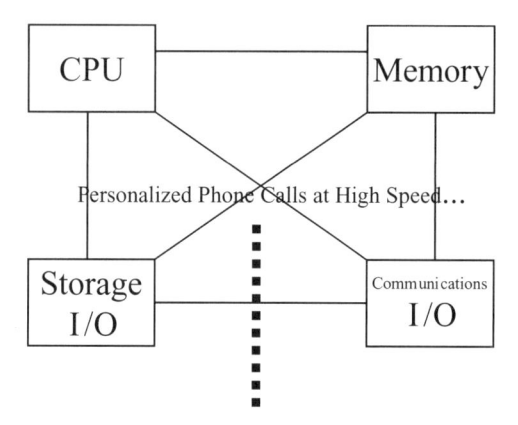

```
CPU — Memory
   \ /
Personalized Phone Calls at High Speed...
   / \
Storage I/O — Communications I/O
```

And data can be sent across the network fabric to be processed on or obtained from other systems

FIGURE 12
Bus versus Switched Data Handling

How powerful is InfiniBand? The InfiniBand switch architecture has been designed to accommodate more than 48,000 simultaneous connections. This means that 48,000 CPUs, memory, storage, and communications subsystems can link together for transaction processing, batch computing, or any other computing task. In a local InfiniBand environment, systems can be linked together if they are within 17 meters using copper connections. Devices up to 100 meters apart can be linked on fiber-optic cable. To move beyond these limits, switches and subnets can be interconnected via routers that can carry IP and InfiniBand data to and from other InfiniBand server environments.

InfiniBand uses up to 12 separate wires, each capable of transferring data at speeds up to 2.5 GBs per second. However, InfiniBand can be configured to use one, four, or 12 wires to reach transfer rates of up to 30 GBs per second.

When delivered en masse, InfiniBand servers will likely be multiple small "1u" servers linked together to form powerful, stacked computer complexes. 1u is a unit of measurement for the size of a rackable or rack-mounted CPU, memory, fan, and network connection put together in a configuration the size of a pizza box. These "stacked" server environments will allow systems designers to pack plenty of computers and related processing power into a small footprint, while also allowing for bandwidth to increase. This is because InfiniBand uses a switched architecture so interaction between the rack-mounted systems does not hit the performance constraints of a bus-based architecture.

Readers should expect InfiniBand-designed servers to impact the computer scene in 2002, delivering significantly increased bandwidth and increased scalability to corporate users of computer systems. Systems designed using the InfiniBand architecture have the potential to deliver from 30 percent to over a 100 percent increase in performance—without requiring major system upgrades or forcing existing systems to be discarded—a value proposition that enterprise computer buyers will find hard to resist!

As for how InfiniBand pertains to the Sensory Virtual Internet, it is important to know that InfiniBand is likely to become the standard that systems builders and network, system, and storage architects use to create highly scalable system architectures. It is reasonable to expect that businesses will use InfiniBand architecture to scale and grow back-end, behind-the-firewall systems that will support the computational and application needs of virtual yous in 3D community, retail, e-learning, and collaborative sites. The long and the short of it is that InfiniBand will likely become the architecture-of-choice that will enable IT managers and people who operate Internet server/storage/networked environments to easily scale their systems, storage, and communications on-the-fly to meet increasing computational and transaction processing needs of the future.

Other Power Computing Options

As mentioned previously, other architectures such as tightly coupled clusters or supercomputers may prove to be useful in helping IT managers muster enough computing power to support hundreds or thousands of avatars in the sensory-rich virtual worlds of the future.

Self-contained clusters, due to features such as workload balancing and security and systems management extensions, may do a better job than today's peer-to-peer-based approach in providing safe, commercially usable systems to IS buyers looking to scale overall computing performance.

> Office-supply retailer Staples, Inc., bought an IBM SP cluster-based supercomputer in order to build a company-wide data warehouse. This data warehouse will help integrate sales information from Web, catalog, and retail channels. This IBM SP is actually 512 separate computers coupled together as part of a scalable cluster configuration.

It is reasonable to expect that clustered systems will also play a role in providing the processing power needed to provide virtual reality scenarios on the Sensory Virtual Internet of the future.

Beware: There Are Some Hurdles with the Peer-to-Peer Approach

The concept of distributed computing has been with us for almost 30 years. IBM's MSNF program of the early 1970s, which allowed multiple mainframes to work cooperatively in a domain, represented potentially the first implementation of distributed and even peer-to-peer processing. Since then, proprietary implementations of peer-to-peer processing such as Digital Equiptment Corporation's (now part of Compaq) VAXcluster and various UNIX cluster architectures (most notably IBM's SP2 cluster) have made their way to market.

In a way, however, the current implementation of peer-to-peer processing is distinctly different from its predecessors. Companies such as Napster, Gnutella, and FreeNet have built their businesses on the concept of peer-to-peer computing, but these companies do not invest heavily in computer infrastructure. Instead, their versions of peer-to-peer processing work by helping users find files on a network (not hosted by each company) and facilitating the file transfer between the host computer and the user's computer. These applications tend to require less security and less systems management than commercial, run-the-business-type systems.

To share files in today's peer-to-peer systems environments implies that these Gnutella, FreeNet, et al., have to be able to steer their users toward files and computing resources. This implies that sophisticated directories must be in place to locate the data (most often music files—certainly a form of sensory communications) on the Internet. Napster, Gnutella, and FreeNet provide such access. Other companies, such as Groove Networks, Xdegrees and others, are also starting to maintain immense directories of where files can be found. Xdegrees is notable because the company also provides access to text and video, adding encryption and compression features in order to help users get the fastest, safest access to a file.

Aside from having to develop sophisticated directories, many companies will have to deal with systems administration issues, security issues, indexing, and a host of other infrastructure-related issues in order to build their own secure and manageable peer-to-peer networks.

Chapter Summary

This chapter was most concerned with discussing the forthcoming market shift toward a more powerful distributed computing networking model. This model will use a peer-to-peer processing and, in some cases, the new InfiniBand architecture to deliver very powerful computational capabilities to back-end servers. In turn, these back-end servers will use this computational processing power to perform the calculations needed to display 3D and logistical information, to process 3D audio, and to transmit and recreate other sensory experiences such as scent, touch, and taste.

The two most important technologies to be aware of when considering processing huge computationally oriented workloads are InfiniBand (a switched network/load balancing architecture) and peer-to-peer processing (a variant of the distributed computing model). Each approach has its positives and negatives—but it is highly likely that one or both of these approaches will be widely adopted in the future to allow for the processing of sensory and logistical data in Sensory Virtual Internet worlds.

CHAPTER 13

THE ROLE OF DATA COMPRESSION

In the previous two chapters we looked at:

1. How PCs, laptops, hand-helds, and such will be redesigned to provide more power for processing complex graphics and sensory data.
2. How back-end computers could be improved to process vast volumes of computationally complex sensory data.

In those chapters, we established that over time, current devices used for the capture, transmission, and playback of sensory data would more than likely have sufficient power to meet increasing demand. Hopefully, I also established how the architecture of back-end systems is going to change to better accommodate the processing of very large streams of complex, computationally heavy sensory data.

What we did not establish, however, is whether the network will be able to handle the millions of continuous, complex, large sensory data streams that will make up the Sensory Virtual Internet. We established that users with access to high-speed network connections will have significant advantages over slow-speed modem users as the new Sensory Virtual Internet age arrives, but what happens when millions of users in the same communities want access to virtual worlds? When asked to map the logistical movements of millions of avatars through virtual vistas, will networks again become the bottleneck? These same networks will be asked to provide users large files consisting of 3D graphics, stereophonic sound, and scent and touch data—and do so smoothly and efficiently.

More than likely the answer to this question is yes, networks will again become the bottleneck. We can expect millions of people to upgrade to high-speed Internet connections over the next few years. However, millions of other people who use standard modem connections won't have this luxury. In order to help people who don't have access to high-speed Internet services, some basic changes such as caching data closer to the user to reduce the number of "hops" the user makes over the Internet to retrieve data will have to be made. This approach would yield better performance for low-speed Internet users while lessening the overall communications load on the Internet.

Another approach is compressing and decompressing data, which will prove crucial in reducing the communications load of sending large sensory-rich files over the Internet. This chapter examines techniques for reducing the heavy data load that sending sensory files will create for Sensory Virtual Internet users. It examines caching and codecs, but focuses on compression and decompression techniques and the ramifications of these techniques on sending complex, large data streams over the Internet.

What Are Caching and Codecs and How Do They Enter the Picture?

Caching is a way of taking some of the processing load off back-end servers. Caching is a process whereby Web pages and search results on servers are stored in a temporary file. Rather than having to search for the most popular, highly used data that a particular site has to offer each time, it is served much more quickly from this temporary filesystem, called the cache. Rather than creating communications overhead and burning additional processing power to provide, for instance, a multimedia stream to a group of remote users, caching makes that data closer to the requestors. It is used to provide data efficiently to end users without burdening servers with heavy streaming media tasks. The data is duplicated and placed on front-end caching servers to streamline data delivery and to relieve performance and network bottlenecks, thus avoiding network slowdowns even if thousands, hundreds of thousand, or millions of people decided to hit the same servers all at the same time.

Caching is most relevant in cases where heavily used data can be offloaded to servers that are logistically closer to the users who need access to that data. Typically these are static Web pages that are heavily accessed or streaming media. When you are on the Sensory Virtual Internet, you will be making use of both static and streamed data but these files pale in comparison to the very large sensory data files that you will use when in virtual worlds. Hence, this chapter does not focus on the merits and benefits of caching technologies.

On the other hand, compression and decompression technologies are critical to our use of the Sensory Virtual Internet. These techniques deal with using mathematical algorithms to shrink down files before transmission and then reconstruct them at the user's end. Software engineers have developed a variety of these codecs (COmpression/DECompression), each of which can significantly decrease the size of files that are to be sent over the Internet. As a result, complex files can be sent in compressed form to sensory Internet users thereby significantly decreasing the network load and reducing potential network bottlenecks.

A Data Compression Discussion

The most important concept that you, the reader, should take from this discussion is that compression is used to shrink the size of files and decompression is used to recreate the original files. The reason that this technique is extremely important to our Sensory Virtual Internet future is because sensory files can be immense. Hundreds of thousands of packets of sensory information may be exchanged in a communications session between a user and back-end sensory servers when visiting virtual worlds. Hence any technology that can be found to reduce the size of these data files to avoid potential network bottlenecks is highly desirable.

How does this technique work? Compression programs are written to look for similarities in a data sequence. If similarities are found (for instance, a video data file may focus on the same object for several frames), these programs capture the first frame and make note of how many times to play that frame. In a short video, hundreds or even thousands of frames would not have to be replicated and stored. A video codec can also handle just the small differences between frames. For instance, if the image is of a person talking in front of a neutral background, the program only records the movements of the person's face and essentially uses a kind of ditto mark for the background. The result? This video data file would be significantly reduced in size, would be easier and quicker to transmit, and would use up less storage space on the sending and receiving computers.

On the receiving end, a PC or other receiving device accepts the compressed file and uses the same algorithms for reinserting the missing frames and background information, thus reconstructing the high-quality video, audio, or other sensory information. See Figure 13 for an illustration of the compression and decompression technique.

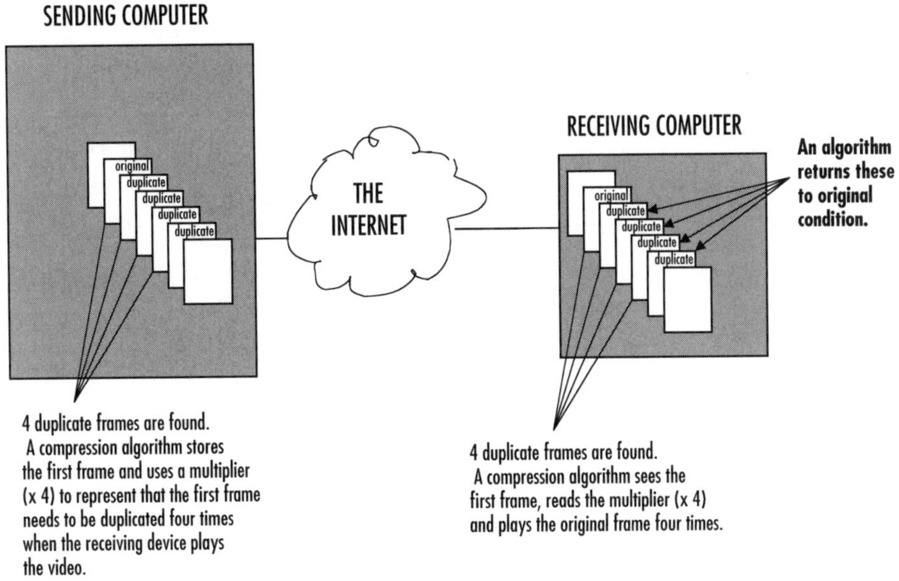
SENDING COMPUTER
original
duplicate
duplicate
duplicate
duplicate
THE INTERNET
RECEIVING COMPUTER
original
duplicate
duplicate
duplicate
duplicate
An algorithm returns these to original condition.
4 duplicate frames are found. A compression algorithm stores the first frame and uses a multiplier (x 4) to represent that the first frame needs to be duplicated four times when the receiving device plays the video.
4 duplicate frames are found. A compression algorithm sees the first frame, reads the multiplier (x 4) and plays the original frame four times.

FIGURE 13
Compression/Decompression

This example above describes a video codec, but this technique can also be applied to the compression of audio. This is actually how MP3 audio files work. Codecs can also be used for other sensory data such as touch or scent data. The basic technique used is the same—find redundant data, note it in algorithmic form, and have the decompression program recreate the original when the file is played. Ultimately, the benefit is the same. By using compression, you save network download time and storage space on your computer.

Lossless and Lossy Compression

The type of compression discussed above is called lossless compression. The object of lossless compression is to allow you to recreate the original file exactly. This type of compression is wholly shrinking file size by reducing files into smaller segments for transmission or storage, then putting those files back together on the other end in exactly its original form.

Another type of compression is called lossy compression. The primary goal of this type of compression is to eliminate unnecessary bits of information, thus making files even smaller. This type of compression is particularly useful when dealing with large graphics files, such as bitmapped images. This compression technique essentially reduces file size while helping to maintain the quality of the original by removing wasted space in the original.

Real-World Uses for Compression Technologies

There are dozens if not hundreds of compression algorithms in use today. Some of the most popular software compression formats include MPEG-1 through -4, motion JPEG, JPEG, BMP, and WBMP. One of the more popular hardware compression products is Intel's Indeo. It is not my intention to provide an exhaustive list of codecs nor spend a lot of time defining what these acronyms mean. Suffice it to say that there are many types of compression/decompression algorithms, all of which deliver different levels of quality and all of which save you storage space and download time.

Many of the most popular codecs are available for download as free or shareware utilities. One such compression algorithm is the zip file. You'll find zip files (which use the ".zip" file extension) all over the Internet. In particular, you'll find them on sites run by software companies as a means to deliver software and software updates to users. All that users need to do is download a file to a certain directory (and pay for that file if necessary). The server sends the zipped file. After that file has been received, the user needs to do is run an "unzip" utility, which will decompress the file. Compression works just as easily. All a user needs to do is compress a file using the zip utility and voilá—the compressed file is often substantially smaller than the original.

A search of my own personal computer (using the Windows search utility found on the Start menu) revealed that I had in excess of 200 zip files stored on my hard drive. And zip is only one of many compression algorithms.

I have over 50 Gb of audio-video presentations stored on my hard drive. One file is particularly interesting. It contains highlights of my son's year 2000 football season. In uncompressed form, it takes up over 23 Gb. However, when compressed using Microsoft's MovieMaker, this same file takes up less than 280 Mb. In other words, the compression algorithms used in MovieMaker reduced the size of one of my files by a factor of almost 10!

In the above example you will note that compression is not just used for transmitting files over a network. It is also important for local desktop use. I store all my video files in compressed form, even though I don't expect to send the files that I create over the Internet. If I need a file, I decompress it, returning it to an original, uncompressed form. Compression can be used to help save storage space on your computer.

Other real-world uses of compression and decompression technologies can be found in streaming media. Microsoft's Media Technologies, Apple's QuickTime, and Real Networks' Media Player are the most heavily used players for streaming audio and video on the Internet. At present, every time you view multimedia over the Net you are using encoding, compression, and decompression techniques.

Compression/Decompression in the Future

Codecs will have a major effect on how sensory systems perform in the future. Good compression/decompression schemes will enable us to send and receive data more rapidly. If the scheme is written well, we will see high-quality replications of the original file. In some codecs, quality is sacrificed in exchange for reducing overall filesize. The goal of compression/decompression algorithms is to maximize the performance of our computer systems and graphics cards while minimizing the amount of data that must be carried across a network. Any technology that helps improve performance while reducing network load will greatly benefit the users attempting to navigate through virtual worlds in the Sensory Virtual Internet. Web Driver from Wild Tangent is a perfect example of such a codec technology. It represents the path that compression/decompression will take in the future.

> Wild Tangent's Web Driver is based on something called virtual bandwidth, a term that the company uses to describe how a computer can use compression technology to create a highly optimized multimedia processing environment for Internet users who use standard modems for access (as opposed to high-speed broadband connections).
>
> The Web Driver product uses a dozen different compression techniques to create a "virtual bandwidth" effect. In other words, by cleverly compressing and optimizing networking, graphics acceleration, and CPU processing Wild Tangent is able to deliver high-quality media streams that rival media stream quality delivered over high-speed broadband connections. Web Driver compresses geometry, textures, bitmaps, audio, and text such that the greatly compressed files can be sent over narrow-bandwidth Internet connections. The product is also designed to adjust content on the fly and to adjust to the processing and network capabilities of the target system.
>
> Source: http://www.wildtangent.com

In addition to improving the delivery speed and quality, compression technologies can be useful in viewing and editing graphics and documents:

> WebGraphics' Optimizer enables users to compress pictures or GIF animations for Internet use, which makes graphics load faster while conserving space on the server. The product enables artists to control the ratio, color depth, dithering, color palette, and file format of their images. Up to five variations of an image can be compared simultaneously, each having different settings and file sizes. Additional information about the image is stored in the file, such as size, file format, bits per pixel, compression ratio, and the number of unique colors used. Zoom, automatic transparency features, 3D text, picture cropping, color manipulation, a multidocument interface for working with multiple images, and a host of other features are also included in the package.
>
> Source: www.plenio.com

As compression technologies improve and faster Internet connections become more widely available, computer makers and software engineers will need to find new ways to optimize their products for the reception and decompression of sensory-rich data files. Users are already demanding better graphical display capabilities, more three-dimensional application environments, and higher quality 3D world venues to visit. And business users already want to sensory-enable some business applications (such as collaborative product development and e-Learning). Home and mobile users already want more places to visit on the Internet. They want these places to accommodate 3D and sensory interfaces, while offering high-quality images that can be viewed in a high-quality mode on receiving devices connected to low-speed lines.

Chapter Summary

Previous chapters sought to establish the idea that computer systems are changing to support the type of computing done in 3D virtual worlds. Front-end PCs are being redesigned to allow for the processing of complex 3D graphics and other sensory data while back-end servers are being linked together in new ways to allow for the processing of vast amounts of computationally intensive data.

Although back-end systems may have the power to process computationally challenging graphics, logistics, and application information and front-end devices may have the ability to process and display complex graphical information, there will still be a network in between back-end servers and personal computing devices. That network may prove to be a performance choke point for large blocks of sensory and Sensory Virtual Internet data. You can rest assured that to reduce network congestion, application makers will have to compress and decompress graphical and sensory files transmitted over the Internet.

At a very basic level, two things have to happen to allow sensory-driven virtual 3D sessions to take place over the Internet. Software engineers will have to become more adept in how they *present* data over the Internet and the Internet pipes (the network itself) will need to be used more efficiently to route traffic to users. What this means is that software engineers will need to write better compression algorithms and that receiving systems will have to be optimized for decompressing the data back to its original state. Furthermore, providers of data files will need to make a concerted effort to locate data close to the user of that data.

The good news is that compression and decompression technologies already exist to allow for the delivery of high-quality sensory information over the Internet—even over relatively low-speed connections. In addition, there's even better news: the software development community has already gotten the message that they need to accommodate the delivery of complex sensory files in an efficient manner, as evidenced by Wild Tangent's Web Driver product.

In the future, expect to see better codec algorithms, improved system and software performance, and better sensory performance from our receiving devices through compression and decompression techniques.

Part V: Web Services

Now that you've spent hours of your valuable time reading well over 250 pages of human interface and computer infrastructure definitions and projections, what would you say if I told you that all of your effort might have gone for naught? It's true. You may now understand how various technologies will enable the formation of a new, sensory-rich Internet environment that I call the Sensory Virtual Internet. You may now have a solid grasp of the changes that need to take place in user interfaces, PC architecture, server design, and other technologies to enable this Internet to become real and viable. But *without useful applications, all of this effort will have gone for naught*!

Of all the observations I have made in this book so far, this one is probably the most important. Without finding some new way to rapidly develop and deploy sensory-based applications, *it may be five years or more until we are able to realize the full potential of the Sensory Virtual Internet.*

The observation that I make in this part is that something important has changed in application development. That something is the arrival of Web Services. I expect the use of standards to create Web Services to radically change the way that applications are built and deployed in the future. This change will make it possible for application developers to more quickly develop sensory-enabled applications than ever before, thus greatly decreasing the time needed to develop and deploy new sensory-enabled applications.

Web Services are new standards for creating and delivering cooperative applications over the Internet. They are crucial to the formation of the Sensory Virtual Internet because these standards will allow application developers to find and use sensory-enabling applications to make applications capable of understanding voice commands. Web Services will also allow common applications to use 3D audio and reproduce scent, touch, and taste sensations. Expect Web Services to create a renaissance in software development that will greatly hasten the arrival of the sensory-enabled virtual Internet.

What This Part Is About

What are Web Services, how do they work, and what will they enable you to do? Web Services are standards that enable applications to find other application, figure out how they work, and cooperate. As to how they work and what they enable you to do, that is the topic of the next chapter.

Chapter 14 describes how applications are developed and how Web Services will streamline the process. You'll learn about the object development model and about the approaches being taken by IBM, Microsoft, and Sun (and many others) to market applications as services. Further, I'll provide examples of how sensory modules will be mixed with core applications to create new sensory-enabled applications.

What I Hope You'll Learn

After reading this part, I hope that you'll understand how important Web Services are to the future development of the Sensory Virtual Internet. These services will have a profound effect on the computing industry as a whole, and on the rapid advance of the Sensory Virtual Internet in particular. It is very important that business executives understand the ramifications of the Web Services model to the strategic development of their companies. *It is also very important that software developers understand that this model will let them build sensory-rich applications far more easily than ever before.* Without sensory-rich applications, the Sensory Virtual Internet will be slow to develop and this whole book will have gone for naught. I sincerely hope that this section acts as a catalyst to get business executives and software developers thinking about ways to rapidly build the sensory-rich applications that will be needed to make the Sensory Virtual Internet a reality.

CHAPTER 14

WEB SERVICES

The world of application development environments can be deadly dull for nontechnical readers, so let me make this simple for you.

In the early days of computing, application code could start short and simple, but as an enterprise added new functions and features to its core applications, the code could become quite large and untenable. Small code changes to these ever-increasing-in-size large, unified applications had the potential to break the entire application. Imagine the effect that a small change could have if it broke a company's accounts receivable or accounts payable application—the company would not be able to send or pay bills.

In the late 1980s and throughout the 90s, application developers started to write modular applications that could be bolted onto (easily attached while leaving the core code intact) existing applications. This made it easier to build and test new applications. New applications modules became known as objects, and this approach to application development is known as object-oriented programming.

Using this modular approach, application developers have been able to write code as reusable objects. For instance, a developer could create a dictionary as an object module for a spell-checker in a word processing program. Because the application developer wrote the dictionary as a discrete object, that object could then also be used to provide the same dictionary function in a graphics, spreadsheet, presentation, or other application that needs to do dictionary look-ups.

But what good is it to have a large library of reusable objects if nobody can find out that they exist, where they are located, and how to link to and communicate with such programs? This is where the idea of Web Services comes in. Web Services are directory, application interface, and communications standards that enable developers to create applications that can find each other, establish ground rules for interfacing with each other, and communicate over the Internet. This new approach presents applications-as-services to each other and enables applications to be rapidly assembled by linking application objects together. Because standards have now evolved to help applications find each other, cooperate with each other, and communicate with each other, I now believe that new, sensory-enabled applications will be able to be brought to market a lot more quickly than most people think. As the Web Services approach becomes more widely adopted, application developers will be able to find the right sensory-enabling applications that they need to enrich current text-based applications. Depending on how the component object has been written, application developers may be able to quickly integrate sensory front-ends with existing core applications.

What Are Web Services?

Web Services are standards for finding and integrating object components over the Internet. What these services enable is a development environment where it is no longer necessary to build complete, monolithic applications for every project. Instead, core components can be written that can be assembled with components from other application sources on the Web to build a complete application portfolio. The important concept here is that under this model, Web-based applications would run as services to core applications.

The goals for Web Services are to provide a means for applications to work seamlessly and cooperatively with each other. To date, there have been several issues that have prevented this from happening:

- **The types of network protocols used**—In the past each computer vendor tended to favor a different network protocol, such as TCP/IP, OSI, SNA, or IPX/SPX. The Internet settled this divergence of protocols by standardizing on TCP/IP for communications and networking.
- **Program-to-program standards**—Applications use programmatic interfaces to communicate with each other. In the past, one vendor would use its preferred interface, while another vendor would use a different interface. The result: Programs were unable to communicate with each other. Web Services creates a common interface that Web-enabled applications can use to talk to each other.
- **Locating application components**—In the past there has been no common directory that enables application developers to find the application components they needed in order to build new applications. Because there has been no common directory, application developers often reinvented objects over and over again (even though a suitable object already existed somewhere—even, for

example, in the same company). Web Services corrects this situation by creating a directory standard that helps developers locate application objects and services on the Internet.

These new standards are UDDI, WSDL, and SOAP, and they will help application developers find needed application services, make it possible for applications to talk to each other, and provide for program-to-program communications over the Internet. Here's what they do.

Newly Evolved Web Services Standards

To find out where available applications services are located, a Web look-up standard has been developed known as the *Universal Description, Discovery, and Integration (*UDDI) standard. A service requestor (either an application developer or an intelligent application) would use UDDI to locate a particular object component or service that could be integrated with a core application.

Web Services Description Language (WSDL) enables applications to be published on the Web so that other applications can become aware of the services it could provide. WDSL is essentially a descriptor standard that provides information about how the listed application could communicate with another application.

SOAP (Simple Object Access Protocol) provides the basic program-to-program glue that enables applications to bind together and commence program-to-program communications.

The bottom technology line is that these Internet standards—UDDI, WSDL, and SOAP—have evolved that allow application components to be listed and located, and harnessed as services over the World Wide Web.

How Do Web Services Work?

Figure 14 illustrates how Web Services work.

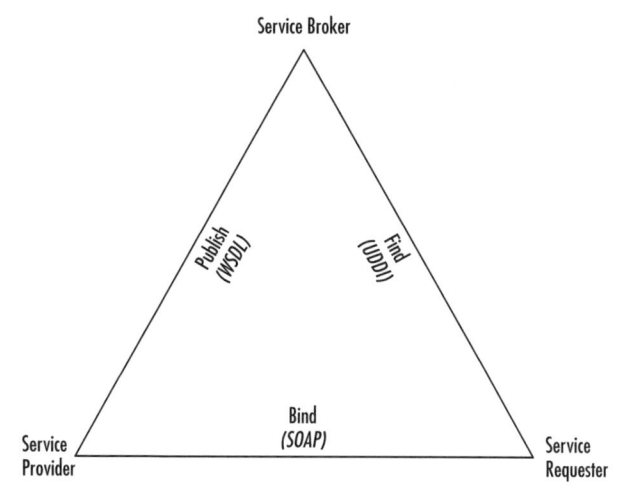

```
                    Service Broker
                        /\
                       /  \
                      /    \
                Publish    Find
                (WSDL)    (UDDI)
                    /        \
                   /          \
                  /_____\
         Service      Bind      Service
         Provider    (SOAP)     Requester
```

FIGURE 14
Activities and Program-to-Program Standards
Source: IBM Corporation. Reprinted by permission of IBM Corporation.

To enable applications to communicate with other applications over the Internet, the following activities need to take place:

1. A service provider (someone who has an application available as a Web Service) needs to publish information about his or her application. For this they need a standard way of describing their application's information (location, functions performed, etc.). This standard descriptor is known as a WSDL record.
2. Applications need to be able to find these services. Some form of directory service is needed that a service requester can use to find a particular application component. UDDI fulfills this need.
3. Once the application is found, the rules regarding how to communicate need to be established and observed. SOAP enables applications to bind together to work cooperatively.

Why Should You Care About Application Components and Web Services?

Why should you care? The answer to this question depends on what your role is and what type of organization you represent. If you are an enterprise business executive (CEO, CIO, IS executive, or line-of-business manager), you will find that Web Services will enable your organization to reduce development costs and expand your application portfolio at a fraction of current costs using traditional application development and deployment methods. You'll be able to bring products to market more quickly and respond to competitive threats with more flexibility. Your organization may also be able to remarket existing intellectual capital and thus generate a new source of revenue.

If you are involved in executive management, strategic planning, marketing, or development at an Independent Software Vendor (ISV), then you are aware that in the past, the traditional approach to application development involved creating large, monolithic applications that had to be ported to several operating systems. Porting to multiple platforms is expensive, as was the concomitant quality-assurance testing and ongoing technical support.

When using Web Services, the operating system and hardware platform no longer matter—they are incidental. What matters is how applications communicate and share information across the Internet. Web Services allow applications to communicate irrespective of platform or operating system. By using Web Services, developers can eliminate major porting and quality testing efforts, potentially saving millions of dollars in both the development process and quality control. *Web Services fundamentally change the way that software developers can and will build applications.*

In addition, using Web Services enables software vendors to deliver applications to market in a new way. Applications can be packaged as services in addition to being packaged for sale by license. This ability to repackage applications will enable software vendors to expand market share, and to find and service new customers using innovative packaging. It may even enable software vendors to grow revenues by hosting applications and providing them as services to existing customers and prospective buyers.

If you are in an executive management, strategic planning, or sales position at a value-added reseller (VAR), you will find that Web Services provide your organization numerous opportunities for expansion and customization of the systems that your company already sells. VARs sell systems with turnkey, optimized solutions. Web Services enable VARs to rapidly add new functionality to existing product offerings or to help customers customize existing applications. By adding new functionality, a VAR can make its products more competitive. By helping customers customize applications, a VAR can increase revenues from professional service consulting, design, and deployment.

If you are an executive manager or a strategic planner at an Original Equipment Manufacturer (OEM) (such as Compaq, IBM, Hewlett-Packard, or Sun Microsystems) or at a company that develops system software (such as Microsoft), Web Services will have the effect of leveling the playing field. In the OEM/systems software game, victory has traditionally gone to the companies that do the best job of capturing and integrating applications on their respective platforms. The more applications a vendor can offer on its platform and the better those applications are integrated, the higher the chances of making a hardware or software sale. Software developers have traditionally focused their efforts on only the industry's largest suppliers (Compaq, HP, IBM, Microsoft, and Sun) because they believe that by going with the big boys they can get the broadest distribution for their products. Now, Web Services make it possible for applications on one vendor's system to work cooperatively with applications on a completely different system from another vendor irrespective of system type or operating environment. This eliminates the need for software developers to specifically tune their applications for particular hardware platforms or operating environments.

As a result of the Web Services approach to application development and deployment, the name of the game for large OEMs and system software vendors will be focusing on building *the most integrated infrastructure environments* (hardware and software) and *the most solid implementation of Web Services—as opposed to focusing on ISV recruitment and integration efforts*. This represents a huge shift from most OEM strategies of the past. The emphasis is changing from the capture of packaged applications to the creation of strong infrastructure environments. Successful OEMs will be the ones that will enable their systems platforms to host Web Services applications most effortlessly.

If you are a portfolio investment manager, you will care because the evolution of Web Services will create a new business model. The metrics that you currently use to evaluate companies in your portfolio (such as Return on Invested Capital [ROIC]) need to change accordingly. The enterprises that exploit Web Services will be better able to adapt to changing market conditions or competitive threats. Software developers that figure out how to repackage their products using Web Services will be able to increase market share. VARs that embrace Web Services will find a new source for revenue growth by being able to both improve existing applications and provide their customers with application customization services. OEMs that focus their attention on building solid infrastructure servers as well as on providing solid Web Services implementations and strong application development environments will be the winners as the computing world adopts Web Services.

The bottom line is that you should care because Web Services will fundamentally change the way that applications are built and information systems are structured. The resulting new business model will fundamentally change the way that business will be conducted in various segments of the computer industry. Failure to understand these services and the resulting changes in the business model will likely result in lost revenue opportunities, vulnerability to competitors, and increased development costs.

Examples of Applications as Web Services

To illustrate how certain sensory applications can be presented as Web Service modules, I've chosen two examples.

Visualize, Inc., is a maker of data visualization software—the kind of software that enables users to view flat, 2D data in three dimensions. This company faces two issues as it seeks to grow its installed base: 1) the cost of hiring a direct sales force is prohibitive (hence the company relies on distributors who also carry other products); and 2) many potential customers and prospects do not want to take responsibility for installing and running data visualization code within their information system infrastructure. They would rather have the data visualization software hosted by someone else and provided to them as a service.

By making some of its data visualization software available as a Web Service, Visualize, Inc., is able to address both issues. Thus it can broaden its sales coverage. By listing its product in a UDDI directory (which they are planning to do) the company will be able to make these services known to other applications, thus increasing exposure while lowering the cost of sales. Because applications find each other in the Web Services model, no sales rep is needed. By using the WSDL and SOAP protocols, Visualize can offer its products to customers in a new way. They are offering their services as Application Service Providers using IBM WebSphere servers. This will increase the appeal of their products to customers.

By using Web Services, Visualize is now able to open new market opportunities while lowering its costs of sales. These are worthy results for any enterprise looking to build marketshare and increase market penetration.

This illustrates how an software vendor can use Web Services as a new way to purchase its product as an Internet-based service.

Visualize is making use of Web Services as a means to more effectively market its product to customers and prospects. Now take a look at this situation from the customer's point of view. Remember that Visualize is taking 2D data and enabling the customer to view that data in three dimensions. In other words, they are sensory-enabling an existing application. This is a perfect example of how additional sensory data can be made available as a service to Internet users. It is also an early manifestation of how sensory-enabled applications will be developed and used on the Sensory Virtual Internet.

Another such example of using modular code to provide a sensory interface to existing applications can be found in the Voice Search Engine offered by Phonetic Systems.

Phonetic Systems, Inc., builds a voice search engine that makes it possible for users to query databases by telephone using speech recognition technology. The beauty of this product is that it has been architected as a building block, which allows developers to integrate the voice search engine with other applications to create value-added services built around voice-access capabilities.

Just suppose that some day Phonetic Systems is able to package its voice search engine as a Web Service. Although this is not the case at the present time, nor is there any indication that the company intends to do so, let's just suppose anyway. If the company offered its product as a Web Service, it might be possible for a prospective customer to structure a business deal with Phonetic to use the company's voice search engine to front-end their data. This would make it possible for customers or authorized internal users to access such data without having to use a keyboard. Expect more and more companies that have such modules to become aware of the potential to grow marketshare using a Web Services approach in 2001. I also foresee that in 2002 and 2003, a landslide of component modules will be developed as makers become heavily involved in repackaging their products as application services. In this way they can market these services to customers whom they currently do not reach using traditional direct and indirect methods of selling.

Source: http://www.phoneticsystems.com

As you can see by these examples, *Web Services application code modules have the potential to be highly instrumental for bolting on sensory enablers* to new or existing application environments. Web Services hold the promise of being the delivery mechanism.

Competitive Positioning: Who's Building Web Services?

Previous attempts to set up standards for accomplishing these same goals have run into difficulties because they were not functionally rich enough, they were too complex to deploy, or they were vendor-specific (as opposed to using open and cross-vendor standards). The use of Web Service standards holds the promise of correcting each of these difficulties.

Some of the past approaches for enabling program-to-program communications included combinations of program-to-program protocols such as Remote Procedure Calls (RPCs) and Application Program Interfaces (APIs) along with architectures such as the Common Object Model (COM), the Distributed Common Object Model (DCOM), and the Common Object Request Broker Architecture (CORBA). Without a common underlying network, common protocols for program-to-program communications, and a common architecture to help applications become aware of each other and negotiate services, it has proven difficult to implement cross-platform program-to-program communications between application modules.

With the advent of the Internet and its protocols, most vendors and enterprises have graduated to a common communications and networking protocol—the Internet's TCP/IP protocol. And with the availability of Web standards such as SOAP, UDDI, and WSDL, most vendors will have a way to enable their customers to publish specifications about application modules, find those modules (either on an internal intranet or on the Internet), and bind applications together to work cooperatively.

The good news on the competitive front is that every major hardware vendor and certain key software vendors are backing the new Web standards for program-to-program communications. IBM, Microsoft, Oracle, Sun, and several other hardware and software companies offer or plan to offer product sets that provide integrated Web Services. IBM has already released a complete soup-to-nuts suite of highly integrated Web Services packaged as part of its WebSphere server. Sun's Open Network Environment (ONE) uses various Sun technologies and third-party products to achieve the same goals. Microsoft is betting heavily on Web Service standards with its .NET initiatives. Oracle has also signed up to deliver Web Services–based solutions.

Chapter Summary

The development of the Sensory Virtual Internet will require the construction of sensory-enabling software modules such as speech recognition software, 3D graphics-enabling software, or scent, touch, and (someday) taste modules. Web Services will allow vendors to package sensory modules for delivery and use as services.

The reason that Web Services are extremely important to the development of the Sensory Virtual Internet is that the *Web Services application development model can be expected to greatly reduce the time it takes to build sensory-rich applications*. In the old days (pre-2000) application designers used to have to build monolithic applications and bolt on sensory applications such as speech recognition. The time it would take to build a sensory application and the amount of work needed to integrate sensory-type modules with core applications frequently made sensory applications uneconomical and unfeasible.

Using a Web Services approach for application development helps condense the time it takes to build sensory applications. It also helps overcome two other obstacles that application developers have faced: 1) getting their products known (UDDI directories will help solve this problem); and 2) finding a low-pain way to integrate sensory-enabled applications with core applications (WSDL and SOAP will help work out application integration issues).

By making use of newly evolved Web Service standards, application builders will be able to easily acquire and integrate applications from other sources, thus reducing in-house development time and expenses. The sudden openness of applications to find each other and communicate will cut the time it takes to bring sensory-enriched applications to market from years to months, thus supporting my belief that we will see sensory-enabled applications come to market more quickly than complex applications from previous generations.

Part VI: Collaboration

When people work together, especially on intellectual endeavors, they are said to be collaborating. But in this Part I'd like the term "collaboration" to also include activities such as:

- Conducting business cooperatively (cross-organizational design, cooperation in modeling, business meetings in virtual space, etc.)
- Commerce (particularly retail shopping)
- Learning
- Consulting
- Various social activities such as building virtual communities together, communicating with each other over the Internet, and even getting married virtually

Basically, I'd like to consider any activity that involves the exchange of ideas with other people—whether those ideas are intellectual, political, religious, or commerce-related—as being collaborative.

If you can accept this definition, then collaborative applications are those applications that enable two people or groups of people to work together, to hold meetings, to share and modify engineering designs, to participate in educational activities, or to pursue other intellectual or commerce-related goals.

Now pause. Think about how you work collaboratively today in business situations. Perhaps you pick up the telephone and orchestrate a conference call (meaning that you can only work collaboratively in one dimension—sound). If you're very lucky, you may be able to arrange for that conference call to be conducted using videoconferencing software. If so, congratulations, you're now using two dimensions (your audio call has now been augmented with additional sensory data in the form of visual height and width views of your fellow collaborators). Notice that as you made the leap from a simple telephone call to videoconferencing technology you were suddenly able to read the expressions on the faces of your fellow collaborators. By adding additional sensory data, you are able to gather more information and work more effectively together—without having to be colocated!

Now take this image of working together and transpose it to a shopping situation. You are in a Middle Eastern bazaar preparing to haggle with a shopkeeper over the price of a jar of curry powder. You can hear the seller, you can read his face (just like in the business meeting example used above)—but you lack other data points that you need to make your decision on the value of that jar of powder. You probably want to smell that curry before you make your decision. You may even want to feel the coarseness or fineness of its texture—just as if you were there at that bazaar.

The problem with collaborative applications in the past has been that collaborative applications have been one or two-dimensional. Real collaborative exercises had to be conducted in person in order to get all the sensory information needed to make decisions. Indeed, telephones help us work collaboratively but using a telephone only enables us to share audio sensory information. We can't examine merchandise over a phone. And videoconferencing enables us to see the people with whom we are collaborating and perhaps share two-dimensional PowerPoint slide presentations. But again, we are denied the use of other important senses when we work in this manner. The new Sensory Virtual Internet is all about using additional technologies to provide collaborators with the ability to conduct joint intellectual and commercial engagements in a virtual reality mode with the added luxury of a full complement of sensory feedback.

By streamlining and automating collaborative processes that are both internal and external to the company, businesses have the potential to save billions of dollars annually. They can make these savings by streamlining interactions with their supply chain partners, by using collaborative software to develop new products and shorten product development cycles, and by reducing overall project costs. Only a few industries make heavy use of 3D modeling and design collaborative applications today—

most notably, aircraft manufacturers and automakers. The Sensory Virtual Internet will enable many more industries to make use of a full complement of sensory data. The hardware and software that will enable more businesses to work cooperatively will be available at affordable prices so that small businesses and even individuals will be able share multisense data and information.

As the use of sensory technologies becomes more pervasive, people will find ways to meet with each other virtually in social and consultative settings. For instance, going to the doctor (and waiting in line in his or her office) could be accomplished in virtual space. You would no longer have to travel to the doctor's office and spend hours in a waiting room. You could use a device in your home to take your temperature, measure your heartbeat, assess your glucose level, and so on—all without needing a nurse. When you meet with that doctor in her virtual office, she would have your latest information, would listen to your symptoms, and be able to recommend a course of treatment, prescribe needed medications, or refer you to a specialist.

The whole point of the Sensory Virtual Internet is to make it possible for us to use our computers to capture, relay, or present sensory data. We no longer have to be on site to gather this rich sensory information. The first generation of hardware and software that will enable business, learning, consulting, and social collaborative activities to take place in virtual space on the Sensory Virtual Internet is already upon us.

What This Part Is About

This section is about the next generation of collaborative applications that we will make heavy use of when using the Sensory Virtual Internet:

- **In business**—We are moving beyond videoconferencing to virtual meeting spaces, where we can actually visit a business partner online and participate in a meeting at that partner's site. The virtual you will be able to walk into reception and meet a virtual receptionist. The receptionist can gather the meeting participants together, find a free conference room, and otherwise facilitate your meeting. Imagine having your sales people conduct business this way. Companies that spend hundreds and thousands of dollars for traveling to and from and arranging meetings will suddenly see their cost of sales drop dramatically. Other examples of how virtual meeting room technology will save time, effort, and money abound.

- **In commercial settings**—The new Sensory Virtual Internet is becoming an ideal place to conduct commerce. Some of the most exciting work is taking place at the retail level, where customers can now examine objects in 3D space before purchase. How long will it be until consumers can touch a velvet blouse or smell a bouquet of flowers over the Sensory Virtual Internet? I would propose not long at all.
- **In consulting**—The same virtual meeting room concept applies for professionals as well. High-priced professionals, such as doctors, lawyers, sales representatives, or consultants, will no longer have to travel to meet with their clients nor ask their clients to travel to visit them. Again, millions of dollars will be saved as people use virtual conference room collaborative applications to meet on the Sensory Virtual Internet.
- **In learning**—Since the time of Socrates and Aristotle—and probably long before that—learning has been a collaborative activity. Over the past three years, a plethora of new e-learning software products have come to market. These products focus on pedagogy, testing-and-measurement, chat-enablement, and other elements that create a classroom setting in virtual space. Again, because students and teachers no longer need to travel to learn but can make use of virtual meeting spaces on the Internet, the costs of providing and obtaining education should drop significantly.

- **In socializing**—If you look at virtual worlds today, you'll find they are mostly occupied by teenagers who chat about virtually anything and nothing. They flirt. They hang. These same uses will soon be available to everyone who uses the Sensory Virtual Internet. Online social activities will soon include group meetings. For instance, parents could meet with teachers at a virtual Parent Teachers Association meeting or car hobbyists could meet with other enthusiasts and maybe even cocreate a virtual auto show.

This part discusses each of these activities in more detail. We will see how the next generation of collaborative applications is about to change the way we deal with geography and locality. Soon it will provide us with a form of electronic geographical and logistical independence.

Chapter 14 ties interfaces, technologies and applications all together. The improvements in interfaces to and from your computer and the enabling technologies such as high-speed networking and peer-to-peer computing are meaningless if there are no meaningful applications at the end of the rainbow. This chapter discusses those meaningful applications.

The Sensory Virtual Internet will come about because new and different virtual applications will attract us to it. Most of these applications will be created out of a need for more virtual collaboration. We are human. We have a built-in genetic need to communicate with our fellow humans. And next-generation collaborative applications will be the force that pulls us into virtual collaboration for business, commerce, learning, consulting, and socializing.

What I Hope You'll Learn in This Part

It is not readily obvious that many of today's collaboration software programs are moving toward virtualization. You would be astounded if you talked to some of the executive management of these software companies and discovered how little time and effort they have spent considering how their products need to go virtual in the future. Therefore, if you work for a software maker, I hope you will learn that sensory virtualization is in your future—a future that is very near. You had better be making strategic plans to allow for the virtualization of your software products.

If you are a professional, my hope is that you'll learn that your world is about to change and that the new geographical independence that the Sensory Virtual Internet is about to bring to you may represent a new (and potentially more profitable) way for you to deliver products and services to your customers. The bottom line is that I hope this chapter will give you cause to embrace Sensory Virtual Internet technologies.

I also hope that all of you will come to understand that the Sensory Virtual Internet will soon provide you with new ways to socialize with your friends, with people who have the same interests, and even with people that you have never met before who reside in far-off places.

Our world is about to go through a radical change. But at this point the clues that this change is coming are subtle and hard to discern. This chapter is meant to get you thinking about the next generation of collaborative software and to prepare you for that change.

CHAPTER 15

THE NEW AGE OF VIRTUAL APPLICATIONS

Imagine a computing environment that would allow visitors to enter virtual vistas that included shopping malls, movie theaters, parks, museums, stores or even virtual homes. Visitors would use these vistas to conduct commerce, be entertained, or to meet with friends, relatives, consultants, doctors, lawyers, or other advisors. These visitors would be able to use directional devices—such as a computer mouse, a game pad, a steering wheel, or other yet-to-be-invented devices—to walk, ride, or even skateboard through virtual stores, parks, or other venues. These visitors would be able to communicate with other avatars of people or avatars of programs designed to simulate sentient beings. Together with their human or programmatic companions, the visitors could embark on journeys to far-off places—

or, for that matter, to nearby places such as churches, stores, or the home next door.

Alone or with companions, visitors would be able to view and examine goods, electronically purchase those goods, and receive expedited delivery from geographically dispersed regional or local warehouses. Product deliveries would take from minutes to a few days, depending on the availability of the product and the shipping terms. Instead of going to the lawyer's office or paying for a consultant to come to visit you, these business functions could be conducted virtually, either face-to-face using streaming video or through the use of other 3D interfaces. The World Wide Web would transform from a being a static, cumbersome-to-navigate computing environment to a more intuitive computing environment that could be navigated using voice, visual affirmation, and the assistance of others (either people or programs)—this virtual Web would be an environment that is more natural to how humans navigate and communicate using visual and audio cues than today's character-driven Web. The new Sensory Virtual Internet age will have a profound effect on how we conduct business (internal to our own organizations as well as with business partners), engage in commercial activities (such as buying, selling, and shopping), learn (all the way from elementary school through our professional careers), are entertained (including increased team play), and how we conduct ourselves socially.

In the years to come, tens of thousands of applications will become sensory- and 3D-enabled. There will be Sensory Virtual Internet–enabled games, shopping, collaborative experiences, social/community experiences, and business applications. All of these will use 3D as a means to provide more sensory feedback to users as well as a way to entertain.

This chapter examines the progression and ramifications of the Sensory Virtual Internet on human collaborative activities. It pays particular attention to how new collaborative applications are being developed to streamline business and commercial activities and to improve education. It also shows how the new generation of collaborative applications will affect us socially and educationally.

Business: A Move Toward Greater Collaboration

In Chapter 8, we discussed the business uses of 3D graphics. It was shown that certain businesses—auto and airplane manufacturing in particular—have invested heavily in the use of 3D graphics technologies to help product designers and modelers ascertain how parts of a plane or auto could work in concert. We also saw how they these manufacturers use these products to look for any design flaws before a product went into a costly physical modeling stage. For example, using 3D modeling programs a designer can ascertain if all the doors in a new car design open and close properly or if they will be obstructed in any way. He can also determine if a driver's seat leaves enough foot and leg clearance room for a rear-seated passenger. As previously stated, using 3D graphics and computer modeling technologies enables companies to produce product designs that can be visualized and tested before entering a modeling/prototyping stage. Prototyping can cost hundreds of thousands or even millions of dollars. 3D modeling reduces this financial exposure while at the same time reducing development time and time to market.

A closer look at many of the programs used for modeling and design in these industries reveals that many visualization programs can be used in a *collaborative mode*. Teams of people can get together and contribute to a virtual 3D product design project. And working this way creates efficiencies in terms of time to bring a product to market as well as lowering the ultimate cost of a project.

> Ford Motor Company recently completed development of its first car to be 100% designed and developed over the Internet—the Ford Mondeo. Ordinarily it takes 40 to 48 months to bring a new car design through development

and into the marketplace. Using a proposed standard for Internet collaboration known as C3P, Ford was able to cut this time to only 16 months. The company saved millions of dollars in design and modeling costs, skipping most of the clay-and-steel mock-ups and prototypes. Because the car is now available years before it would have been, Ford will be able to capitalize on opportunities that may previously not have been open to the company without this specific car design.

What is exciting about Ford's use of the C3P initiative is the way that Ford used 3D modeling techniques in a collaborative fashion over the Internet. By making use of CAD/CAM and collaboration software, Ford was able to capture, store, and share information over the Internet. By so doing they cut down the amount of time wasted by large groups trying to communicate effectively. With its Mondeo effort, Ford has proved the point that visually based, sensory-driven computing combined with collaborative computing can and will play a huge role in the development of the Virtual Internet of the future.

Finally, in addition to acting as the poster-child for 3D/Internet/collaborative computing, Ford has found a new way to save its investors and its customers money. This will ultimately improve stockholder value while potentially reducing purchase and service costs for Ford buyers.

Source: http://library.northernlight.com/DL200100270500/0362.html?Cb=0&SC=0#doc

In short, Ford's CP3 initiative demonstrates that that economies in project cost and time to market can be realized through the clever use of collaboration technologies for collaborative product design and program management.

New Virtual Colocation Products

One of the things that many people like least about conducting business is the constant stream of meetings that need to take place. People show up late or can't be found. Some people step up on soapboxes and drone on about topics tangential to the main topic of the meeting. Sometimes the people or the background data needed to solve the problem are not in the room at all. Wouldn't it be nice if someone invented software that would enable us to virtually attend a meeting? This way we could shut off or leave if the meeting strays to topics that are not pertinent. Wouldn't it also be nice to have software that would help us page other people who weren't invited to our meeting who might have pertinent information that we need to conduct our meeting, whether those people are located in our facility or in some remote location halfway across the world?

To date, people have used videoconferencing software to help address a few of these problems, namely:

- Getting people together who are remotely located as if those people were in the same virtual conference room
- Sharing documents and other presentation materials or files

If you want to spontaneously connect attendees who are not in the videoconference room, many videoconferencing software products will leave you hanging. Some products are awkward to use when sharing data, whiteboarding, or viewing product or application demos, and some are just not well integrated, such as when voice and video are out of synch, which is distracting.

Data/videoconferencing products have generally fallen into two categories: products that are session-centric, such as PlaceWare and WebEx, and those that are document-centric, such as eRoom and Lotus Notes. Very recently a third category has emerged known as virtual space or colocation conferencing. This category integrates the best of both worlds by combining the abilities of the session-centric applications to manage sessions with the document-centric applications' abilities to share documents simultaneously in virtual meeting rooms (see Figure 15).

Four players that are architecting virtual meeting places are Groove Networks (founded by Ray Ozzie, one of the original

296 VISUALIZE THIS

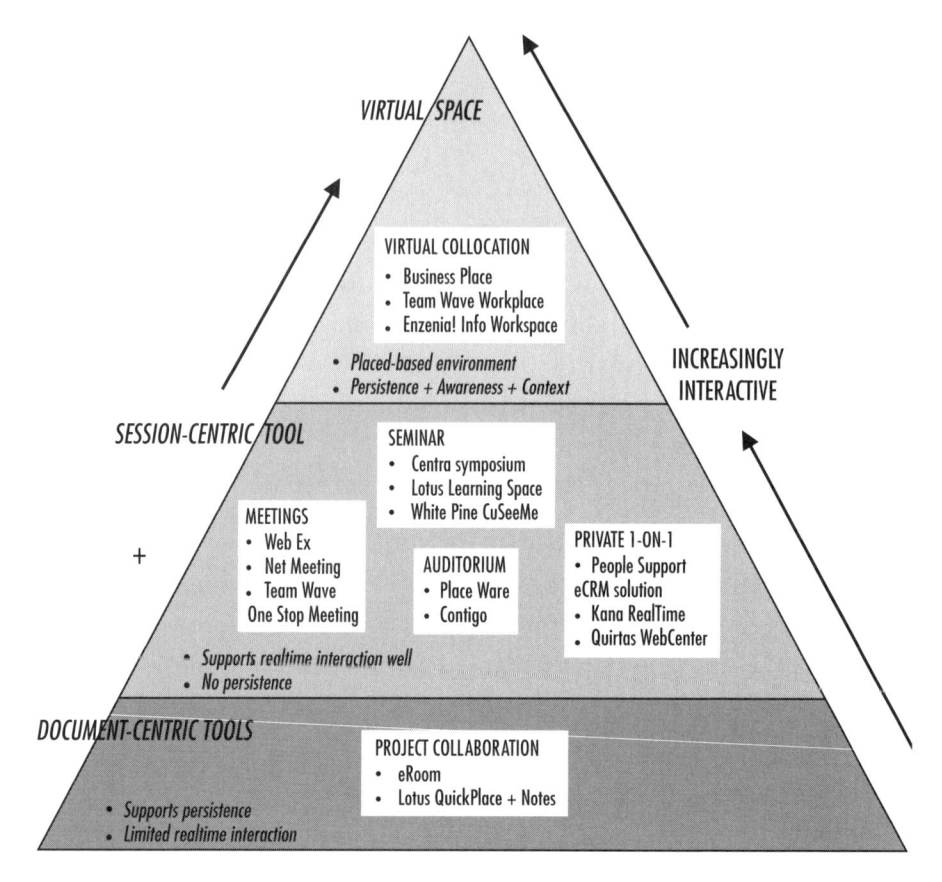

```
                    VIRTUAL SPACE

                 VIRTUAL COLLOCATION
                  • Business Place
                  • Team Wave Workplace
                  • Enzenia! Info Workspace
               • Placed-based environment            INCREASINGLY
               • Persistence + Awareness + Context   INTERACTIVE

  SESSION-CENTRIC TOOL      SEMINAR
                             • Centra symposium
                             • Lotus Learning Space
              MEETINGS       • White Pine CuSeeMe
               • Web Ex                           PRIVATE 1-ON-1
       +       • Net Meeting    AUDITORIUM         • People Support
               • Team Wave       • Place Ware        eCRM solution
               One Stop Meeting  • Contigo         • Kana RealTime
                                                   • Quirtas WebCenter
           • Supports realtime interaction well
           • No persistence

  DOCUMENT-CENTRIC TOOLS       PROJECT COLLABORATION
                                • eRoom
                                • Lotus QuickPlace + Notes
           • Supports persistence
           • Limited realtime interaction
```

FIGURE 15
Virtual Space/Colocation: The Basis for Next-Generation Collaborative Applications

Source: e-Global Reach. Reprinted by permission of eGlobal Reach.

founders of Lotus Development Corporation); IBM Corporation with its Sametime conferencing, messaging, and integration services; Microsoft with NetMeeting; and a small, evolving company by the name of eGlobalReach.

> eGlobalReach uses a place-based metaphor combined with key concepts of persistence, online awareness and context, eGlobalReach's BusinessPlace product set enables companies to set up mirror image virtual meeting places. Customers and business partners can visit these places in virtual space to meet with company officials,

customer service representatives, or any authorized individual from the company president to a janitor.

BusinessPlace uses a physical building metaphor that helps people feel their way around an organization. A prospective customer can go to a virtual company's "reception desk." There they would be guided to the right resource to help address their issue or request. Customers and company representative can go to virtual conference rooms to have a one-on-one chat. Audio and video streams allow the customer and the customer service representative to see each other. The customer service representative can call other members from within his/her company if additional assistance or information is needed to help the customer.

eGlobalReach has also taken into account human-interface elements in its product design. To quote: "BusinessPlace is very human-centric in its approach, recognizing the importance of the softer side of human-to-human interactions. We have modeled BusinessPlace after a building/room metaphor as a way to help users make a smoother transition from the physical to the virtual world. Over a familiar room background, the ability to see pictures of room participants and know who is the current speaker humanizes that virtual experience. This intuitive, secure, and easy-to-use environment reinforces natural social behavior, making users feel comfortable enough to engage in interactions and share information, ultimately building trust relationships, which is the key to successful widespread adoption."

Complex problems require more people and more interaction to resolve. This drives up the overhead costs dramatically. These resources must be fully utilized to compete effectively on a billable basis. Encounters are often very dynamic, requiring periods of intense, continuous interactions, quick ad hoc gatherings for resolving urgent problems, scheduled meetings to coordinate and resolve issues, as well as the ability to asynchronously access a myriad of shared documents to work individually. They involve a broad range of experts and cross-functional teams from different companies. These people are often dispersed geographically and when called upon to contribute, can participate almost instantly and from anywhere. BusinessPlace has positioned virtual meeting places for conducting business-to-business and business-to-consumer activities.

Source: http://www.eGlobalReach.com

The reason that products such as BusinessPlace are so exciting is because they go above and beyond the ability to hold scheduled on-line meetings, which is typically the focus of most of today's data conferencing products. The integration of session-centric and document-centric tools—built around the three key concepts of persistence, context, and awareness—distinguishes BusinessPlace from those products. Let's take a look more closely at these key concepts.

BusinessPlace facilitates the colocation of participants within the virtual environment and provides for:

- **Persistence**—By ensuring that the room contents are left intact. Documents and other materials can be stored in a room's virtual file cabinet for access at a later time. Participants can now reside in the virtual workplace throughout each workday from wherever they are physically, access shared information, interact continuously with team members, or be found by others almost instantly.
- **Context**—We all understand what a room is and we all know that there are many types of rooms that can be used for many different purposes. This room-based metaphor acts to frame the focus of interaction, allowing that focus to be changed as one navigates from one type of room to another. For instance, as you move from a conference room to an auditorium, you would expect a different type of audience and you would also change how you behave according to the new context.
- **Awareness**—Participants can find out who is available for interaction, whether in the same virtual facility or elsewhere. Dynamic and *ad hoc* interactions, previously not

possible in videoconferencing software environments, can now be supported. New meeting attendees can be easily paged or visited. This means that you can use this new virtual space software to conduct *ad hoc* meetings by first paging a person to see if he or she is available—and then (if permission is granted) dropping in. It doesn't matter if you are in the next office or halfway across the world. The room you'll be sitting in is only a virtual representation of someone's office.

This combination of context, persistency, awareness, and flexibility will provide a powerful new way for people to collaborate. Metaphors for project team rooms, conference rooms, personal offices (for private chats), training facilities, auditoriums, and other rooms common to real-world organizations can be built. However, ultimately the bottom-line result of this type of collaborative software is that it enables internal groups, customers, and business partners to conduct meetings using audio and visual cueing without having to be physically present!

Groove Networks is another example of this new category of software creating virtual space meeting places.

> Groove allows workgroups of people to share information, such as documents and calendars, as well as to interact in a shared space. Groove replicates information in shared space and makes that information available to all participating clients. When changes are made to one document, the changes are synchronized with all clients in the shared space. The architecture of Groove is peer-to-peer, which is radically different from the client-server architecture employed by many existing videoconferencing product providers. Groove's marketing target appears to be personal workgroups as well as businesses. The appeal of the peer-to-peer concept is that it does not require a server. This means that many business functions can be performed without further burdening the IT department and their servers.
> Source: http://www.eGlobalReach.com

Another company worth observing is IBM. IBM has made huge investments in building peer-to-peer products—in voice technology, collaborative computing, and mobile computing—and many of these investments manifest themselves in IBM's Lotus Sametime collaborative environment.

> IBM classifies Sametime as a real-time collaborative environment that enables instantaneous, live electronic communication between two or more people. Sametime services fit into three categories: 1) Conferencing services; 2) Secure Instant Messaging; and 3) Integration services.
> - Conferencing services consist of a server-based meeting center where users can schedule online meetings and store meeting materials. Users can whiteboard (draw upon shared electronic objects) and share documents and meeting materials online.
> - Secure Instant Messaging services include awareness of individual attending the meeting, instant messaging, and chat capabilities.
> - Integration Services enable Sametime to be integrated with other applications such as help desks, training/information delivery and e-commerce type applications.
>
> Sametime is also compatible with Microsoft's NetMeeting software, which allows individuals to send video and audio interactively over the Internet.
>
> As this type of software matures and becomes even further integrated, expenses related to travel for communication between distributed teams will be reduced; distributed teams will be able to work more effectively; and most importantly, the sharing of knowledge that can improve an enterprise's responsiveness, innovation, compentency, and efficiency across departments and between business partners will be improved.
>
> Source: Lotus Software, IBM Software Group. Reprinted by permission of IBM Corporation.

Microsoft's free NetMeeting client has been distributed with Windows and via Microsoft's Web site. NetMeeting capabilities have recently been redesigned and released as Microsoft Conferencing Server, a component of Microsoft Exchange 2000.

This product is a highly structured meeting scheduler integrated with Exchange calendaring and e-mail.

In addition to the installation of Exchange 2000, Microsoft Conferencing Server requires the installation of several other Microsoft products: a Windows operating system, Outlook 2000, and MSN Instant Messenger services. To perform multiparty audio and videoconferencing, NetMeeting uses IP multicast, a technology not readily available on the public Internet. Although the Conferencing Server is accessible on the Internet, the target of the server is corporate intranets. Microsoft Conferencing Server appears to be positioned as value-added capability aimed at encouraging corporations to adopt more Microsoft software. These software prerequisites together with the dependency on IP multicast make Conferencing Server a much more suitable product for internal corporate communications rather than intercompany communications on the Internet.

Other evolving products in the new virtual space category include TeamWave's WorkPlace and General Dynamics' Info-Workspace, which is modeled, like e-GlobalReach's Business Place, after MITRE's CVW virtual workspace program.

Commerce (e-Tailing) and the Sensory Virtual Internet

If the business of business is to make money, then commerce is at the very heart of conducting business. However, not every business is commerce-based. For instance, many nonprofit organizations rely heavily on volunteers to provide services. No buying or selling transactions take place.

Most businesses are commerce-based, which means that these businesses need to have plans in place to attract customers and provide merchandise or services for sale to their customers.

We are all familiar with how businesses—particularly retail businesses—attract customers today in the real world. Advertisements in newspapers, on television, through the mail, and over the telephone are designed to lure new customers and inform existing customers of clearance sales or discounts. More recently, more and more organizations have been making use of electronic mail to send advertisements and information to their existing customers and to new prospects.

As we move toward an Internet that is capable of providing increased sensory data, it is reasonable to expect that businesses—especially retail businesses—will be the first to use the unique sensory potential of the virtual Internet to find and attract new customers as well as to entice existing customers. To this end, I expect retail businesses to use the Sensory Virtual Internet in several ways.

Shopping malls will be established in virtual space. Clever application service providers (ASPs) with Internet experience and virtual site-building expertise will soon proliferate. These virtual mall ASPs will be leaders in sensory experimentation. It is at these sites that you'll find leading-edge virtual technologies such as scent, touch, and perhaps taste being demonstrated. These ASPs will provide virtual malls where smaller businesses can gather to present their wares to passing visitors as well as community members who may have a fondness for a particular mall. Large retail businesses may participate and buy virtual space in these electronic malls. However, it is more likely that large businesses will concentrate their efforts on improving their own direct retail Web sites before focusing on virtual mall sales.

Eventually these malls will get aggressive and begin building "customer service avatars." These are virtual sales clerks that may be actual people using a 3D façade or may be computer programs designed to provide customer assistance. Large business will also jump on this trend. At first, these avatars will seem gimmicky but over time we will all come to accept and even rely on these avatars to assist us in our shopping endeavors. In effect, many of us currently use text versions of these customer service avatars today when we use shopping bots such as Ask Simon to find the best prices on merchandise.

An example of one such avatar can be found at Hugo Boss in New York City:

> In 2001, Hugo Boss, a clothing retailer, introduced "Cameron"—a virtual sales assistant. Cameron, made by Virtual Characters, Inc., is a hologram—a 3D projection. Customers who trip a motion sensor launch Cameron into action. Right now Cameron can only inform shoppers of new products or sales, but Cameron will eventually be able to interact with and serve customers who visit Hugo Boss stores.
> Imagine a worker who will not require a raise, does not need a fancy car, and who does not need medical benefits, sickness time, or maternity leave.
> Source: http://www.virtualcharacters.com

From a buying and selling perspective, shopping can easily be viewed as a collaborative activity. A buyer is looking to obtain an object or service; the seller is looking for a particular price for that product or service. Some form of give-and-take takes place to arrive at a purchase price. In other words, a form of collaborative activity takes place as two parties work collaboratively toward a common goal. Even if you choose not to haggle for a particular price, your assent to buy a product is a form of passive collaboration. You went to a market and chose a product, a seller informed you of the price, and you tacitly agreed to pay that price.

Expect retailing, or e-tailing as the Internet version of e-commerce is often called, to undergo aggressive change as sensory technologies converge with collaboration software to create electronic 3D virtual malls complete with sight, sound, scent, and tactile attractions.

E-learning and the Sensory Virtual Internet

E-learning involves taking traditional methods of teaching and training, such as classroom teaching and seminars, and virtualizing them. As such, e-learning plays on two themes that I have been focusing on in this book.

- The Sensory Virtual Internet will eliminate our need to physically travel to settings (such as classrooms and offices) to obtain services (such as instruction).
- The applications that run on the next-generation Sensory Virtual Internet will be collaborative in nature.

E-learning is a form of collaboration. It represents a way in which the Internet will enable teaching institutions to run more efficiently while reducing course delivery costs. E-learning reduces travel time and expense and enables organizations to deliver knowledge to the point where it is needed most in a timely and expeditious fashion.

The e-learning market is expected to grow from a $3 billion market today to over $11 billion in three years. Part of this growth will be businesses looking to find alternative ways to cut education costs and universities seeking to find new ways to deliver existing and chargeable educational content to more paying customers (students).

One could argue that the explosive growth in e-learning is occurring because educational e-learning software has finally matured, high-speed Internet connections are finally more available to a broader segment of the population, and virtual technologies are finally in place that can deliver rich and interesting sensory data that can retain student interest. Until recently, the e-learning involved posting HTML pages with words and graphics on Web sites and then streaming in live audio. At one point, the industry also tried including a streaming video of the instructor teaching the course, but most students found this approach to be superfluous. Looking at a talking head for hours on end can be rather boring. As technology has progressed and more bandwidth has become available, e-learning has become more dynamic and more sensory-oriented, with features such as 3D modeling and simulations, full-motion video, live testing, raise-your-hand Q&A, and other features that mimic a live classroom—only in virtual space.

Today, e-learning software suppliers have focused on creating courseware that better supports animation, interactions, chat, conferencing, and real-time audio and video. In the future it is reasonable to expect that e-learning software suppliers will also focus on adding sensory experiences to their virtual classroom environments.

Learning can be conducted as a collaborative activity or as an individual exercise. Regardless of which type of learning you choose to engage in, the Sensory Virtual Internet will service your needs. Should you choose to embark on a self-learning program, the Internet will eventually be chock full of virtual worlds to explore—worlds designed to mimic real-world environments that will be sensory-rich with tactile, audio, visual, and olfactory sensations. Today's computer-based training courses generally provide guided learning activities using text and 2D graphics. However, you will learn better using the Sensory Virtual Internet because it will provide you rich 3D graphics and touch and scent experiences. The more sensory data you can gather, the richer your educational experience is likely to be.

Businesses and universities are treating e-learning as a collaborative activity. Access to expert teachers is core to many courses taught in business and at the university level. Both types of organizations are now actively and aggressively seeking alternatives to traditional classroom training. They are starting to focus on alternative, technology-based training (TBT). These are approaches other than classroom-based training that use computers, the Internet, television broadcasts, audio tapes and videotapes to deliver classes, seminars, and the like. The Sensory Virtual Internet will provide the ideal environment for the delivery of TBT services.

Reducing Costs Related to Employee Training: A Major Driving Force

The training of employees represents a huge expense for businesses today. Travel and living expenses while attending physical classrooms can be exorbitantly expensive, consuming up to 40 percent of the average corporate training budget. The total cost of training can include up-front costs for developing training courses and materials as well as the ongoing costs of delivering the training, setup costs, and classroom lecture fees.

Other factors also influence the cost of delivering traditional classroom training. Businesses experience nonbillable time and lost opportunity costs, which happen when employees cannot work because they are on the road or in a classroom.

There are strongly compelling economic reasons to find alternate means to educate. Virtual training can greatly reduce the cost of training.

> In November, 2000 at the Orlando, Florida, TechLearn conference, more than 3,000 attendees heard Deloitte & Touche LLP describe how the company used online curricula to reduce executive training costs from almost $1,000,000 to about $30,000. Deloitte & Touche developed an online curriculum to provide a company orientation course for new partners, eliminating the need for 200 newly appointed partners to travel to New York City. This saved hotel and other travel expenses, thereby significantly reducing this annual and recurring expense item.
> Source: http://www.techlearn.net

There are clear benefits to physical classroom settings such as developing camaraderie and a sense of team play and team spirit—but many companies are closely examining the costs of such intangible benefits, weighing the social benefits of physical classroom attendance against bottom line course logistics and delivery costs. Many are deciding in favor of distance learning or e-learning.

Speed of Delivery

Another factor that works against the traditional classroom method of training is the speed of delivery of course material. Bringing hundreds of people to headquarters over several months may not only be costly, the course material for those who attend at the end of the training cycle may have become stale, invalid, or competitively inaccurate. Most trainers would agree that traditional classroom training methods have difficulty keeping up with the speed of delivery that well-architected Internet e-learning courses can deliver.

As an example of how important timely delivery of course material is, consider the following scenario. Imagine that a software company releases a new, vastly changed, and highly innovative software module to the marketplace. Wouldn't it be wise to ensure that the company's sales and support staff is fully trained on the day a new software application hits the market—not weeks or months after the release? Failure to deliver training in a timely fashion can most definitely result in lost market opportunity as well as failures in customer service. Deploying classroom training in geographically dispersed locations can be ineffective and time-consuming, ultimately not achieving the result that a business is looking to achieve.

Schools and Universities: New Ways to Deliver Existing Content

Informational content is a very valuable commodity. Content has the remarkable characteristic of being able to be repackaged in a number of consumable forms. People seem to be willing to pay good money for good content. For instance, this book could be packaged into smaller, chargeable pieces or even repackaged as Web site material that could draw advertising money. Funny thing about content—once you have it there are a lot of ways to resell it.

This example holds true for colleges, universities, and other educational institutions. Once you've created a course, you can deliver it at your educational facility and capture revenue from as many students as you can jam into a particular physical classroom. But how much more effort is actually required to move that content beyond the classroom walls to paying external electronic customers (or even nonpaying customers receiving public education) who can access this same material over the Internet? As it turns out, very little extra effort is required. And the rewards can be great. With very little extra effort, the educational institution could "Internet-ize" its content, and then could provide education to a wider group of people who may otherwise not have access to your course material. Voilá—a new source of revenue from existing content!

Courses can be expanded beyond geographical boundaries to serve the needs of students who cannot physically attend the school where a course is being taught.

> On January 8, 2001, in a pilot educational project, the State of Illinois launched its Illinois Virtual High School (IVHS), a virtual school created with the goal of giving students a chance to take courses they could not get in their own school districts. "This will afford schools who have been unable to offer a wide array of courses such as foreign languages or advanced courses outside the main curriculum that opportunity," Illinois Governor George Ryan (R) said.
>
> Initially, this pilot project was been designed to handle a maximum of about 1,700 students, but over time Illinois hopes to build a system that can handle as many as 600,000 students. Those students who attend each semester-long course pay $300 for the privilege. Each advanced placement review course costs $49.
>
> This project demonstrates two things: 1) how content can be scaled to serve thousands of people who otherwise would not have access to the virtual high school courses because of logistical difficulties; and 2) how new revenue opportunities can be created for existing content. Inci-

dentally, the content for the courses was purchased from other suppliers but is taught by Illinois teachers.

Source: http://www.State.il.us

In addition to remarketing courses, education can be used as a way to retain existing employees, or to obtain and retain recruits.

> The U.S. Army is now using e-learning to recruit and retain soldiers. With partner PricewaterhouseCoopers, the army has set up Army University Access Online, an e-learning service that lets soldiers earn college degrees and technical certifications while serving in the military. This builds on the army's previous approach of offering recruits funds for college after those recruits served their tour of duty.
>
> Why is the army doing this? According to military personnel, a record numbers of prospective soldiers are opting for college instead of the army, making army recruiting a tough assignment. The army identified that classroom-based training interferes with most soldiers' schedules and by setting up an electronic means to earn a degree, a recruit can be all he can be, both a soldier and a student.
>
> PricewaterhouseCoopers is the prime contractor on this $453 million electronic university contract. The company is working with 29 accredited higher education institutions as well as other software and service providers such as Saba Software, PeopleSoft, and Blackboard to deliver its electronic university. During the next five years, the army expects up to 80,000 soldiers to take advantage of its new e-learning university offer.
>
> Source: http://www.dtic.mil/armylink/news/Dec2000/a2001214earmyu/200.html

ISSUES SURROUNDING THE E-LEARNING CONCEPT

Although e-learning lends itself nicely to delivery on the Sensory Virtual Internet, a number of critics have raised some valid concerns about virtual learning. Some of the issues to be considered include:

- E-learning isolates students.
- E-learning is too passive and does not motivate students.
- It's hard to keep students involved and online for the extended periods of time needed to deliver the course content.

However, each of these issues is easily corrected with the proper course structure and level of teacher involvement. The colocation technology described earlier in this chapter enables students to sit in a virtual classroom where they can see and interact with each other, thereby reducing the isolated feeling they might get when researching or engaging in a self-learning exercise. The remedy for the first problem is creating a virtual classroom environment, where students can meet and engage each other.

The colocation software described earlier in this chapter also helps overcome the passive-learning issue by allowing students to share their work in a virtual forum. They can use audio, graphics, and someday touch and scent technologies. In addition, many new e-learning software packages actually create a virtual classroom environment where students can raise hands to ask questions, see each other, view course material, and otherwise be fully engaged.

Finally, the issue of keeping students online and focused—and monitoring their progress—can also be dealt with using colocation software as well as some of the new e-learning pedagogical software now available. Many new e-learning packages can provide instantaneous details about whether the class is following the topics being presented and measure in real time the class's understanding of those topics. This is done through quick, online tests and quizzes. The software automatically calculates the class grade, which helps teachers ascertain whether they are being effective. If they're not, then it enables them to take corrective action while the audience is still present.

Perhaps all of these issues will fade when the Sensory Virtual Internet makes "v-learning" a reality.

New Consulting Approaches and the Sensory Virtual Internet

Today, professionals frequently set up their own Web sites for the purpose of providing information about the service that they provide. Some professionals occasionally offer chat sessions. Most answer e-mail sent to their sites by interested customers. These sites are static but informational: More often than not they are also boring.

Colocation software will move today's static sites into the world of virtual interactivity by allowing professionals to deliver real-time, in-person, virtually face-to-face services to clients. This is a radical departure from the formal and staid professional sites of today. It represents a chance for professionals to see more clients, thus increasing revenue streams by serving more people. In addition, it allows customers a way to avoid having to travel to see a professional in order to receive a service.

Intel Corporation has set up a concept demonstration to illustrate how doctors can make use of Pentium processors, speech recognition technology, authentication technology, diagnostic tools, and high-speed networking to share medical content, communicate privately with patients and other doctors. Doctors in this demo can get online access to comprehensive medical resources, including access to medical training, private (physician-only) clinical and general discussions, secure e-mail, and online access to lab results. 3D visualization and animation technologies are used for teaching as well as diagnostic purposes. Intel claims, as I do, that the combination of these technologies will greatly increase doctors' efficiency while enabling them to share diagnostic results with patients and colleagues.

Club Medical Expand—A Concept Demo

Consider visiting Intel's "concept demo" at their http site, *developer.intel.com/software/idap/media/doc/clubmedical/doc/clubmedical.doc*. At this site, you will find an aging document about one of the first online medical communities developed in France (launched in October, 1998). What is salient about this online community is that Club Medical Expand (CME)—the community—made early use of many of the sensory technologies described in this book to build a private communications environment for doctors and health practitioners.

Note that CME made early use of:
- 3D technology (using a programming language called VRML that is extremely useful in developing 3D animation) to facilitate online collaboration and training. The example cited for the use of this 3D technology refers to complex medical subjects like "mitral valve surgery."
- 3D technology was also used to help render data into graphics form—such that data could be more easily interpreted by physicians—this data visualization is similar to the Visualize, Inc., example from the Web Services chapter of this book.
- Speech recognition—such that doctors/physicians could dictate to a machine rather than having to use a human to transcribe thoughts.

This site was also meant to showcase the power of Intel's Pentium III processor as well as advances in multimedia processing. It is my guess that if we were to rebuild this site today, we'd see even more powerful speech- and data-processing capabilities, more advanced multimedia presentations, and richer 3D animation. These advances would be largely attributed to faster processors (now Intel's Pentium IV generation that includes a sophisticated multimedia instruction set), better speech technology, better compression/decompression algorithms, more sophisticated visualization software, and more sophisticated collaboration software—the infrastructure and programmatic improvements that we've spent most of this book exploring. This site was a harbinger of things to come and represents a way to track how the Sensory Virtual Internet is progressing.

Source: http://developer.intel.com/software/idap/media/doc/clubmedical_background.doc

This is the Sensory Virtual Internet in action!

Colocation software allows us to create virtual malls, schools, churches, or virtually any building that you can think of. The Sensory Virtual Internet will, over time, enable you to visit these virtual sites, to swap full-sensory information with your service provider of choice (a doctor, lawyer, consultant, etc.). Millions of hours of travel and waiting time will be saved yearly throughout the world, as people no longer have to travel to receive or provide services. This will provide all of us with more time to spend doing other, more productive activities.

The Sensory Virtual Internet and Socializing

There are many virtual worlds ready for you to explore: Virtual Prague, Amsterdam, Paris, Berlin, and other cities; Virtual Raleigh Durham IBM's RTP development site; and historical re-enactments of Gettysburg and Apollo IX on the moon. What is most interesting about the existing 3D virtual worlds on the Internet is how these worlds are being used—and by whom. As the virtual you visits these sites, you will observe that people are using these sites to chat and to share ideas. Many sites offer visitors the opportunity to join and become members of a community. Within this community, members can acquire real estate (virtual space that is, in reality, disk space) upon which they can build their own 3D world, vista, home, shop, or other environment.

Once meeting places have been architected, community members tend to congregate in their favorite venues, meeting friends or striking up conversations with complete strangers. And one of the nicer qualities of these 3D worlds is that many of these conversations take place between avatars, giving the visitor a certain degree of anonymity. Conversely, bad people could also be hiding behind avatars—so, just like in the real world you'll need to be careful about the kind of personal information you give out.

The key point about these virtual worlds is that these worlds are being used for social and collaborative purposes, primarily by adolescents and adults looking to hang with friends in non-2D, nontraditional, nonstatic, 3D computing environments. It does not take a lot of imagination to visualize adults coming to these sites to use them for more pragmatic purposes.

The Sensory Virtual Internet and Entertainment

As the Sensory Virtual Internet evolves, it will offer us a new way to interact because we will be able to use a full complement of senses to speak with each other. We will be able to see each other, to touch each other (yes, I do know what you're thinking and we are not going to go there), and even to smell someone's perfume.

In the entertainment world, there will be two driving forces that will require the use of technologies that form the Sensory Virtual Internet: community game playing and pornography.

As distasteful as pornography is to some people, it would be hard to deny that pornography has played an important role in pushing various technologies that we now use every day on the Internet. Pornography has served to influence downloading, compression, storage, network design (to accommodate large numbers of hits on the same files), caching, and more. The moral issues aside, it is reasonable to expect the pornography industry to be particularly aggressive in pushing the envelope for increased (and chargeable) sensory experiences on the Sensory

Virtual Internet. It is also reasonable to expect the pornography market to find a way to use newly available collaborative applications for various purposes.

The New Game-Socialization Trend

From a game-playing entertainment perspective, we will be using the Sensory Virtual Internet to play virtual collaborative games with each other. This trend has already started as players go to Sony, Microsoft, and a dozen other sites to participate in adventure games, strategy games, card games, and more. But some interesting changes are taking place. Games are evolving toward more team play as well as offering individual competition as new games like the Sims have come on the scene. These games replicate what our behavior will be like in virtual communities on the Sensory Virtual Internet in the future.

Collaborative Games

On the team-play front, parents and educators have long worried that game playing has been a reclusive activity that could be considered antisocial in nature. But with the introduction of Internet game playing, suddenly games as a whole are taking on a new dimension. Game players are now able to find other players at community sites and are able to initiate game play and to compete on an individual basis (which develops self-confidence) as well as a team basis (which develops teamwork, requires social skills for interaction, develops leadership abilities, and expands creativity). What is really interesting about this multiplayer/Internet trend is that game playing is moving beyond merely being a competitive activity. It is becoming a *collaborative* activity! As was the case in the business world, once 3D technologies and the Internet come together, people start to gravitate toward collaborative activities.

The use of multiplayer games over the Internet is growing rapidly as indicated by the growth in popularity of Microsoft's zone.com, Mplayer's Gamers community, Battlenet's Battle.net gaming service, and Aries Games' Gamestorm environment. This trend is particularly interesting because it shows that game players want company (a trend toward socialization and collaboration activities). Multiplayer games are expected to help triple the number of PC game players over the next two years. Data Monitor, a game market research firm, predicts that by 2003, the game market will reach $17.2 billion in revenues and number 45 million gamers.

> Despite the fact that it is a killing game, "Half-Life: Counter-Strike" by Sierra Studios is a fine example of collaborative game playing on the Internet. The theme of this PC game is to pit counterterrorists against terrorists. The purpose of this game is to foster player teawork. You need to work together to eliminate terrorists (or vice versa). For instance, a single player cannot singlehandedly remove a good sniper. That player must work as part of a team in order to flush a terrorist from his position. Each player plays an individual role, each of which can contribute to a team's success. If a player is eliminated, that player can still follow the activities of her team through a view-camera that follows the remaining players around until the game ends.
> Source: www.sierrastudios.com

As game consoles allow for Internet play, expect more team-oriented collaborative games will make an appearance on the game market, driven yet again by the desire of people to work together collaboratively on projects (or in this case, in a team-sport environment).

Simulation Games

Other games mirror our future on the Sensory Virtual Internet. These have avatars that move about in virtual spaces (homes, offices, and communities) and perform certain tasks.

> One game series that is illustrative of how games are acting as precursors to future Sensory Virtual Internet

worlds is "The Sims" series from Electronic Arts. Sims is short for "simulations." The game uses simulated characters that can socialize and coexist in home, neighborhood, and work settings and allows users to create venues, architect homes and surroundings, and interact with 3D characters. In effect providing users with a simulated 3D community experience.

Source: www.thesims.ea.com/index/phtml

The reason that this experience is so noteworthy is that playing The Sims game is very similar to the experience that you will find on the Sensory Virtual Internet of the future. You will be able to architect your own domicile, invite visitors to your virtual home, traverse vistas, visit other avatars in various settings, and otherwise participate as a member of a virtual community. If you want to experience a virtual community without having to go to the Internet, the Sims "Living Large" software program is a good place to start.

Chapter Summary

The Internet was started by the defense community as a collaborative effort. It was then used by the higher education community to share files, to post information, and to correspond in a more efficient manner than physical mail. But the Internet to date has not moved very far beyond its original position as a repository for static information and a method of sending mail electronically.

What has been missing to prevent the Internet's evolution to bigger and better things? I have identified the impediments earlier in this book.

- User interfaces have been inadequate.
- Navigation/manipulation peripherals are not necessarily natural tools to grasp or manipulate objects in virtual reality.
- Lack of network bandwidth has prohibited the sending and receiving of rich sensory data files.

- There has not been enough processing power on the desktop and on back-end servers to handle the computationally heavy workload of processing virtual world and sensory data.

But once these obstacles are overcome, we will still have problems moving to the next-generation Internet if we don't get access to new sensory-rich applications. These next-generation applications will be closely linked to the original founding purpose of the Internet—collaboration. This next generation of collaborative applications will include rich sensory data that will enable us to actually enter the Internet as virtual humans to conduct business, to learn, and to socialize in new ways.

The Sensory Virtual Internet is a new medium, and it's the most powerful communications tool we humans have developed since the telegraph and telephone. In the future, we will use this new medium to communicate with each other in a full sensory manner, finally making videophone calls to each other and picking up a variety of sensory clues when engaged in conversation.

Ever since the Jetsons cartoon of the 1960s, I've been waiting for videophone services to arrive. Today we can place a phone call to just about anywhere in the world but that phone call is sensory-limited. It transmits analog sound in the form of voice over twisted pair wiring to a receiver at the other end of the line. The new Sensory Virtual Internet will move us into a 3D world where we will be able to see the person to whom we are speaking (not a flat picture, but three dimensions—height, width, and depth); hear that person; perhaps even feel a handshake (if wearing a sensory glove or some other body apparatus); or maybe even smell the flowers in the background at that person's vista. And we can do all this without having to personally and physically travel to that person's locale.

The Sensory Virtual Internet will heavily feature the use of public virtual meeting areas, where we will congregate to share ideas, to shop, and to conduct business. But this Internet will also provide for private virtual meeting areas where one can expect that people will go to party with friends, maybe go on a date, or even get married.

> As far back as 1996, people recognized that the Internet could be used as a place to congregate for private parties. On May 8, 1996, at 9 p.m. Central Standard Time, the first Internet wedding took place at Alphaworld—a virtual world site. The bride, groom, members of the wedding party, and guests all attended—dressed appropriately for the occasion—as virtual world avatars. According to the Internet site that I browsed for this information tidbit, "a special pavilion was built for the event by Laurel. Best man was AlphaWorld Chief of Police Net-Guy. Bridesmaid was Yellow Rose. The honorable minister presiding was New World Times Editor Dataman."
>
> Using the technologies available today, it is reasonable to expect that that first ceremony would have been improved with better graphics, and better mobility and navigation due to improved network performance. It could have been augmented with Voice-over-IP so that voice and graphics could be sent to attendees simultaneously.
>
> No follow-up information could be found on how the couple (Janka and Tomas) are doing today.
>
> Source: http://www.web3d.org/www-vrml/hypermail/1996/9605/0279.html

On the flip side of marriage, the Sensory Virtual Internet will also be used to keep families together in the event of a divorce:

> TRENTON, NJ—A state appeals court recently announced that a divorced woman could move with her daughter to California and use the Internet to enable the girl to keep in touch with her father who will remain in New Jersey—thus making use of the Internet as a "visitation tool."
>
> Kyron Henn-Lee indicated to her ex-husband that she desired to take their nine-year-old daughter, Katherine, from New Jersey to Brea, California—and that she would build a Web site for the father and daughter to

communicate. Although her ex-husband objected, the Appellate Division of New Jersey's state Superior Court said the Internet would provide a "creative and innovative" way for the father and child to remain in communication with each other after a move.

David Levy, president of the Children's Rights Council, an advocacy group for children of divorce, indicated that the New Jersey case is the first one in the United States to involve and allow for Internet visitation.

Source: http://library.northernlight.com/ED20010105130000029.html?cb=0&sc=0#doc

The whole point of this story is that the Sensory Virtual Internet will make it possible for you to stay in closer communications with your family and friends. There has been plenty of press over the past 30 years about the break-up of the extended family as family members move to all corners of the globe in search of jobs or adventure. The Sensory Virtual Internet will make communications between family members as effortless as picking up the phone. And with a full complement of sensory services, this Internet will make the prospect of phoning home more rewarding and enjoyable.

The most important concept in this chapter is the concept of virtual colocation. As new collaborative applications evolve, their focus will be on enabling us to meet with business partners, seek consultative services, sit or stand in virtual classrooms, play team games virtually, or converse with family members over long distances. The need to be colocated for full sensory input and output will someday be eliminated. What will change is our need to be physically present to communicate with the outside world. We will find ourselves able to collaborate with others making use of the full range of our senses (3D vision, 3D surround sound, scent, touch, and taste) from virtually any remote location (provided our personal computing device is equipped to handle the display of such data and that we have the right peripherals for producing sound, scent, touch, and taste sensations). We will, in essence, be logistically free.

Part VII: Where Do We Go from Here?

CHAPTER 16

SUMMARY OBSERVATIONS

We are surrounded with clues in the technology press, from the news media, from Internet news sources, from hardware and software suppliers, and from various research and analysis firms that a major shift is under way in the way that mankind interacts with and uses computers. The technology press is writing about peer-to-peer computing, grid computing, and 3D graphics. The news media are talking about exciting sensory technologies like digital scent. Hardware and software suppliers are actively marketing Web Services for application development. And research analysts and consultants are issuing reports and forecasts that describe how high-speed networking, systems infrastructure, and applications are adapting to accommodate greater-bandwidth applications. Unfortunately, this information is being presented to us in bits and pieces that don't seem to relate to each other. But, in fact, these changes in user interfaces, infrastructure, and application development are all interrelated. There is an end game and a big picture—it's called the Sensory Virtual Internet.

Look closely at the world around you—at evolving business practices, game playing, retailing, and education—and you will find clear evidence that the technologies needed to build the Sensory Virtual Internet are moving from the drawing board into real life. We are quickly moving from the first-generation, static Internet to a highly interactive, virtual, sensory-based Internet that will allow us to communicate with each other and collaborate with each other in radically new ways.

The premise of this book is that the convergence of five technologies is enabling us to enter a new age in computing—the "Sensory Virtual Internet" age. This age has been created by the convergence of human interface input and output systems, infrastructure improvements to networks and systems architectures, the evolution of Web Services standards, and the arrival of virtual-space-based collaborative applications. It is my belief that the resulting convergence of these technologies will result in the formation of a new kind of Internet—a vibrant, interactive, sensory-based Internet I've called the Sensory Virtual Internet. This new Internet will change forever the way that people communicate, learn, conduct business, socialize, and are entertained.

In this book I've put forward the argument that strong advances in speech recognition and artificial intelligence technologies are creating better user interfaces. Finally, we will be able to use our computers in a more natural manner. Keyboards will eventually be replaced by speech-based systems. Someday track pointers and mice may be replaced (or at least augmented) by other devices that provide a more natural way to navigate through 3D vistas and manipulate objects therein.

I've also told you that as we become better able to receive 3D graphics and 3D sound on our personal computing devices and as new sensory peripherals become available to provide us with scent, touch, and taste feedback, computer-to-human output will undergo a significant change. I observed that we learn better when we have multimodal learning experiences, which means being able to use more than one sense to gather information and data about the environment that surrounds us. Soon, the Sensory Virtual Internet will be able to deliver to us such rich sensory data.

But in order for us to get access to rich sensory data, three infrastructure changes need to occur:

1. Our networks need to be able to handle the transfer of the very large files of complex sensory data quickly.
2. Our computers are going to have to be optimized to handle the computationally challenging tasks of presenting such data to us in a high-quality fashion.
3. We are going to have to get more clever about how we compress and decompress data so that we can send these large files at high speed over the Internet.

The more efficiency that we can build into networks, CPUs, GPUs, and codecs, the richer our Sensory Virtual Internet experience will be.

Even with the availability of better infrastructure, all of our efforts will go for naught if sensory-enriched applications fail to make it to market quickly. For over 23 years I've watched the computing industry try to make cross-platform program-to-program communications easy to accomplish. In addition, I've watched each previous effort fail due to vendor arrogance, complexity, or technical issues. But the evolution of Web Services—new standards that allow modular applications to be located on the Web and integrated into the core application portfolios of enterprises—has given me great hope that we finally will have a way to rapidly build sensory-based applications and release them to market more quickly than previous attempts. It is this concept of applications-as-services that leads me to believe that the Sensory Virtual Internet will evolve more quickly than most informed observers and analysts currently believe.

As for the types of applications that will be most popular on the Sensory Virtual Internet, it is my belief that the Sensory Virtual Internet will be used primarily for collaborative purposes. Whether people are playing games, working, learning, conducting business, or socializing, the Sensory Virtual Internet will enable people to gather sensory information that will make such electronic experiences far more realistic.

For me, the biggest benefit of this Sensory Virtual Internet will be the saving of precious time. The Sensory Virtual Internet will introduce the concept of locale independence. Soon you will have access to a host of services that will enable you to gather or share information from a variety of sources *without having to be physically present*! The next-generation sensory Internet will make your life simpler while expanding your access to consultative and collaborative experiences. The convergence of these technologies will enable us to coexist and collaborate in vibrant 3D electronic worlds without having to be colocated. This makes finding and communicating with people easier and more natural. It also enables this communication to take place between locations that may be very far apart. The effects of these developments will be felt in our business as well as personal lives. Businesses will save billions in travel expenses while individuals will save hours and hours of wasted travel and wait time—leaving the real you with more time in your life to do the things you really want to do.

After the Sensory Virtual Internet Age

The Sensory Virtual Internet age will bring us the ability to communicate and collaborate in virtual electronic environments. The technologies that we will need to participate are well defined. Development is already well under way. There is a clear, three-year roadmap for the roll-out of these technologies.

Less clear at this point are certain developments related to sensory display—specifically the use of holographs. I refer to possible future advances in laser holography that might make possible representations of people or objects that can be projected into real-world space as opposed to on a computer or projection screen.

Holographs

To me, holographs are just another way to display sensory visual information. I doubt that in my lifetime I'll see holography become a highly available sensory display technology. But it would be really cool to see a fully sensory-enabled 3D football game played on my living room floor rather than having to go to the stadium.

This technology is actually quite advanced at this stage—it is just very expensive to implement. This is why I don't see holography becoming commercially available to consumers for the next 10 years or so. The projection of images in real space is done today (go to DisneyWorld's Epcot center for a showing). It has even started to be used in certain business environments for modeling and for flashy retail purposes. Remember, to generate 3D holographic images you need devices on the capture side that can capture and compute the dimensions and movements of a holographic image. On the receiving side you need laser and other technologies to display that image. At this point, laser technology is extremely expensive to acquire and there are very few practical uses planned for this technology in either business or consumer markets.

Holodecks

After researching and writing this book, I've gained a new appreciation for the "Star Trek" concept of "holodecks" (virtual space that the real you can traverse). Holodecks will require large 3D surround-sound and displays as well as the ability to replicate topography and other touch sensations. But hardware and software to build this type of environment is being worked on today. Expect holodecks to evolve over the next 10 to 20 years.

I'll See You There

The change from physical to virtual communication will be the most significant advance in technology that I'm likely to see in my lifetime (and I've already witnessed the creation and evolution of the computer and of the Internet). The advancement of computer technologies, sensory technologies, human interfaces, and high-speed networking are interesting to watch, but ultimately its what we do with these technologies that counts. The Sensory Virtual Internet will include collaborative applications that will enable us to conduct business, to learn, to be entertained, and to socialize without having to be colocated. We are entering a new dimension in communications—a sensory-based virtual dimension. This dimension will radically change our world—more so than any other occurrence that I've witnessed in my lifetime.

In the new virtual worlds that we are about to enter, our physical concepts of venue and locality are about to change. New technologies and new applications will enable us to interact in a more organized and efficient fashion without having to be physically present to conduct a business meeting, to go shopping, or to consult with a doctor, lawyer, or some other consultant or advisor. Millions of hours in travel time, waiting time, and wasted time will be saved because the need to be there physically at doctors' or lawyers' offices or at other professional sites will be tremendously diminished.

The Sensory Virtual Internet will be almost inescapable. It will affect you, how you deal with your everyday world, how you shop, how you gather information, and how you seek advice. Soon strategic placement of speech-driven kiosks will provide people who are Internet- and technology-resistant with access to Internet services without having to learn how to use a computer. In fact, the new speech-driven applications developed for mobile phones and other wireless devices will be transparent in nature. Most people will either be unaware they are using them or just not care that they are using the Internet to get the data, graphics, music, or other information they seek.

Thanks to the convergence of five technologies and the advent of new collaborative colocation applications, we will soon be able to communicate in a natural and multimodal fashion over the Internet. We will be able to meet in virtual worlds to conduct business, learn, socialize, and be entertained.

I look forward to someday meeting the virtual you in one of these virtual communities of tomorrow.

Bibliography

Most of the research conducted in the writing of this book was performed by accessing publicly available Web sites as well as by subscribing to newsfeeds and newsletters readily available from several technology news sites. The following is a list of my personal favorites for gathering information about sensory and computing/networking technologies on the Web.

ExtremeTech, *http://www.extremetech.com*—A newly evolved offshoot of *PC Magazine* (part of the ZDnet series of publications) that gets down-and-dirty into technology details related to PCs, microprocessors, peer-to-peer processing, and the like. An excellent source for discussions on the futures of advanced technologies.

KenRadio, *http://www.KenRadio.com*—One of the best sources for condensed news clips on worldwide happenings that affect the development of the Sensory Virtual Internet. I highly recommend that if you wish to continue to follow advances in technologies related to the Sensory Virtual Internet that you consider subscribing to Ken's daily newsletter (available for free). To view the daily tech news coverage, visit *www.KenRadio.com/today.asp*.

NUA Internet Surveys, *http://www.NUA.com*—One of my primary sources for information about Internet communications and new technologies evolving in Pacific rim and Asian countries.

TechTV, *http://www.TechTV.com*—Provides insightful articles about how computing environments work; about new gadgets coming to market and how they are competitively positioned; as well as providing topical coverage on technology advances.

Wired, *http://www.wired.com*—Particularly valuable source for information on the telecommunications industry.

Red Herring, *http://www.redherring.com*—*Red Herring* (the magazine) has a solid Web site that provides a diverse perspective on a variety of technologies and technology markets (such as computer games and mobile computing).

University of California—Davis, *http://phosphoric.cpic.ucdavis.edu*—Provides access to excellent analysis of sensory technologies—especially audio technologies. Of all of the universities that I visited while investigating audio sensory research, UC Davis was the best. Check it out for outstanding audio research.

ZDnet, *http://www.ZDnet.com*—A solid source of information for topical, day-to-day topical coverage of technolgy events and advances—and archives information on all of the areas-of-convergence in this book (human interfaces to and from computers, high-speed networking, peer-to-peer infrastructure, compression/decompression, Web Services, and collaborative computing).

A Special Mention:

Shortly after I started writing *Visualize This*, Micheal L. Dertouzos, the former director of the Massachusetts Institute of Technology's computer science lab, an early influencer of Internet communications, and a leading advocate for improved human interfaces for computers, published *The Unfinished Revolution: Human-Centered Computers and What They Can Do for Us* (New York: HarperBusiness, January 2001; ISBN: 006620678). This book closely examines how human interfaces to and from computers and how applications can be improved to create human-centered computing environments. *The Unfinished Revolution* makes an excellent companion read to *Visualize This*. Mr. Dertouzos died shortly before the publication of this book—a great loss for all of us in the Internet research and analysis community.

INDEX

A

access speed, 50
accuracy in speech recognition, 103
ADSL, 196–198
Advanced Micro Devices, 230–231
advanced virtual world sites, 47–50
AI. *See* artificial intelligence
anti-aliasing, 125–126
application code, 116–117
application components, 271–272
application development
   environments, predictions for, 67
   Sensory Virtual Internet, 32–33
   in 2002, 70–72
   in 2003, 73
   in 2004, 75
artificial intelligence
   computer-to-human speech input
      issue, 94–95
   overview, 88–90
audio technologies
   current state of, 163–164
   file size, 164–165
   state-of-the-art virtual technology, 51
   3D sound, 165–166
   virtual worlds, 15
avatars, 13

B

back-end modifications, 179
bad graphics, 126–127
bandwidth, 187–188
binocular stereopsis, 122–123
Bluetooth technology, 209–210
body positioning and physical input
   devices, 91
broadband technologies
   ADSL, 196–198
   cable Internet access, 199–202
   common broadband technologies,
      195
   described, 188–189
   DSL, 195–196
   Hughes Network Systems, 203–204
   overview, 193–195
   satellite Internet access, 202–204
   SDSL, 198–199
   wireless LAN, 204–210
building applications, 40–41
business
   collaboration, 152–153, 293–294
   colocation conferencing, 294–301
   customer service avatars, 302–303
   e-tailing, 301–303
   modeling, 148–150

business (*continued*)
  retailing, 150–152
  videoconferencing software, 295
  visualization, 148–152
business executives and Sensory Virtual Internet, 22–23
business model and Web Services, 274–277
BusinessPlace, 296–299

C

cable Internet access
  overview, 199–200
  success of, 200–202
caching, 255
Click-to-Meet, 18
clustered systems, 250
codecs, 255–256
collaborative applications
  in business, 293–294
  predictions, 67
  in the present, 69
  Sensory Virtual Internet, 8, 33–34, 41–42
  in 2002, 72
  in 2003, 73–74
  in 2004, 75
collaborative games, 315–316
colocation conferencing
  BusinessPlace, 296–299
  consulting and, 311–313
  described, 295
  e-learning, 304–307
  eGlobalReach, 296–299
  entertainment and, 315–317
  Groove Networks, 299
  NetMeeting, 300–301
  Sametime, 300
command-and-control systems, 86–87, 93–94

common broadband technologies, 195
computer architecture, 38–39
computer hardware and speech recognition, 99–100
computer infrastructure, architecture and computing techniques, 8
computer interfaces with humans, 8
computer mice, 114–115
computer-to-human speech input issue
  artificial intelligence, 94–95
  speech recognition, 92–96
consulting and colocation conferencing, 311–313
consumers and Sensory Virtual Internet, 24–25
continuous dictation products, 87, 97
control sequence memorization, 91
convergence of technologies creating, 31–34
CPU speed, 227–228
creation of 3D graphics, 124–126
CRTs, 138–139
customer service avatars, 302–303

D

data compression
  codecs, 255–256
  future issues, 260–261
  lossless compression, 258
  lossy compression, 258
  overview, 256–257
  real-world uses for, 258–259
  types of, 258–259
  Web Driver, 260
data transmission, 31–32
DataSynapse, 240–241
dialogue systems, 87–88, 95–96, 102–103
DigiScents, 169
digital content, 153

INDEX

disbelief in creation of Sensory Virtual Internet, 34–35
disorganization of Sensory Virtual Internet, 7
distortion in speech recognition, 98
Dr.Goodwell.com, 25
DSL, 195–196

E

e-learning
  costs related to employee training, reduction of, 306–307
  obstacles to, 310–311
  overview, 304–306
  schools and universities, 307–309
  speed of delivery of course material, 307
  state-of-the-art virtual technology, 58–59
e-tailing, 301–303
eGlobalReach, 296–299
electronic communications
  evolution of, 5
  historical progression, 3–4
Elsa 3D Revelator, 141
Elumens Corporation, 143–144
enrollment, 98, 103
entertainment
  collaborative games, 315–316
  digital content, 153
  manipulation, 116–119
  navigation, 116–119
  pornography, 315
  simulation games, 316–317
  special effects, 153–154
Eye Control Technologies, 114

F

First Virtual Corporation, 18–19
front-end modifications, 178–179
FTTH, 211–213

G

games industry
  advantages of game consoles, 155–157
  disadvantages of game consoles, 157–159
  manipulation, 116–119
  navigation, 116–119
  overview, 154–155
  PC architecture compared to game consoles, 155–160
  Xbox, 156–157
gloves, 116
GPU speed, 228–229
graphics
  described, 50
  files, 51
  handling issues, 55–56
  3D. *See* 3D graphics
Groove Networks, 299

H

handwriting recognition, 106–107
haptic technology. *See* touch technologies
HDTV, 146
head-mounted displays, 139–140
health challenges and physical input devices, 91
healthcare industry use of 3D technology, 159–161
high-speed networking
  access, 176–177
  ADSL, 196–198
  bandwidth, 187–188
  broadband. *See* broadband technologies
  cable Internet access, 199–202
  common broadband technologies, 195
  consumer market for, 213–214
  cost, 177–178

high-speed networking (continued)
  DSL, 195–196
  FTTH, 211–213
  Hughes Network Systems, 203–204
  latency, 188
  modems and, 191–193
  options for, 189–191
  powerlines, 210–211
  reasons to have, 185–186
  satellite connections, 190
  satellite Internet access, 202–204
  SDSL, 198–199
  Sensory Virtual Internet, 17, 31, 39–40
  standard modem over twisted pair, 190
  state-of-the-art virtual technology, 53–54
  terminology for, 187–191
  wire-based broadband interconnect, 189–190
  wireless communications and, 190–191
  wireless LANs, 190, 204–210
  Zoom Telephonics, Inc., 192
Hitachi Corporation, 144
holodecks, 328
holographs, 327
hot applications, predictions for, 67
Hughes Network Systems, 203–204
human interfaces with computer systems. *See also* user interfaces
  artificial intelligence. *See* artificial intelligence
  described, 7, 30–31, 42
  manipulation. *See* manipulation
  navigation. *See* navigation
  predictions, 67
  speech recognition. *See* speech recognition

I
IBM Model 170 UNIX workstations, 220–221
Immersion Corporation, 132–133
improvements to virtual worlds, 50–52
InfiniBand architecture
  overview, 246
  power of, 248–249
  as standard, 245
  switch-fabric architecture, 246–250
infrared technologies, 114
infrastructure
  improvements, predictions for, 67
  in the present, 68–69
  in 2002, 70
  in 2003, 73
  in 2004, 74–75
interface sickness, 126–127
intuitive movement, 113–114
Intuous 4D mouse, 115

J
Juno, 241–242

L
latency, 188
LCDs, 138–139
lossless compression, 258
lossy compression, 258

M
Maddox, Mitch, 20
mainstream applications for speech recognition, 100
manipulation
  application code, 116–117
  computer mice, 114–115
  current technology, 114–115
  games and entertainment, 116–119
  gloves, 116

Intuous 4D mouse, 115
natural motions, 115–116
Sensory Virtual Internet, 17, 31
state-of-the-art virtual technology, 51
MechDyne Corporation, 144–145
Metabyte Inc., 141
mice, computer, 114–115
modeling, 148–150
modems, 191–193
modular integration of speech with mainstream applications, 101
multimodal communications, movement toward, 4–7
myIVAN, 102–103

N

natural motions, 115–116
navigation
 application code, 116–117
 devices, 112–114
 Eye Control Technologies, 114
 games and entertainment, 116–119
 infrared technologies, 114
 intuitive movement, 113–114
 Sensory Virtual Internet, 17, 31
 state-of-the-art virtual technology, 51, 54–55
NetMeeting, 300–301
network protocols and Web Services, 271
networking, high-speed. See high-speed networking
NHS Online, 24
Nuance Communications, 101

O

One Voice Technologies, 47

P

PC architecture compared to game consoles, 155–160
PC bus architecture, 224–225
PC bus speed, 229–231
PC graphics processing, 222–223
peer-to-peer computing
 big business' application of, 244
 DataSynapse, 240–241
 examples, 238–243
 future of, 243–244
 Juno, 241–242
 obstacles to, 250–251
 overview, 237–238
 SETI@home, 238–240
performance optimization, 227–231
personal computing devices
 portable/laptop computers, 231–232
 stationary computers compared to mobile/portable computers, 218–219
 stationary devices. See stationary computing devices
Phonetic Systems, Inc., 278–279
physical input devices
 body positioning, 91
 control sequence memorization, 91
 health challenges, 91
 overview, 90–91
 proximity, 91
 usability issues, 91
pornography, 315
portable/laptop computers
 overview, 231–232
 stationary computers compared, 218–219
powerlines, 210–211
predictions
 application development environments, 67
 collaborative applications, 67
 hot applications, 67

predictions (*continued*)
  human interfaces with computer systems, 67
  infrastructure improvements, 67
present day
  collaborative applications, 69
  infrastructure, 68–69
  user interfaces, 68
problems with speech recognition, 97–99
processing techniques, 31
productivity and speech recognition, 103–104
professionals and Sensory Virtual Internet, 23–24
progress in state-of-the-art virtual technology, 52–59
progress of Sensory Virtual Internet, 6–7
projected roll-out of Sensory Virtual Internet, 66–68
projector-based displays, 143–145
proximity and physical input devices, 91

R

recognition of Sensory Virtual Internet, lack of, 5–6
retailing, 150–152

S

Sametime, 300
satellite connections, 190
satellite Internet access, 202–204
scent technologies
  companies/organizations involved in, 168–170
  current state of, 167–168
  DigiScents, 169
  how it works, 130
  overview, 130
  virtual worlds, 16

SDSL, 198–199
sensory data received from computer
  overview, 14–15
  scent technology, 130
  taste sensation technology, 130–131
  3D audio, 128–129
  3D visualization, 122–128
  touch technology, 131–134
sensory input, 36–37
sensory output, 37–38, 42–43
Sensory Virtual Internet
  application development, 32–33
  building applications, 40–41
  business executives and, 22–23
  collaborative applications, 8, 33–34, 41–42
  computer architecture, 38–39
  computer infrastructure, architecture and computing techniques, 8
  computer interfaces with humans, 8
  consumers and, 24–25
  convergence of technologies creating, 31–34
  data transmission, 31–32
  disbelief in creation of, 34–35
  disorganization of, 7
  Dr.Goodwell.com, 25
  effects of, 21–25
  entertainment and, 314–317
  factors in creation of, 36–42
  high-speed networking, 17, 31, 39–40
  human interface technologies, 7, 30–31, 42
  manipulation, 17, 31
  navigation, 17, 31
  NHS Online, 24
  processing techniques, 31
  professionals and, 23–24
  progress of, 6–7
  projected roll-out, 66–68
  recognition of, lack of, 5–6

sensory input, 36–37
sensory output, 37–38, 42–43
socializing and, 313–314
speech recognition, 16–17
stimuli, 43–44
systems architecture, 31
technologies, 7–9
Telemedicine, 24
three years from now, 20–21
videophone service, 18
virtual collaboration, 19
virtual shopping, 17–18
Web services-based model for application development, 32–33
SETI@home, 238–240
shutter glasses, 140–143
Simple Object Access Protocol, 71
simulation games, 316–317
64-bit computing, 223–224
SOAP, 71, 272
social issues and speech recognition, 105–106
socialization and virtual worlds, 313–314
sound, 3D, 165–166
special effects, 153–154
speech recognition
  accuracy, 103
  achievability of, 99–105
  command-and-control systems, 86–87, 93–94
  computer hardware, 99–100
  computer-to-human speech input issue, 92–96
  continuous dictation products, 87, 97
  demand and supply, 104–105
  dialogue systems, 87–88, 95–96, 102–103
  distortion, 98
  enrollment, 98, 103
  mainstream applications, 100
  modular integration of speech with mainstream applications, 101
  myIVAN, 102–103
  Nuance Communications, 101
  overview, 86
  problems with, 97–99
  productivity, 103–104
  Sensory Virtual Internet, 16–17
  social issues, 105–106
  speech synthesis, 88
  transcription, 88
  types of, 86–88
  Wildfire, 100
  Windows XP, 93–94
  wireless communications market, 101–102
speech synthesis, 88
standard modem over twisted pair, 190
state-of-the-art virtual technology
  access speed, 50
  advanced virtual world sites, 47–50
  audio files, 51
  categories list, 45–46
  graphic files, 51
  graphic handling issues, 55–56
  graphics, 50
  high-speed networking, 53–54
  improvements to virtual worlds, 50–52
  manipulation, 51, 54–55
  navigation, 51, 54–55
  One Voice Technologies, 47
  overview, 45–47
  progress in, 52–59
  transaction processing, 57–58
  virtual learning, 58–59
  VoIP, 56–57
stationary computing devices
  Advanced Micro Devices, 230–231
  CPU speed, 227–228

stationary computing devices
(*continued*)
  GPU speed, 228–229
  IBM Model 170 UNIX workstations, 220–221
  PC bus architecture, 224–225
  PC bus speed, 229–231
  PC graphics processing, 222–223
  performance optimization, 227–231
  portable/laptop computers compared, 218–219
  64-bit computing, 223–224
  storage access, 226–227
  UNIX workstations, 219–222
stimuli, 43–44
storage access, 226–227
switch-fabric architecture, 246–250
systems architecture and Sensory Virtual Internet, 31

T

taste technology
  current state of, 170–171
  overview, 130–131
  virtual worlds, 16
Telemedicine, 24
3D audio, 128–129
3D graphics
  business use of, 147, 148–153
  CRTs, 138–139
  Elsa 3D Revelator, 141
  Elumens Corporation, 143–144
  entertainment industry use of, 147, 153–154
  games industry use of, 148, 154–159
  HDTV, 146
  head-mounted displays, 139–140
  healthcare industry use of, 148, 159–161
  Hitachi Corporation, 144
  LCDs, 138–139
  market use of, 146–147
  MechDyne Corporation, 144–145
  Metabyte Inc., 141
  projector-based displays, 143–145
  shutter glasses, 140–143
  types of presentation displays, 138
  Virtual Research Systems, Inc., 142–143
3D sound, 165–166
3D visualization
  anti-aliasing, 125–126
  bad graphics, 126–127
  binocular stereopsis, 122–123
  creation of 3D graphics, 124–126
  described, 15
  interface sickness, 126–127
  overview, 122–123
  users, large groups of, 128
touch technologies
  current state of, 166–167
  overview, 131–134
  virtual worlds, 15–16
transaction processing, 57–58
transcription, 88
transmission of data, 31–32
2004 (predictions for year)
  application development, 75
  collaborative applications, 75
  infrastructure, 74–75
  user interfaces, 74
2003 (predictions for year)
  application development, 73
  collaborative applications, 73–74
  infrastructure, 73
  user interfaces, 72–73
2002 (predictions for year)
  application development, 70–72
  collaborative applications, 72

infrastructure, 70
user interfaces, 69–70
v-commerce, 72

U

UDDI, 71, 272
Universal Description, Discovery, and Integration, 71
UNIX workstations, 219–222
usability issues and physical input devices, 91
user interfaces. *See also* human interfaces with computer systems
  in the present, 68
  in 2002, 69–70
  in 2003, 72–73
  in 2004, 74

V

v-commerce, 72
videoconferencing software, 295
videoconferencing technology, 28–29
videophone service, 18
videophone technology, 28–29
virtual collaboration, 19
virtual learning. *See* e-learning
Virtual Research Systems, Inc., 142–143
virtual shopping, 17–18
virtual worlds
  audio technology, 15
  avatars, 13
  3D visual technology, 15
  described, 13–14
  scent technology, 16
  sensory data, 14–15
  taste technology, 16
  touch technology, 15–16
visualization, 148–152
Visualize, Inc., 277–278
VoIP, 56–57

W

Web Driver, 260
Web Services
  application components, 271–272
  business model and, 274–277
  examples, 277–279
  how it works, 273
  network protocols, 271
  obstacles to, 271–272
  overview, 269–272
  Phonetic Systems, Inc., 278–279
  program-to-program standards, 271
  SOAP, 272
  standards for, 272
  UDDI, 272
  Visualize, Inc., 277–278
  WSDL, 272
Web services-based model for application development, 32–33
Web Services Description Language, 71
Wildfire, 100
Windows XP, 93–94
wire-based broadband interconnect, 189–190
wireless communications
  high-speed networking, 190–191
  speech recognition, 101–102
wireless LANs
  companies licensed to deliver, list of, 208–209
  high-speed networking, 190
  overview, 204–208
  wireless PANs, 209–210
WSDL, 71, 272

X

Xbox, 156–157

Z

Zoom Telephonics, Inc., 192

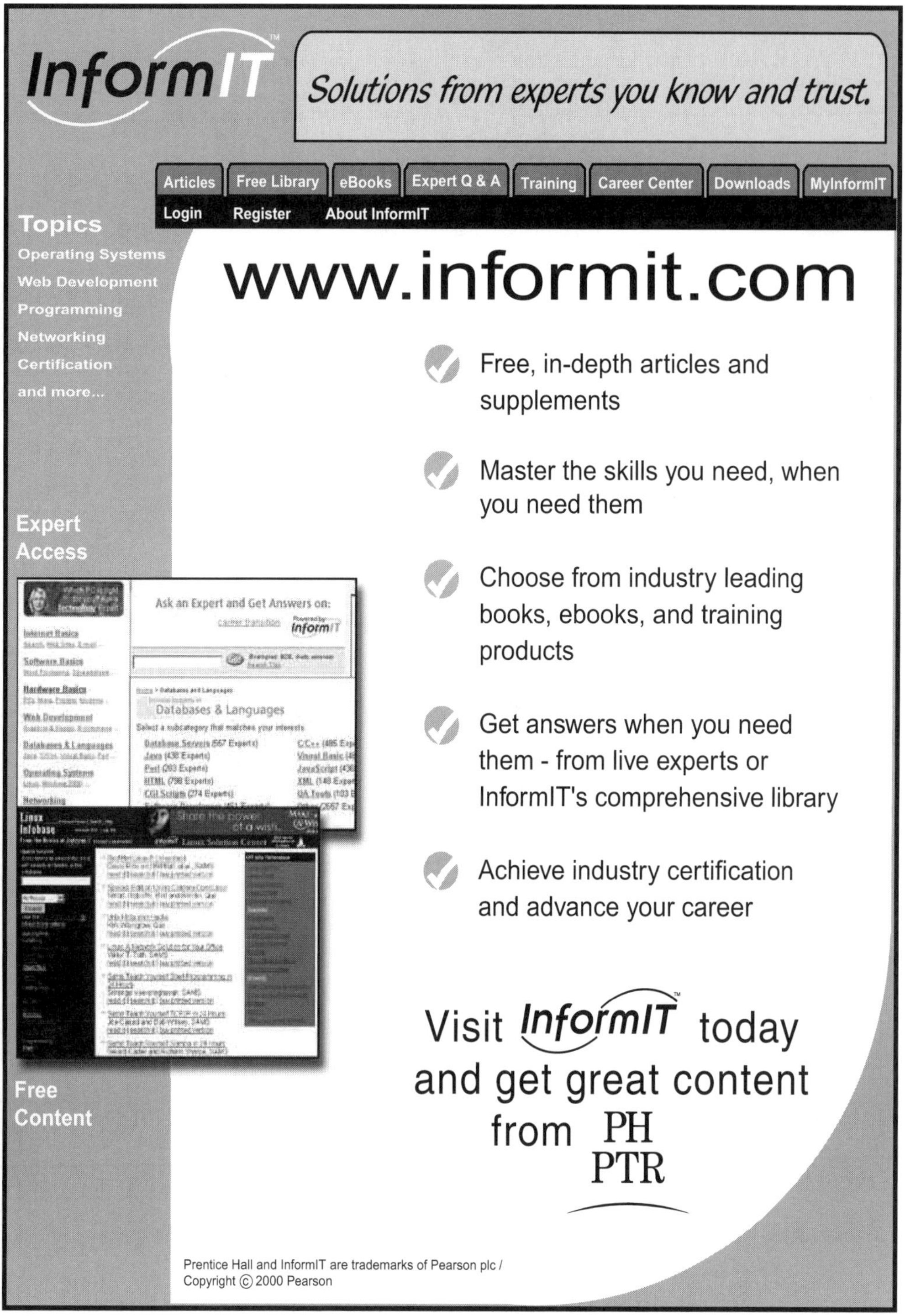
InformIT™
Solutions from experts you know and trust.
Articles
Free Library
eBooks
Expert Q & A
Training
Career Center
Downloads
MyInformIT
Login
Register
About InformIT
Topics
Operating Systems
Web Development
Programming
Networking
Certification
and more...
www.informit.com
Free, in-depth articles and supplements
Master the skills you need, when you need them
Choose from industry leading books, ebooks, and training products
Get answers when you need them - from live experts or InformIT's comprehensive library
Achieve industry certification and advance your career
Expert Access
Ask an Expert and Get Answers on:
Databases & Languages
Free Content
Visit InformIT today and get great content from PH PTR
Prentice Hall and InformIT are trademarks of Pearson plc / Copyright © 2000 Pearson

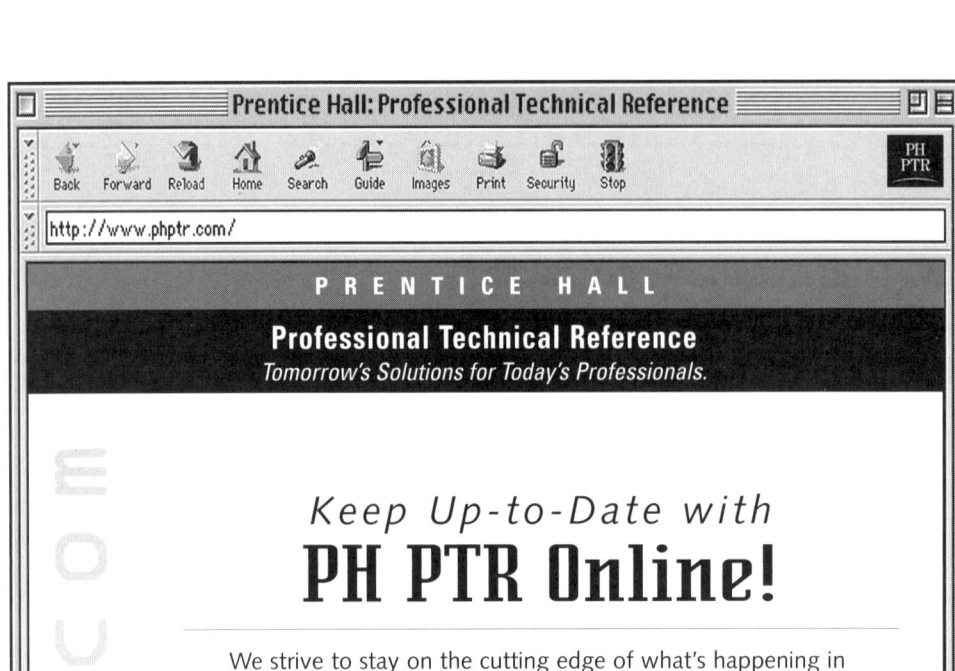

PRENTICE HALL
Professional Technical Reference
Tomorrow's Solutions for Today's Professionals.

Keep Up-to-Date with
PH PTR Online!

We strive to stay on the cutting edge of what's happening in professional computer science and engineering. Here's a bit of what you'll find when you stop by **www.phptr.com**:

Special interest areas offering our latest books, book series, software, features of the month, related links and other useful information to help you get the job done.

Deals, deals, deals! Come to our promotions section for the latest bargains offered to you exclusively from our retailers.

Need to find a bookstore? Chances are, there's a bookseller near you that carries a broad selection of PTR titles. Locate a Magnet bookstore near you at www.phptr.com.

What's new at PH PTR? We don't just publish books for the professional community, we're a part of it. Check out our convention schedule, join an author chat, get the latest reviews and press releases on topics of interest to you.

Subscribe today! **Join PH PTR's monthly email newsletter!**

Want to be kept up-to-date on your area of interest? Choose a targeted category on our website, and we'll keep you informed of the latest PH PTR products, author events, reviews and conferences in your interest area.

Visit our mailroom to subscribe today! **http://www.phptr.com/mail_lists**